D1087969

Charting an Independent Course

CHARTING AN INDEPENDENT COURSE

Finland's Place in the Cold War
and in U.S. Foreign Policy

Edited by

T. Michael Ruddy

Regina Books
Claremont, California

Library of Congress Cataloging-in-Publication Data
Charting an independent : Finland's place in the Cold War and in U.S.
   foreign policy / edited by T. Michael Rudday.
       p.   cm.
   Includes bibliographical references and index.
   ISBN 0-941690-83-0 (alk. paper). -- ISBN 0-941690-84-9 (pbk. : alk.
paper)
   1. Finland--Foreign relations--1917-1945. 2. Finland--Foreign
relations--1945- 3. Cold War. I. Ruddy, T. Michael.
DL1066.7C43   1998
327.4897--dc21   98-5995
                                             CIP

Regina Books
Post Office Box 280
Claremont, California 91711
Tel: (909) 624-8466 Fax: (909) 626-1345

Manufactured in the United States of America.

Contents

Acknowledgments

I would like to thank both the Finlandia Foundation and the Mellon Faculty Development Fund, St Louis University, College of Arts and Sciences, for their generous support that made publication of this volume possible.

Contributors

R. Michael Berry received his doctorate from the University of Wisconsin. He now resides in Finland and is a senior lecturer at the Turku School of Economics and an adjunct professor of history at the University of Tampere and the University of Turku. His publications include *Political Parties in Finland: Essays in History and Politics* (1987) and *American Foreign Policy and the Finnish Exception: Ideological Preferences and Wartime Realities* (1987), as well as articles on U.S.-Finnish relations.

Jussi M. Hanhimäki received his undergraduate degree in history and politics from Tampere University, Finland, and his Ph.D. in American history in 1993 from Boston University. He is currently a lecturer in international history at the London School of Economics. He has published *Containing Coexistence: America, Russia, and the "Finnish Solution", 1945-1956* (1997) and articles on U.S.-Finnish relations.

Robert W. Matson is an associate professor and chairperson of the history department at the University of Pittsburgh at Johnstown. He received his Ph.D. from the University of Oregon in 1981. His publications include *William Mulholland: A Forgotten Forefather* (1976) and *Arctic Twilight: Old Finnish Tales* (1982).

George Maude received his Ph.D. from the University of London. He currently holds the position of docent in international relations in the Faculty of Law at the University of Turku, Finland. Maude has published widely in the area of Finnish international relations including the critically acclaimed *The Finnish Dilemma: Neutrality in the Shadow of Power* (1970).

Keith W. Olson is professor of history at the University of Maryland, College Park. He received his Ph.D. from the University of Wisconsin. His publications include *Biography of a Progressive: Frank K. Lane,*

1864-1921 (1979) and *The G. I. Bill, the Veterans, and the Colleges* (1974), as well as articles on Finnish and Scandinavian history.

T. Michael Ruddy is professor of history at St. Louis University. He received his Ph.D. in diplomatic history at Kent State University. His publications include *The Cautious Diplomat: Charles E. Bohlen and the Soviet Union, 1929-1969* (1986) and articles on American foreign policy and Finnish-U.S. relations.

Charles Silva is currently a researcher at the University of Stockholm where he is preparing his doctoral dissertation on Sweden and the Marshall Plan. He has published articles on contemporary history in journals including *Historians of Contemporary Europe* and the *Journal of Scandinavian Studies*.

Introduction

T. Michael Ruddy

With the end of the Cold War and the collapse of the Soviet Union, historians have expended a great deal of effort reassessing this critical period. Blessed with the wisdom of hindsight, these scholars can now more accurately analyze major developments and conflicts. More often than not, this reassessment has led to a more nuanced and complex explanation of historical events. Such is the case with Finland and its relationship with the United States. Through much of the Cold War, historians paid little attention to this small and relatively insignificant country situated in the shadow of the Soviet Union. When they did, their examination was often clouded by stereotypes, images of the honest Finns who steadfastly paid their debts from World War I while other countries defaulted or of the Finns who staunchly resisted the Soviet invasion during the Winter War of 1940-1941. Such impressions remained strong despite Helsinki's decision to support the Axis during the Continuation War.

As the Cold War evolved, negative stereotypes also surfaced. "Finlandization" rather simplistically made assumptions about the Soviet-Finnish relationship premised exclusively on the bipolar rivalry between the superpowers with little consideration for the reality of the circumstances Finland found itself in. Finlandization viewed the Finnish experience as a bad example for other countries facing Soviet pressure, its connotation being of a country whose foreign and domestic policies willingly sacrificed sovereignty for the sake of preserving felicitious relations with the Kremlin. This image appeared early in the Cold War, but was popularized in the 1970s by Walter Laqueur, who feared that other European countries might succumb to this course and, therefore, benefit the Soviet Union.[1]

---

[1] Walter Laqueur, "Europe: The Specter of Finlandization," *Commentary* 64 (December 1977): 37-41.

Admittedly, there were a few scholars—including some of the contributors to this volume—who looked more closely at the Finnish situation and tried to explain its complexity and uniqueness. But by and large, historical treatments of Finland fit into these stereotypes, and consequently the U.S.-Finnish relationship was often interpreted in this light as well. However, now as historians look at the events since the end of World War II in a different light with the passing of the Cold War, more attention can likewise be focused on Finland, its place in European history, in the bipolar struggle between the U.S. and USSR, and in the evolution of American policy. Some scholars have already begun this process. John Lukacs in a 1992 article in *Foreign Affairs* took a post-Cold War look at Finlandization and argued that the outcome has "vindicated" Finland. He judged Finland's solution to its relationship with the Soviet Union as appropriate and successful and derided the image of Finlandization as "nonsense." Further, he emphasized the uniqueness of the Finnish situation and argued that Finland's solution could not be viewed as a precedent for other nations. [2]

The articles in this volume follow in this vein. They attempt to give equal weight to Finland and the Finnish situation as well as the Cold War and the role of the United States. The goal is to shed new light on Finland's place in the Cold War and in American foreign policy. A lot of attention has been focused on the unique relationship Finland crafted with the USSR, but the seemingly atypical relationship that developed with the United States has largely been overlooked. The authors interpret events by drawing on Finnish—and in one case Swedish—history as well as international relations and U.S. foreign policy to explain the situation.

Keith W. Olson begins with an historiographical overview of how American historians have neglected Finland. In "American Historians and the History of Finland since 1939," he traces how historians have treated and more often failed to treat Finland's struggle with the USSR during the Winter War, World War II, and the Cold War. The two earlier conflicts certainly add to the historical understanding of Finland's situation in the Cold War. He detects a lack of serious consideration for the Finnish experience and in part attributes this to an ubiquitous shortcoming of historians of foreign relations. "Unlike social historians who have neglected centers to concentrate on marginalized groups," Olson contends, "historians of foreign relations have done just the

---

[2] John Lukacs, "Finland Vindicated," *Foreign Affairs* 71 (Fall 1992): 50-63.

opposite. The profession has devoted insufficient attention to small nations on the periphery of the two superpowers during the Cold War."

Finland to Olson clearly illustrates this failure. Olson argues that serious consideration of the Finnish case would add insight and perhaps even lead to a modification of generalizations of past historical understandings about the Cold War struggle. One example, Olson suggests, is that closer scrutiny of the Winter War might provide a more appropriate paradigm for analyzing Stalin and the USSR than the more common analogy of the Munich Conference. The Winter War demonstrated that Stalin respected and responded to military power.

In contrast to the traditional tendency to place postwar events mainly in a geopolitical context, George Maude's "The Cold War as an Episode in Finnish History" explains the Finno-Soviet relationship in terms of Finnish history and politics. To him, the relationship coincided with Finland's responses to outside forces dating back to the beginning of the twentieth century and earlier. Traditional Finnish ruling elites, in the person of the president, tended to form a modus vivendi with foreign executives, powerful foreign states like Russia, which persistently seemed to be on Finland's border. He calls this situation a "quasi-constitutionalism of international relations." "While the Finnish people have sometimes been stirred up by foreign events and ideas," he concludes, "in the end, it is the elite, through the traditional domestic executive, that deals with the foreigner, in the name of a defense of democracy, more particularly parliamentary democracy." In turn, this modus vivendi facilitated the elites' efforts to keep down the left.

This tendency had long-ranging effects, all of which were reflected in Finland's Cold War international relations. Politics became personalized around the presidency. Juho K. Paasikivi and Urho K. Kekkonen manipulated to preserve Finland's independence. They, not parliament, controlled relations with the foreign executive. Consensus became "if not the goal, the catch-word and modus vivendi of the system in the second half of the Cold War." This, to Maude, made understandable the "consensual work" Finland engaged in during the 1970s with such initiatives as the Conference for Security and Cooperation in Europe.

Whereas Maude examines the origins of the so-called "Finnish Solution" in the context of Finnish history and politics, R. Michael Berry studies it from the standpoint of World War II diplomacy. In "The Ideology and Politics of Midwifery in American-Finnish Relations," he maintains that to understand what transpired in the Cold War one must "read history forward through the prism of American ideological preferences for a multilateral world." Prior to World War II, American policymakers advocated an informal international order based on principles of political and economic liberalism and saw the USSR as the enemy to this order. During the war, however, American policy shifted to Soviet-American cooperation. Furthermore, there were competing strategies advocated by the allies. The Anglo-Soviet preference for spheres of influence contrasted with the U.S. preference for an open, multilateral world order.

As for Finland, the U.S. was preoccupied with the postwar era. In 1943-44, Washington formulated a policy as if the U.S. was above spheres of influence and hoped to come to terms with the USSR through postwar United Nations cooperation that would lend itself to a multilateral world order. As policymakers shifted from a paradigm of Soviet-American conflict to one of Soviet-American cooperation, Finland's fate was caught up in the effort to achieve a balance between Soviet security requirements and Finnish self-determination. On the eve of the Yalta Conference, the U.S. and USSR shared a common concept of democratic and friendly neighbors in the case of Finland. At least, Berry argues, the convergence of perceptions outweighed the divergence. It was by its own initiative that Finland survived the war, Berry declares, and postwar Finland carried its own weight. The U.S. conceded Finland to the Soviet sphere, but remained on the sidelines, like a midwife, pursuing a policy supportive of Finland within the context of UN cooperation.

Jussi M. Hanhimäki, in "We Are Not Czechs," moves the analysis of Finland's Cold War position forward to the time of the all important Treaty of Friendship, Cooperation, and Mutual Assistance (FCMA) negotiated by Paasikivi in 1948. He points out that this treaty had an impact on the whole outlook of the Cold War. From the Finnish perspective, Paasikivi succeeded in manipulating the agreement so that to a large extent it included most of what the Finns wanted. Nevertheless, the U.S. response was ambivalent, in part because it did not conform to the view of Soviet intentions that had become the basis of the containment policy, a view that was particularly prevalent in American politics at the time.

The American perspective on the FCMA treaty was colored by the fact that it was negotiated in the wake of the 1948 Czech coup, leading to the assumption that Finland might face the same fate as Czechoslovakia. But, as Hanhimäki asserts, there were clear differences between the

Czech and Finnish situations. Unfortunately for Americans who preached distrust of the Soviet Union, the Finns were not Czechs. Nor were they Yugoslavs, another scenario for relationships with the USSR that offered an opportunity to combat Soviet expansionism and control of Eastern Europe. American policymakers approached Finland flexibly, often revising their strategies to meet the challenges posed by Finland's unique circumstances. At the root of it all, however, was the American determination to contain the Soviet Union. Hanhimäki laments the fact that these policymakers failed to seriously consider that the Finnish solution might have represented a shift in Soviet policy.

In "If Finland Weren't Finland, Would Sweden Be Finland?" Charles Silva examines the "Finland argument" used by Swedish diplomats and politicians to justify Sweden's adherence to neutrality. This argument that Sweden's continued neutrality would insure continued Soviet mild treatment of Finland and assure Finland's continued independence had a significant influence on Finland's relations with its neighbors in the Nordic region and was an important factor in the deliberations of American policymakers at the time. In a detailed analysis of Sweden's domestic and foreign policies, Silva exposes how this argument related to the Finnish situation and affected Sweden's relations with the two superpowers. He concludes that the evidence suggests that the argument was largely rhetorical, aimed at avoiding heated debate over foreign policy at home and winning support for Sweden's nonalignment in the West.

The Finnish argument became particularly pertinent to U.S.-Swedish relations during discussions leading to the North Atlantic Treaty. Sweden used it to justify its refusal to join this alliance. Silva identifies evidence that Washington's attitude toward Sweden had shifted in a positive way by 1951-52, but contends that the Finnish argument was not a significant factor in this shift.

T. Michael Ruddy carries the discussion into the 1950s. In "The Road to Nowhere," he places Finland within overall U.S. policy formulation for Europe in the critical decade and a half after the end of World War II. Starting from the premise that Finland was not a priority and that, at any rate, little could be done to alter Finland's position vis-à-vis the USSR, American policymakers constructed a realistic and mutually beneficial relationship. This relationship was largely determined by Helsinki, which measured its every move according to how it would affect the delicate balance with its Soviet neighbor. The U.S. respected this.

But, according to Ruddy, the evolution of this relationship cannot be explained in isolation from America's geopolitical interests. As Washington refined its policies toward Finland, officials realized that Finland fit into America's plans and goals for Europe. Through the Nordic Balance, Finland contributed to Western Europe's collective security by assuring a stable and peaceful northern flank. Although it was a slow process, Finland ultimately became a participant in the European economic and political integration that reinforced collective security. And as a bonus, Finland's continued independence proved a diplomatic advantage for the U.S. in its rivalry with the USSR. As Ruddy argues, this relationship began to take root during the Truman years and matured during Eisenhower's tenure in office. The policy in place in 1961 contained the essential elements that would guide the U.S.-Finnish relationship to the end of the Cold War.

Robert W. Matson's "Finlandization: A Retrospective" concludes this volume with an evaluation of Finland's Cold War experience from the perspective of the 1990s. He suggests that the Finno-Soviet relationship represented one of the few instances where Franklin D. Roosevelt's World War II vision for postwar Europe actually emerged. That being said, Matson discusses two contrasting interpretations of Finland's experience.

The first, that the Paasikivi-Kekkonen Line was a success, was understandably the view of virtually all Finns. Paasikivi in shaping Finland's relationship with the USSR was responding more to his own analysis of the international situation than to Soviet pressure. Kekkonen adopted Paasikivi's successful policy and with his propensity to activism took Finland more fully into the international community. The line these two presidents adopted represented successful coexistence.

The second contrasting interpretation was the Finlandization charge that became particularly prevalent during the 1970s. Matson maintains that Finlandization was less about Finland itself and more a critique of American and European leaders who employed détente as a realistic means to deal with the Soviet Union. The fact that Kekkonen had a role in the emergence of détente—Matson describes a convergence between Kekkonen's long held goals and Richard Nixon's foreign policy—led critics to use Finlandization to challenge contemporary policy trends. Matson questions whether Finnish sovereignty was reduced by this alleged Finlandization any further than the constraints of geography and history dictated. "The implication that a sinister process was under way," he contends, "rested on ethnocentric and ahistorical commentary."

Some common threads run through all of these studies. Although one can easily argue that every nation's circumstances are unique, clearly the Finnish situation was more unique than others. Building upon its distinct position, Finland to a remarkable degree exercised its independence and shaped its own foreign policy, a policy that pragmatically adapted to the situation it occupied. The course Helsinki pursued was not without precedent in Finnish history and tradition. And now, from the perspective of the post-Cold War era, one can say it succeeded.

As for the United States, circumstances largely dictated the realistic, consistent relationship that transpired. On the one hand, as would be expected, the exigencies of the Cold War played a large role in determining Washington's position. And Finland certainly served a purpose in this Cold War rivalry. On the other hand, as in the case of some of the other European neutrals, the relationship that the U.S. devised transcended the traditional Cold War framework. Finland may have been a low priority for American policymakers, but Finland was not absent from American plans. Furthermore, as the case of Finland illustrates, U.S. policy was far more complex and diverse than previously recognized.

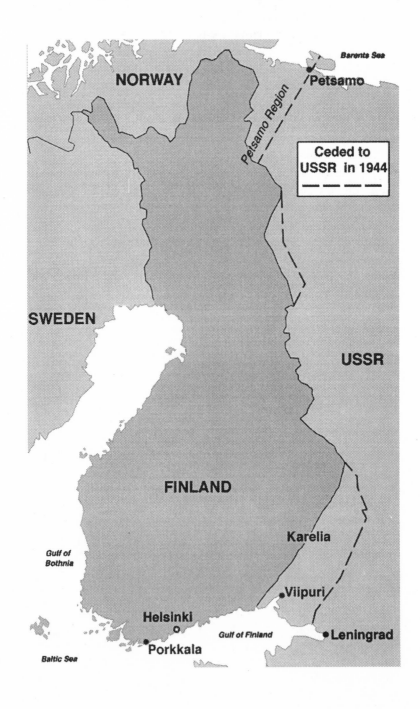

1

American Historians and the History of Finland Since 1939

Keith W. Olson

The American historical profession has paid scant attention to Finnish history. Not a single member of the American Historical Association lists Finland as a primary interest. Of the more than seventeen hundred members of the Society for Historians of American Foreign Relations (SHAFR), only two have fundamental interests in the history of Finnish-United States relations. One teaches in the United Kingdom and both list their current research as Nordic, not Finnish.

American historians, of course, cannot research, write, and teach about all countries and all societies throughout all ages. Traditionally American historians have devoted most of their attention to the history of European nations and the origins of the religious, political, legal, and societal institutions that form the bedrock in the development of the United States. By American standards Finland is a small country with a tiny population located in perhaps Europe's most remote corner.

Finland, contrary to its size and location, however, merits attention because its experiences, conditions, and institutions offer insights into the broader sphere of the history of the western world. Of universal value is an understanding of Finland as a border between East and West, religiously, culturally, economically, and politically. Integral to Finnish history, moreover, is the accommodation of two languages within one country. One of the languages, closely associated with class and region, is the home language of less than ten percent of Finns. In its treatment of its Swedish linguistic minority and its Eastern Orthodox religious minority of less than two percent of the population Finland sets a model for the western world. Finland also has importance as one of the five Nordic countries that together have developed the world's most successful regional cooperation and integration. Finnish history links to Scandinavia and the western world and affords opportunity for a trans-national approach to the study of history. Despite the potential benefit of studying Finnish history, American history departments rarely include historians with that interest.

During the mid-1940s, three developments stimulated an unprecedented American interest in Finland's giant neighbor, the Union of Soviet Socialist Republics (USSR). First, at the end of World War II the United States basked in its new status as the world's preeminent industrial, economic, military, and scientific power with the appealing political ideology of democracy and individual rights. Paralleling the United States' rise to preeminence was the rise of the USSR to the status as the world's second power, although a distant second. The new status of these two countries resulted in a third development, a Cold War.

For the past five decades the United States has committed massive research, publication, and symposium resources to the attempt to understand the Soviet Union, the Cold War, and the legacy of the Cold War. Scholars in universities, research institutes, and elsewhere might have gained additional insights had they examined the relationship between the Soviet Union and its neighbor nearest to Leningrad and Moscow. This relationship included a common border 789 miles long, two wars between 1939 and 1944, "The Treaty (in 1948) of Friendship, Cooperation, and Mutual Assistance between the Republic of Finland and the Union of Soviet Socialist Republics," and a Finnish policy of neutrality during the Cold War. During the latter decades of the Cold War the Soviet Kola Peninsula, adjacent to Finland's northeast border, gained in importance with the development of ballistic missile submarines and the expansion of the Soviet navy. In December 1982, American Secretary of the Navy John E. Lehman, Jr., categorized the Kola Peninsula as "the most valuable piece of real estate on earth."[1] Three years later Norwegian State Secretary Tøbjorn Frøysnes of the Ministry of Foreign Affairs reminded his audience in Washington, D.C., that the Kola Peninsula served "as the base for two thirds of Soviet ballistic missile

---

[1] *Washington Post*, 29 December 1982, A1.

submarines, most long-range radars for detection of western strategic retaliatory forces."[2]

Finland's relationship to the Soviet Union offered historians an inviting and potentially fruitful field of research. American historians who specialize in the World War II and Cold War periods, however, have not taken advantage of this opportunity. Examination of the Finnish-Soviet relationship during three wars illustrates this conclusion.

I

On the surface, a history of the Finnish-Soviet Winter War seems uncomplicated. On November 30, 1939, the Soviet Union unleashed its army, navy, and air force against Finland—a contest between a totalitarian nation of 180 million persons and a democratic country of 3.9 million inhabitants. After 105 days of winter combat, the uneven match ended with an armistice and with large Finnish concessions. As European wars go, the Finnish Winter War proved short in duration and straightforward in terms of settlement. Few international conflicts exhibit such clear-cut lines of innocence and guilt. In reality, every decision Finnish leaders made, from the spring of 1938 until the armistice of 1940, involved consideration of complex contemporary European conditions and assessment of wide historical patterns. In writing about the Winter War, therefore, historians face a complex, interesting, and important subject.

American historians have an easier assignment than their Finnish counterparts when writing about the impact of the war on their countries, but American historians, nevertheless, have differed among themselves in their conclusions. This is particularly true regarding the impact of the war on American isolationism, the subject of Robert Sobel's book, *The Origins of Interventionism: The United States and the Russo-Finnish War*. Sobel concludes that during the Winter War, "the basic positions of isolationist and internationalist were examined, attacked, found wanting and, to a degree, discarded." The war, he continues, "was an important milestone in the turn to interventionism."[3] When Sobel's book appeared, Selig Adler, the profession's senior authority on isolationism, disagreed. He believed

---

[2] *News of Norway* 42 (13 November 1985): 1.

[3] Robert Sobel, *The Origins of Interventionism: The United States and the Russo-Finnish War* (New York, 1960), 177, 183-4.

that Sobel was "prone to over simplification," that the realignment of isolationists and interventionists was "ephemeral," and that "the Finnish crisis was a prototype for future inaction."[4]

David L. Porter, who utilized "a case-study approach," in his *The Seventy-Sixth Congress and World War II, 1939-1940*, maintains that the Seventy-Sixth Congress "journeyed through isolationist, internationalist, interventionist, and preparedness stages and enacted three major measures."[5] The Winter War, he concludes, caused the congressional shift from the internationalist to the interventionist stage and accounted for The Brown Act, the second of the "three major measures." Porter highlights The Brown Act of 1940, which extended to Finland a twenty million dollar credit for the purchase of non-military supplies, as "the first time the Seventy-sixth Congress authorized a federal agency to intervene directly in a specific European conflict to aid a particular democratic country."[6] Although careful in his research and presentation, Porter places too much symbolic importance on The Brown Act. In 1983, when Wayne S. Cole published his definitive study, *Roosevelt and The Isolationists, 1932-1945*, based on research in more than 100 manuscript collections, he made no mention of The Brown Act and no mention of an impact of the Finnish Winter War on American isolationism.[7]

In his solid study, *America and the Winter War, 1939-1940*, Travis Beal Jacobs lends support to the conclusion that the Winter War provided Roosevelt "with an opportunity to gain support throughout the country and weaken the forces of isolationism." Jacobs believes Roosevelt could have done more. To close his book, he writes that had the United States really aided "the victims of aggression during the Winter War, even though it would not have altered the outcome of the Russo-Finnish conflict, [it] might have had a profound impact on the World War."[8] Both Jacobs and Porter offer detailed narratives

---

[4] *American Historical Review* 66 (July 1961): 1086.

[5] David L. Porter, *The Seventy-Sixth Congress and World War II, 1939-1940* (Columbia, MO, 1979), 185.

[6] Ibid., 174.

[7] Wayne S. Cole, *Roosevelt and the Isolationists, 1932-1945* (Lincoln, NB, 1983).

[8] Travis Beal Jacobs, *America and the Winter War, 1939-1940* (New York, 1981), 238. Andrew J. Schwartz, *America and the Russo-Finnish War* (Westport, CN, 1975), reprint of (Washington, 1960), has 92 pages of text of which only 19 cover the

regarding the complexity of the formulation of United States foreign policy during the early years of World War II.

The Winter War placed conservatives, liberals, isolationists, and interventionists in a dilemma. Conservatives and isolationists leaned toward aid because of their anti-Soviet feelings and their respect for Finland as a democracy and as the only country that paid its World War I era debt. To support aid, however, meant cooperation with President Franklin D. Roosevelt whom they disliked and distrusted. They feared he later would use a Finnish precedent to aid France and Britain, then engaged in a "phony war" with Germany. Liberals and interventionists, on the other hand, feared that providing aid to Finland would detract from possible future aid to France and Britain, their major foreign policy priority.

Historians who have examined American public opinion present an almost united front regarding their sympathies toward Finland. Ralph B. Levering, in *American Public Opinion and the Russian Alliance, 1939-1945*, concludes that "except for the Daily Worker, probably every newspaper in America denounced Russia's attack."[9] Jacobs finds that "the religious press unanimously condemned the USSR," and that "nearly everyone on Capitol Hill expressed pro-Finnish or anti-Soviet sentiments."[10] In his poll of December 14 to 19, 1939, George Gallup found that 88% of Americans sympathized with Finland while only 1% sympathized with the Soviet Union, with 11% neutral or with no opinion.[11]

The only person who could have transformed such exceptional sentiments into aid for Finland was Roosevelt. Porter, for example, concludes that "in retrospect, Congress probably would have complied if Roosevelt had publicly supported direct American military assistance to Finland."[12] Historians who have analyzed his actions offer different emphases. In their authoritative study, *The Challenge to Isolation, 1937-1940*, William L. Langer and S. Everett

---

chapter "The U.S. and the Winter War." Schwartz's book did not add to the existing knowledge at the time of its publication.

[9] Ralph B. Levering, *American Public Opinion and the Russian Alliance, 1939-1945* (Chapel Hill, NC, 1976), 32.

[10] Jacobs, *America and the Winter War,* 73.

[11] George H. Gallup, *The Gallup Poll: Public Opinion, 1935-1941* (New York, 1972), 197.

[12] Porter, *The Seventy-Sixth Congress,* 176; see also 126.

Gleason label Roosevelt's record "unimpressive" regarding aid to Finland.[13]

Robert Dallek, in his comprehensive study, *Franklin D. Roosevelt and American Foreign Policy, 1932-1945*, views Roosevelt's performance more favorably. Dallek plays down the strength of public sympathy for Finland and interprets in a favorable light Roosevelt's refusal to provide strong leadership in the movement to aid Finland. Roosevelt, Dallek points out, was "reluctant to do anything that would drive Moscow into closer cooperation with Berlin" and "believed that pressure for a large armaments loan would revive charges that he intended to offer guarded assistance to Britain and France, and would weaken his chances for reelection in 1940, if he decided to run again."[14] Dallek and Langer and Gleason wrote detailed volumes that included relatively few pages (seven and thirty-seven) on Roosevelt and the Winter War.

Jacobs, on the other hand, devoted his entire, well-researched book to the United States and the Winter War. Although even-handed in his judgments, his conclusions question Roosevelt's leadership. In his "Preface," Jacobs notes that presidential speech writer "Robert Sherwood described the autumn and winter of 1939-1940...as the 'one crisis in Roosevelt's career when he was completely at a loss as to what action to take.'" The Winter War illustrates Sherwood's point. Jacobs concludes that Roosevelt just "did not deem Finnish aid sufficiently necessary to exert the influence of the executive branch in Congress." Jacobs reasons that "a demonstration of America's willingness to aid positively the victims of aggression during the Winter War, even though it would not have altered the outcome of the Russo-Finnish conflict, might have had a profound impact on the World War."[15]

By focusing initially on Sherwood's analysis of Roosevelt, Jacobs raises a question that Roosevelt's biographers need to examine in greater detail. Did Roosevelt's "loss as to what action to take" affect his thinking, understanding, and actions in other areas? Dallek, unlike Sherwood, Jacobs, and Langer and Gleason, saw a masterful Roosevelt

---

[13] William E. Langer and S. Everett Gleason, *The Challenge to Isolation, 1937-1940* (New York, 1952), 340.

[14] Robert Dallek, *Franklin D. Roosevelt and American Foreign Policy, 1932-1945* (New York, 1979), 209-10.

[15] Jacobs, *America and the WinterWar*, x, 234, 238.

in full command and aware of the nuances of domestic and world conditions. All historians agree, however, that Roosevelt recognized he faced limits when formulating his foreign policies.

James MacGregor Burns, in his prize-winning, two-volume biography of Roosevelt, does not analyze precisely the president's control over foreign affairs during the winter of 1939-1940. Burns does suggest, however, that Roosevelt "must have felt keenly the hopeless inadequacy of United States aid to the little nation—inadequacy stemming from Hull's caution and from Roosevelt's fear of American isolationists." Other than this sparse assessment, Burns does not consider Roosevelt's leadership in the attempt to aid Finland. Regarding Roosevelt's attitude toward the Soviet Union, Burns paints a picture of Roosevelt more hostile to the Soviet Union than Dallek's portrait. Although the Winter War ended in March 1940, Roosevelt maintained throughout 1940 the "moral embargo" he had proclaimed when the Soviet Union launched its invasion. Burns characterizes United States relations with the Soviet Union throughout 1940 as "remote and unfriendly."[16] Only in January 1941 did Roosevelt lift the embargo as part of an "eleventh hour...counter-coalition to stop the surging Nazis."[17]

The American historian who has written the most sophisticated study of Finnish-American relations is Michael Berry, who lives and teaches in Finland. His book, *American Foreign Policy and the Finnish Exception: Ideological Preferences and Wartime Realities*, is more than a narrative of American-Finnish relations; it also "introduces a conceptual approach to the examination of American policy toward Finland" and "includes an overview of the dominant prewar ideological preferences in both countries." More than any other historian, Berry stresses the importance of Finnish images in the United States, "not just because they are related to Finland but also because they are associated with important American values and assumptions about how the world should be organized and states should act." Berry places the Winter War in the larger flow of United States history. He points out, for example, that immediately after the war the Treasury Department and the Department of State both drafted plans to help rebuild the Finnish economy, "a prototype

---

[16] James MacGregor Burns, *Roosevelt: The Lion and the Fox* (New York, 1956), 415.

[17] Burns, *Roosevelt: The Soldier of Freedom, 1940-1945* (New York, 1970), 94.

'Marshall Plan' in 1940."[18] Berry devotes the heart of his book to the period of Finland's Continuation War, but his explorations into the roots of the Finnish-American relations during 1941-1944, offer a framework that yields new insights in understanding America and the Winter War.

Whatever the degree of their differences regarding isolationism, public opinion, and President Roosevelt, all American historians of the Winter War brand the Soviet Union as the aggressor and conclude that America easily perceived the meaning of the conflict. Politicians, journalists, and others who employ analogies and draw lessons from the past have a clear corpus of publications to consult when considering the Winter War. Few such persons have done so despite the vivid image of a valiant Finland fighting an expansionistic Soviet Union. "Finland was the epitomization of everything that the Americans admired—independent, a republic based on free elections, frugal, businesslike, upstanding, and moral," historian Edward M. Bennett concluded in his study, *Franklin D. Roosevelt and the Search for Security: American-Soviet Relations, 1933-1939.*[19] The reason that the post-World War II generation failed to use this vivid epitomization stemmed from the next phase of Finnish-Soviet relations, the Continuation War of 1941-1944.

II

The armistice that ended the Winter War brought Finland little sense of security. Four months after the fighting stopped, Moscow accepted the "requests" of Estonia, Latvia, and Lithuania to become constituent republics within the Soviet Union. The increased Soviet military presence north of Leningrad added to the Finn's long-standing fear of the Russians. With Germany occupying much of Europe, especially the south shore of the Baltic Sea and Norway, Finland was isolated between two giant, totalitarian powers. Traditionally Finland, as well as Sweden, looked to Germany to counterbalance the threat from Russia. If the Soviets invaded again, Finland's only hope lay with Germany, not the western powers. When Germany secretly indicated an interest to talk with Finnish leaders,

---

[18] R. Michael Berry, *American Foreign Policy and The Finnish Exception: Ideological Preferences and Wartime Realities* (Helsinki, 1987), 9, 35, 83.

[19] Edward M. Bennett, *Franklin D. Roosevelt and the Search for Security: American Soviet Relations, 1933-1939* (Wilmington, 1985), 183.

they listened. In December 1940, German and Finnish military officers started planning joint operations against the Soviet Union.

On June 22, 1941, Hitler hurled his surprise attack, Operation Barbarossa, against the Soviet Union. Three days later the Finnish army launched its own campaign against the Soviets. Although Germany and Finland coordinated their military moves they never became allies; instead, they remained cobelligerents, two countries fighting a common enemy. Unlike Germany, Finland had limited war objectives, to regain the territory lost during the Winter War and to occupy sound defensive positions. To Germany's annoyance, Finland refused to lend support to break the American supply line that ran south from Murmansk or to break the siege of Leningrad. When the military balance shifted from Germany's to the Soviet Union's advantage, Finland sought to extricate itself. An armistice with the Soviet Union in September accomplished this, but with one provision calling for Finland to drive the German divisions from northern Finland. From September 20, 1994, to April 24, 1945, therefore, Finland fought yet another war. As the Germans retreated northward to cross into Norway they left a scorched earth as they moved. The harsh armistice terms included heavy war reparations to the Soviets.

The Finnish Continuation War presented problems for President Roosevelt. At Stalin's insistence, the United Kingdom declared war on Finland in December 1941. In June 1944 the United States broke diplomatic relations with Finland. Roosevelt remained sympathetic to valiant Finland, but also wanted to maintain cordial relations with the Soviet Union. At the Teheran Conference in November 1943 Roosevelt and Churchill both urged Stalin to offer Finland lenient terms to end its war.

The Finnish Continuation War attracted little attention in the United States. Most Americans seemed unaware that Finland fought first the Soviet Union and then Germany. Placed in the context of the magnitude of World War II, this lack of awareness was understandable.

For this same reason American historians likewise have failed to include the Continuation War in their treatment of Roosevelt and World War II. Neither Burns, Cole, Dallek, Frank Freidel, nor Warren F. Kimball mention the Continuation War in their well-received studies of Roosevelt. Even specialized studies touch only briefly on the subject. Gabriel Kolko in his *The Politics of War: The World and United States Foreign Policy, 1943-1945*, for example, devotes slightly more than a page to Finland during World War II.[20] The most valuable American discussion of the Continuation War relates to the policy of unconditional surrender. In his book, *Diplomacy for Victory: FDR and Unconditional Surrender*, Raymond G. O'Connor explains how and why Finland, although at war with both the United Kingdom and the Soviet Union proved an exception to this policy.[21] First enunciated in January 1943 by Roosevelt at the Casablanca Conference, the policy continues as a subject of debate among historians. This is especially true about the surrender of Japan in August 1945. Even so, the Finnish exception to the policy of unconditional surrender concerned a small nation, geographically remote, of little military or political importance except to Finland itself and, indirectly, to Sweden. After the great power leaders reaffirmed the policy at the Yalta Conference in February 1945 and the Potsdam Conference in July 1945, historians apparently find the Finnish exception not relevant. When he discusses the Japanese surrender in his impressive biography of Harry S. Truman, Alonzo B. Hamby, for example, fails to the mention the Finnish exception, even in a footnote.[22]

Roosevelt, and his successor Truman during the closing months of the war, portrayed World War II as a struggle between the moral forces of right and wrong. On January 6, 1942, in his first wartime State of the Union address, Roosevelt concluded that "no compromise can end that conflict. There never has been—there never can be—successful compromise between good and evil. Only total victory can reward the champion of tolerance, and decency, and freedom, and faith." The policy of unconditional surrender, which Roosevelt announced a year later, should have surprised no one. In a world of such stark contrasts, there were only two sides. As historian Robert Sobel noted, "The wave of pro-Finnish sentiment which had engulfed the nation during the winter of 1939-1940 was forgotten by 1944, as was much of the anti-Soviet sentiment of that period."[23] Finland's

---

[20] Gabriel Kolko, *The Politics of War: The World and United States Foreign Policy, 1943-1945* (New York, 1968), 138-9.

[21] Raymond G. O'Connor, *Diplomacy for Victory: FDR and Unconditional Surrender* (New York, 1971), 61-2.

[22] Alonzo B. Hamby, *Man of the People: A Life of Harry S. Truman* (New York, 1995).

[23] Sobel, *The Origins of Interventionism*, 173.

participation in World War II did not fit the one-dimensional interpretation of that conflict that the United States leaders, media, and press presented at the time. In their work historians should explain complexity.

III

Finnish-Soviet relations during the Cold War became increasingly stable to the long-term advantage of both countries. Thanks to three leaders—Carl Gustaf Emil Mannerheim, Juho K. Paasikivi, and Urho K. Kekkonen—who held the Finnish presidency from 1944 to 1981, Finland recovered from a devastating war and harsh armistice terms to enjoy friendly relations with its giant eastern neighbor; a western market economy; a Protestant national church; and a constitutional, democratic political system. Finnish presidents proved singularly successful in satisfying "Finland's desire to remain outside the conflicting interests of the Great Powers," as stated in the preamble of "The Treaty of Friendship, Cooperation, and Mutual Assistance between the Republic of Finland and the Union of Soviet Socialist Republics," signed in April 1948. Like any two countries with differing cultures, political systems, and values, the Finnish-Soviet relationship evolved and changed during the decades of the Cold War. An examination of this relationship offers a unique opportunity to understand Soviet Cold War history.

The American literature on the Cold War is immense, but strikingly thin on the Finnish-Soviet relationship. The title *Silk Glove Hegemony: Finnish-Soviet Relations, 1944-1974,* by John P. Vloyantes, promises more than Vloyantes intended and more than the book delivers. In his preface Vloyantes states that "this study of three decades of Finno-Soviet relations was undertaken for the purpose of employing, testing, and refining the soft sphere model." Vloyantes does not read Finnish or Russian and never meant to write a historical description of events.[24]

Books in Finnish, of course, are available, but also some excellent studies are available in English by non-Americans, including Max Jakobson, *Finnish Neutrality: A Study of Finnish Foreign Policy Since the Second World War*; George Maude, *The Finnish Dilemma: Neutrality in the Shadow of a Power*; Tuomo Polvinen, *Between East*

---

[24] John P. Vloyantes, *Silk Glove Hegemony: Finnish-Soviet Relations, 1944-1974* (Kent, Ohio, 1975), viii-ix.

and West: Finland in International Politics, 1944-1947; Roy Allison, *Finland's Relations With The Soviet Union, 1944-84;* and David Kirby, *Finland in the Twentieth Century: A History and an Interpretation.*[25] Important aspects of Finnish Cold War history have appeared in various issues of *Cooperation and Conflict* and *Yearbook of Finnish Foreign Policy.*

A discerning American historian with no knowledge of Finnish, therefore, would be able to obtain adequate knowledge to add insights and nuances to any study of the Cold War contest between the United States and the Soviet Union, perhaps even sufficient information to modify generalizations. This has not been the case. Two of the profession's finest scholars, Walter LaFeber and Stephen Ambrose, have written two exceptionally successful surveys of foreign relations.[26] Originally published in 1967, LaFeber's *America, Russia, and the Cold War, 1945-1992* appeared in its seventh edition in 1993 and contains only one meaningful reference to Finland. He wrote that in the time context of mid-1945 "Stalin agreed to an independent, non-communist regime in Finland if the Finns would follow a foreign policy friendly to Russia. An 'iron fence' by no means encircled all of Eastern Europe. There was still room to bargain if each side wished to avoid a confrontation over the remaining areas." Despite the implication of Stalin's position for the course of the Cold War, LaFeber never returns to this point. In 1971 Ambrose published his *Rise to Globalism: American Foreign Policy Since 1938*; twenty years later the sixth edition appeared. He made no mention of Finland.

The failure to incorporate the Finnish-Soviet relationship and the character of Finnish institutions and the scarcity of related specialized studies reflect limitations within the American historical profession. Unlike social historians who have neglected centers to concentrate on marginalized groups, historians of foreign relations have done just the opposite. The profession has devoted insufficient attention to small

---

[25] Max Jacobson, *Finnish Neutrality: A Study of Finnish Foreign Policy Since the Second World War* (New York, 1968); George Maude, *The Finnish Dilemma: Neutrality in the Shadow of a Power* (London, 1976); Tuomo Polvinen, *Between East and West: Finland in International Politics, 1944-1947* (Minneapolis, 1986); Roy Allison, *Finland's Relations with the Soviet Union, 1944-84* (London. 1985); David Kirby, *Finland in the Twentieth Century: A History and an Interpretation* (Minneapolis, 1981).

[26] Walter LaFeber, *America, Russia, and the Cold War, 1945-1992*, 7th ed. (New York, 1993); Stephen Ambrose, *Rise to Globalism: American Foreign Policy Since 1938*, 6th ed. (New York, 1991).

nations on the periphery of the two superpowers during the Cold War. Finland is the prime example.

In other ways the profession has become narrower in its outlook. During the past three decades, department after department across the country has reduced or eliminated the two-language requirement once standard for graduate students in American history. Departments also have reduced requirements for a substantial body of work in a second department or a secondary, or minor, field of history. Increased enrollments have meant larger departments that, in turn, have permitted greater specialization. In large departments American historians often teach only one-half of the United States survey. Another type of narrowness manifests itself in hiring patterns. In 1986 the history department at the University of Maryland, for example, hired a senior professor of French history although the department of fifty already had four tenured historians with specialties in French history. At the time the department had no faculty with either a Scandinavian or Spanish specialty and only a handful of graduate students in French history. Tony Smith, in his influential book, *America's Mission: The United States and the Worldwide Struggle for Democracy in the Twentieth Century,* commented that Robert Dallek and John L. Gaddis, both former presidents of SHAFR and among the giants of the profession, "are examples of the American insularity they deplore."[27]

The historical profession is not solely responsible for its degree of narrowness. Lynn Eden, Senior Research Scholar, Center for International Security and Arms Control, Stanford University, has posed the question: "In the context of the Cold War, how did universities, foundations, and the government shape diplomatic history?...What were Cold War funding patterns? What kind of disciplinary work was encouraged, what was not, and why?"[28] The authors of *The Cold War and the University: Towards an Intellectual History* concluded that during the Cold War universities fostered a conservative agenda rather than championing intellectual freedom.[29]

---

[27] Tony Smith, *America's Mission: The United States and the Worldwide Struggle for Democracy in the Twentieth Century* (Princeton, NJ 1994), 354.

[28] Lynn Eden, "The End of U.S. Cold War History? A Review Essay," *International Security* 18 (Summer 1993): 205.

[29] See the review by Hanna Holborn Gray, president of the University of Chicago 1978-1993, in *Foreign Affairs* 76 (March/April 1997): 147.

IV

Though not an American, Jussi Hanhimäki earned his Ph.D. in American history at Boston University and as a graduate student taught at M.I.T. and Boston University. His book *Containing Coexistence: America, Russia, and the "Finnish Solution," 1945-1956* illustrates both the benefit of an international history approach to the study American of foreign relations and the contribution Finnish history can make in understanding United States history and the history of the Cold War. A native Finn who started language training early, Hanhimäki came to the United States on a one-year exchange program and stayed to earn his Ph.D. His teaching in the United States, a one-year appointment at Bishop's University in Quebec, Canada, a lecture series in Finland, and his current position in the department of international history at the London School of Economics, has enhanced his multinational perspective. His book and his current research on European neutrals in american foreign and security policy shows the benefit of such a perspective.

Hanhimäki's conclusions in many areas should interest American historians of the Cold War. He titled chapter one, for example, "Where Yalta Worked," and points out that Finland maintained a democratic government, which Roosevelt and the British Prime Minister Winston Churchill wanted, and a government "friendly" toward the Soviet Union, which Stalin had demanded. Of particular interest is Hanhimäki's assessment of United States foreign policy toward Finland: a "generally cautious policy conducted throughout the postwar period." Elsewhere he adds, "By keeping quiet the United States made it much easier for the Finns to perfect their efforts at reducing tensions in Northern Europe, maintaining good relations with the Soviet Union, and polishing their neutral posture in a divided world." On the broad European scene, he concludes that "Northern Europe was the most conflict-free area in Europe throughout the Cold War. The Finnish solution...was one of the deciding factors behind such a peaceful arrangement at a time of high international tension." To understand the Cold War and the Soviet Union American historians must consider the Scandinavian subsystem and especially its eastern most member, Finland.[30] In a review of Hanhimäki's book,

---

[30] Jussi M. Hanhimäki, *Containing Coexistence: America, Russia, and the "Finnish Solution," 1945-1956* (Kent, OH, 1997), 198, 205-6. Hanhimäki, "The First Line of Defense or a Springboard for Disintegration? European Neutrals in American Foreign and Security Policy," *Diplomacy and Statecraft* 7 (1996): 378-403.

Harvard University professor of international history Akira Iriye recognizes the importance of the book's depiction of Moscow and Washington "as having been more pragmatic than ideological." He evaluates Hanhimäki's book as "a landmark in the historiography of the cold war."

With the disintegration of the Soviet Union and the opening of some of its archives, as well as some Chinese archives, American historians face the challenge of reexamining the history of the Cold War. That disintegration, the new sources, the reunification of Germany, and the new status of the Eastern European countries means modification of perspectives and approaches to research. Multiarchival research will be common; historians appointed to teach foreign relations will have to command at least one foreign language. Historiographical controversies over the Cold War will continue and intensify. With the above changes and the passage of time, historians will reexamine World War II and the Cold War in a broader time span. After all, between 1939 and 1949 Americans and their government switched their feelings from hostility toward Germany to friendship and from hostility to friendship to renewed hostility toward the Soviet Union. Japan, too, went from enemy to friend. Historians already are researching United States support of totalitarian nations as part of the Cold War containment of communism.

In a more open intellectual climate perhaps historians will integrate the experiences of small European nations into the broader framework of World War II and the Cold War. Too often American historians of the Cold War era, consciously or subconsciously, have viewed the World War II years through the prism of the Cold War. This is especially true for historians who repeatedly have used the September 1938 Munich Conference and the subsequent German take-over of Czechoslovakia as the prime symbol illustrating the failure of the policy of appeasement. The Munich Conference and the later German conquest of Czechoslovakia did incite American condemnation of Germany, but the reaction pales drastically compared to the magnitude and intensity of American condemnation of the Soviet Union's invasion of Finland. George Gallup took no survey to measure American attitude toward the German occupation of Czechoslovakia. During the Cold War with the Soviet Union as the enemy the example of the Finnish resistance during the Winter War would have provided a more appropriate symbol to illustrate that the Soviet Union understood and respected only military force. The examples of Estonia, Latvia, and Lithuania offered the symbol of self-inflicted appeasement and subsequent Soviet take-over. Nevertheless, American historians did not utilize the Finnish experience and the Baltic states example to illustrate the nature of Soviet expansion.

Finland's participation in three wars since 1939 directly influenced United States foreign policy. For the early Cold War years, Hanhimäki's book demonstrates the rich potential of a study of Finnish-United States relations as does Michael Berry's book of the World War II years. No comparable study exists for the Winter War period. The works of Berry, the American who had taught in Finland a decade before he published his book, and Hanhimäki, the Finn with an American Ph.D. and broad professional experience, have provided excellent examples of the type of studies American historians need to conduct.

2

The Cold War as an Episode in Finnish History

George Maude

I

What is Finnish history? Listen to this. In 1906, in a public meeting in Seinäjoki in Ostrobothnia, a teacher named Väinö Kivilinna delivered, to the applause of all present, a speech against "the common enemy." Since Finland, an autonomous Grand Duchy of the Russian Empire, had by that time endured several years of direct assault by Russian tsarism upon its constitutional, legal and other institutional structures, an outside historical observer might be tempted to assume that Kivilinna's "common enemy" was, in fact, Russia. But Kivilinna was not referring to Russia at all. In castigating a "foreign-minded and foreign-language speaking upper class" of bureaucrats and financiers, he did not mean the ruling circles of St. Petersburg. He meant the Swedish-speaking upper class of Finland and a number of Finnish-speaking hangers-on.[1]

The venue to which Kivilinna brought his contribution was a rallying point for the formation of an agrarian party in the forthcoming elections for the new unicameral legislature, based on a truly universal franchise of one citizen (including women), one vote. This startling reform, sweeping away the old Diet of Four Estates, was a product of the disorders of the previous year, especially of the Great Strike of November 1905. But these disorders, in their turn, had followed in the wake of the Russian Revolution of that same year, precipitated by the near collapse of the Russian state in the Russo-Japanese War. Kivilinna's bold words about his own society were thus

---

[1] Urho Kittilä, "Huomioita maalaisliiton synty—ja kehityshistoriasta," *Heräävä Maaseutu* (Porvoo, 1956), 6:30.

expressed in a milieu reflecting the diverse aspects of the impact of Russia on Finland. Russian pressure on Finnish autonomy had disturbed the established position of the upper class of the Grand Duchy and driven at least a section of this class to look for allies in the commonalty, a fact which encouraged the hitherto cowed elements among the latter to strike out on their own against the leadership of the Grand Duchy's establishment.[2] Russian pressure helped to release new political forces in Finland, which, with the right response—the reconstruction of the legislature that had now occurred—might still be constrained within a Finnish system of advanced constitutional democracy. In 1906 and 1907 Russia was in retreat and the Finns were afforded a breathing space to attempt to sort out their own social problems.

The constitutionalism assumed by Russia itself during these years was most fragile. Ominously, the general trend of the Russian impact on Finland, being an outcome of a desperate endeavor to renew a vast and atrociously inefficient empire, and producing revolution and counter-revolution in the process, imposed itself upon the minds of the Finnish upper class in terms of contrasting but equally threatening images, those of the chaos of revolution or its alternative, a powerful militarized state. In either scheme, so ran the fears of many responsible Finns, Finland would be lost. The traditional political-bureaucratic forces in Finland trembled between these two extremes. As matters were to turn out, however, the increasingly despised Russian state was still to perform one great service for the maintenance of the power of the Finnish upper class, though the effect of that service was a dubious one.

It is worth underlining at this point how much of Finnish political life, even independence, has been reactive. Historical forces of change have often been perceived as foreign and potentially destructive. Change came from the actions of alien states like Russia and when identified with Russia was viewed as a shift backward. Change resulting from the impact of the international *economic* system on Finland was imperceptible to the members of the Finnish ruling class

---

[2] In 1899 the socialist leadership in Finland was not considered important enough by bourgeois circles to be invited to join in the protest against Russian measures of unification. Yet by 1905 the socialist forces were so powerful as to compel the bourgeoisie to accord a unicameral legislature and universal franchise as a means of sidestepping the demand for a constituent assembly. The Agrarian Union, too, was born in 1906.

until pointed out by worried "agrarians" like Santeri Alkio or Hannes Gebhard,[3] or by the Social Democrats of the early twentieth century. The Finnish upper classes, like the European upper classes in general, saw capitalism as an *economic* "good" that should bring prosperity; only when new *political* forces emerged in the country was the traditional elite confused and, ultimately, alarmed.[4]

Finnish social democracy was revolutionary in tone. It is true that its inspiration came from Germany and Central Europe rather than Russia[5] and that even the Finnish social democratic leaders knew little of Lenin's writings before 1918.[6] Nonetheless the Finnish upper class and bourgeoisie were confronted in 1905 and 1906, and even more in 1917, with manifestations of fraternity between Finnish social democracy and Russian revolutionary forces, with most of the latter in military garb. Before the Russian Bolshevik Revolution of autumn 1917, the Finnish upper class and bourgeoisie were all too aware of a threat arising from a potential coalescence of Russian revolutionary forces and a discontented Finnish left.

Thus an external danger could turn into an internal one. The Finnish upper class and middle class had not wanted to be overwhelmed by a centralizing Russian state, but these classes had certainly no wish to be engulfed by a combination of Russian and Finnish revolutionary forces either. In July 1917, when the Finnish unicameral legislature passed an Enabling Act granting itself supreme power in internal affairs, the last minister state-secretary of Finland in St. Petersburg,[7] Carl Enckell, informed Alexander Kerensky, the newly appointed head of the Russian Provisional Government, of how

---

[3] On Santeri Alkio's attempt to find an alternative to both capitalism and socialism, see David Arter, *Bumpkin Against Bigwig* (Tampere, 1978), 57. Gebhard was never a member of the Agrarian Union, but his influence on it was great. For his antipathy to the dominance of the wood exporting firms and sawmill owners see Kittilä, "Huomioita mealaisliiton synty—ja kehityshistoriasta," 20.

[4] On the perplexity caused by the emergence of socialism for the traditional Fennoman movement, see Vesa Vares, *Konservatiivi ja murrosvuodet. Lauri Ingman ja hänen poliittinen toimintansa vuoteen 1922* (Helsinki, 1993), 85, 101-3, 108, 126, 151.

[5] Hannu Soikkanen, *Sosialismin tulo Suomeen* (Porvoo, 1961), 28, 101-12.

[6] Timo Vihavainen, "Suomalaisten arviot Leninistä," in *Lenin ja Suomi*, ed. Jaakko Numminen (Helsinki, 1990), 3:10.

[7] The minister state-secretary of Finland had traditionally presented Finnish matters for the consideration of the tsar and the office had been the symbol and practical component of Finnish autonomy.

much he disapproved of the legislature's action. It did not take long for Enckell, Kerensky, and the Russian governor-general in Finland, M.A. Stakhovitch, jointly to pressure the Finn's to dissolve this overly radical legislature.[8] If any one Finn may be said to have precipitated the subsequent civil war in Finland, by helping to fulfil lurking fears, it was Enckell.[9]

The largest single party in the Finnish legislature was the Social Democratic Party, which, despite its rhetoric of revolution, had a strong commitment to parliamentarism. This was natural enough. The party's Central European mentor, Karl Kautsky, had himself suggested that revolution might be accomplished through parliamentary means.[10] Here was the rub for the members of the Finnish upper class. The Social Democrats and their Agrarian allies, along with the few activists of the right who supported them,[11] would have brought Finland to the verge of independence by creating a new state in which the legislative organ would exercise executive powers, thus recalling the dreaded eighteenth-century Age of Liberty in Sweden, a country Finland had at the time been an integral part of.[12]

In justifying his action, Enckell later argued that, had he not helped secure the dissolution of parliament, Russian troops in Finland might have been used to destroy every trace of Finnish constitutionalism either at the behest of the Russian Provisional Government or through the machinations of the revolutionaries.[13] The core of his thinking remained the desire to preserve a fairly separate and powerful executive in Finland. For this purpose he was prepared to call upon the protective force of an alien executive.[14]

---

[8] Vares, *Konservatiivi ja murrosvuodet*, 233-4.

[9] Ibid., 235, where the author refers to Arvo Tuominen's opinion that this action destroyed the faith of the young radicals in parliamentarism.

[10] Karl Kautsky, *Erfurtin ohjelma*, Foreward to 5th edition (1904) (Helsinki, 1974), 12.

[11] Unlike the majority of the right, the activists were openly committed to the proclamation of Finnish independence and its attainment by force if necessary.

[12] Carl Enckell, *Poliittiset muistelmani*(Porvoo, 1956), 1:127.

[13] Ibid., 91, 94-5, 220.

[14] This is the traditional closing of ranks of executive power across frontiers when revolution threatens.

He was not alone.[15] It was the Bolshevik Revolution that severed this connection with Russia and compelled Finland to be free. The Bolsheviks provided the factual situation for *de jure* recognition.[16] The Finnish right could hardly claim credit. On the one hand, they felt that the Bolshevik regime might not last and that some future Russian government of a different kind would try to take Finland back. On the other hand, the Bolsheviks themselves might do the trick by fomenting revolution in Finland, a view that became an essential part of the right-wing explanation of why a civil war broke out in Finland in January 1918.[17] The search was on for a linkage with an alternative "foreign executive." Imperial Germany fit the bill, its military forces aiding in the task of destroying the revolutionary Finnish radicalism that sought issue in the civil war. (Germany's action was a parallel to the Russian Provisional Government's application of pressure to dissolve the radical Finnish parliament in July 1917.) Imperial Germany also served as a bulwark against Bolshevik Russia—or against any other Russia.

The economic concessions granted to Germany for its aid were enormous.[18] Most of the Finnish Whites, the victors in the civil war, were prepared to internalize the foreign executive power by adopting a German monarch. Prince Friedrich Karl of Hesse, the brother-in-law of Kaiser Wilhelm II and former governor of the Cameroons, was to become "Väinö I." This internalized foreign executive gave the Finnish elite a means to manipulate the real foreign executive in imperial Germany.[19] Overlooking the economic concessions already made to imperial Germany, this solution had the appearance of being even better than the pre-1899 situation, when the imperial power, remaining in "distant" St. Petersburg, had still been able to impose its own governor general on the Grand Duchy of Finland.

---

[15] On the influence of Ernst Nevanlinna on Enckell, see Vares, *Konservatiivi ja murrosvuodet*, 233.

[16] The three volumes entitled *Lenin ja Suomi* (Helsinki, 1987-1990) were a final and belated recognition of this fact by the Finnish Ministry of Education.

[17] Hence the favorite right-wing designation for this war has been the "War of Independence" as if the main enemy were Russia.

[18] Hannu Rautkallio, *Kaupantekoa Suomen itsenäisyydellä* (Helsinki, 1977), 132-42, 300.

[19] On the role of the Finnish Senate, see Rautkallio, *Kaupantekoa Suomen itsenäisyydellä*, 361.

The sudden collapse of Germany in the autumn of 1918, however, removed all chance of having a German monarch on a Finnish throne. From one point of view, therefore, the breakdown of the Russian and German empires as a result of World War I made the fact of Finnish independence seem comparatively easy, much easier than many of the bourgeois leaders of the Finnish state had anticipated.[20] There hardly appeared to be a need for a protective foreign executive. For those who wanted it, the League of Nations might serve as protector.[21]

In this vacuum of great power relations, the main threat seemed to be the international revolutionary movement. But at home, with much of the extreme left disenfranchised after the civil war, it was possible to go on stifling the radical left by treating the Socialist Labor Party (the Socialist Workers' Party), for example, as a conspiracy right from the start, hardly giving it a chance to develop as a parliamentary party.[22] The changes wrought by capitalism upon Finnish agriculture, given political expression in the rural right backlash known as the Lapua movement of 1929-1932, were politically contained by blaming—as the Lapua movement did—the Communist conspiracy and by enacting further anti-Communist legislation. In fact, the agrarian interests behind the Lapua movement had as much reason to lay the blame on the vagaries of international capitalism as the Communists did.[23] Only instead of being allies, these groups were opponents. In its internal politics Finland continued to lack a radical left. There are strong grounds for arguing that a radical left of sorts survived, albeit

---

[20] Jaakko Nousiainen, *Suomen poliittinen järjestelmä* (Porvoo, 1980), 126, points out that in the proposal for the Finnish constitution, originally drafted by the Ståhlberg committee and laid before the Finnish parliament on December 4, 1917 (two days before the Declaration of Independence), a loose connection with Russia would have been maintained.

[21] Kari Selén, *Genevestä Tukholmaan* (Helsinki, 1974), 336. Characteristically, Carl Enckell played a role in trying to make use of this "executive machinery."

[22] In spite of the fact that this party treated parliament as a forum for class war agitation, its help in securing the passage of constructive legislation, such as the *Lex Kallio* proposals for agrarian reform, was sometimes considerable. On this party, see Jaakko Mäkelä, "Suuri leikkaus 1923" (licentiate dissertation, University of Turku, 1980), 102.

[23] Instead it was a case of dog eat dog. The price of timber (an important source of income for Finnish farmers) fell on the international market, but the agrarian interests were protected by the government through a taxation that bore heavily on the workers. For a general analysis, see Timo Soikkanen, *Kansallinen eheytyminen—myytti vai todellisuus?* (Porvoo, 1984), 15.

with the greatest of difficulties, the repression of the civil war, but could not survive the onslaughts of the Lapua movement.[24]

This meant that a segment of the Finnish population was not truly represented in Finnish democracy. It also meant that critical alternative political bases were silenced. The superfluity of an extreme right wing remained,[25] while the country's essential constitutionalism, still in the hands of a set of interlocking elites, moved towards a policy of modest social reform at the end of the 1930s.[26]

But by the mid and late 1930s Germany and Russia had again achieved considerable power, with the latter feeling an inferiority to the former that compelled it to pressure Finland for defensive territorial concessions, among other things, for the protection of Leningrad, a repetition of the old tsarist fear for the safety of St. Petersburg. No political force existed in Finland that could have spoken for such concessions, and any force that had done so would have been immediately denied legitimacy. By the autumn of 1939 the Soviet Union was prepared to offer in return vast tracts of East Karelia, namely the parishes of Repola and Porajärvi, an area more than twice the size of the lands and islands to be ceded[27] and an area long coveted by the quasi-irredentist Finns of the Academic Karelia Society.[28] Those who saw the military danger of refusing territorial concessions to the Soviet Union, negotiators J.K. Paasikivi and Väinö Tanner as well as Marshal Mannerheim, were acting like far-sighted bureaucrats with no hint of a constituency to whom to appeal. It would have been disloyal to do so. Finnish political life had been rounded smooth upon a narrow base.

The symbiosis between Finnish ruling circles and the Finnish nation could only be broken by *force majeure*, either an ultimatum,

---

[24] The various forms of repression conducted by the Lapua Movement against the radical left are carefully documented by Juha Siltala, *Lapuan liike ja kyyditykset 1930* (Helsinki, 1985), 171-5, 222, 226-7, 235, and 246 ff.

[25] Superfluous, because the constitutionalists did "what was wanted." Thus even Ståhlberg, who had fallen victim to Lapuan excesses, supported the anti-Communist laws; ibid., 160.

[26] Heikki Waris, *Suomalaisen yhteiskunnan sosiaali-politiikka* (Porvoo, 1961), 34-5.

[27] Max Jakobson, *The Diplomacy of the Winter War* (Cambridge, MA, 1961), 116.

[28] Founded in 1922, the Academic Karelia Society was a patriotic and authoritarian society of male academics and students, deeply anti-Russian and working for the attachment of East Karelia to Finland. That area had never been part of a Finnish state.

which the Helsinki government might have been waiting for, or a march over the frontier. The latter took place. Finland fell into a war with Russia, the Winter War of 1939-40, on the third day of which the Russians established a puppet Finnish government at Terijoki, just over the Finnish-Soviet border, seemingly confirming the fears of the Finnish rulers (and undoubtedly, by this time, of the majority of the Finnish people) that there had all along been a conspiracy between the Soviet state and the Finnish Communist underground to wreck forever Finland's independence. Under these circumstances, Russia, an avowed revolutionary state, was exposing its true colors. [29] There could be no thought that Russia would in any way provide a prop of foreign executive support for Finland. On the contrary, any alleged prop would turn out to be a wedge, the thin end of which would be hammered in to bring down Finland's carefully structured parliamentary democracy.

To the delighted surprise of Finland's ruling circles, the overwhelming majority of the concealed or half-concealed Finnish radical left did not support the Terijoki government. Nonetheless a Finnish "home-grown" extreme left movement did not become any the more palatable to the traditionalist constitutionalist forces in Finland. Especially in the period before the outbreak of the Continuation War (1941), when Russian pressure on Finland was again evident, relations between the extreme left and the country's administration were tense.[30]

The felt need was to call upon the services of the alternative foreign executive, Nazi Germany. In joining the German invasion of Russia in June 1941, the Finns claimed not to be in alliance with Germany but only to be Germany's "cobelligerents," an expression cleverly invented by Finnish propagandists to maintain a certain distance between constitutionalist Finland and totalitarian Germany and to emphasize the limited goals of the Finnish war effort.[31] This did not stop the Finns from doing quite a bit for Germany, sending their troops over the old frontiers of the lands lost in 1940 and into East Karelia—to the distaste of many ordinary Finnish soldiers. In

---

[29] Most opinion openly expressed in Finland in the years before the Winter War regarded the Russians as simply waiting their chance to spread Bolshevism wherever they could. See Jakobson, *The Diplomacy of the Winter War*, 48.

[30] Anthony F. Upton, *Finland in Crisis, 1940-41* (London, 1964), 130-2.

[31] These goals were never actually defined.

return the new Nazi order was prepared to do a great deal for Finland. For one thing, Hitler intended to wipe out Leningrad, as Finnish President Risto Ryti was fully aware. Ryti concocted a scenario in which the Germans would occupy a strip of territory between an extended Finland and what would be left of the Russian state, hence separating Finland forever from its troublesome neighbor.[32] So a German empire, headed by Hitler's military-political executive, provided the milieu within which Finland could live its own autonomous life.

However, the West and the Soviet Union began to win the war. Germany and Finland did not even succeed in wearing Russia down enough for Finland to retain its East Karelian conquests[33]; nor after the war, which ended for Finland in 1944, did the West and the Soviet Union turn on each other, as large sections of the Finnish establishment, especially the military establishment, had expected and hoped. (The military, in fact, had cached arms for this eventuality.[34]) Finland's ruling circles were proved wrong on several counts. This being the case, the conclusion of hostilities in 1944 inevitably precipitated a move away from politico-bureaucratic rule and led to a reinvigoration of parliament. Finland's entry into the Continuation War in 1941 and the dispatch of troops beyond the old frontiers a few weeks later had never been debated in parliament. Now "the old gang" were to be ousted.[35] This policy did not merely mean the war trials of discredited political leaders, but also changes in many administrative organs, even if the bureaucracy and its supporting elites

---

[32] Tuomo Polvinen, *Barbarossasta Teheraniin* (Porvoo, 1979), 68-9.

[33] The idea was that of the necessity of a "natural frontier" for Finland—along the Svir (Syväri) River in East Karelia. A current defender of the wartime government's policy has recently maintained that had the government made peace even as late as the spring of 1944 at the cost of handing back all East Karelia, civil war might have ensued in Finland. See Erkki Pihlaja, "Sodasta irtautumiseen vähän mahdollisuuksia" (letter), *Helsingin Sanomat*, 25 July 1994, A23.

[34] These soldiers, condemned by the then Finnish political leadership, were described by the minister of defense, Elisabeth Rehn, in a talk to the War College on March 2, 1992, as "patriots."

[35] Paasikivi, when prime minister in 1945-46, had first hoped that the war leaders would themselves retire voluntarily from positions of authority. See J.K. Paasikivi, *Päiväkirjat 1944-1956* (Porvoo, 1985), 1:120.

conducted quite a good rearguard operation, safeguarding what they could.[36]

The principal agent of change was the Soviet Union, which, having defeated Finland, was not going to sit back and see "progressive forces" in Finland relegated to obscurity.[37] Indeed, the victorious presence of the Soviet Union, working through the Allied Control Commission until 1947, insured that a radical left (including Communists) was back in parliament; and in this sense the Soviet victory enhanced Finland's parliamentarism.

As in 1905 and 1917-1918, Russia's impact on Finnish political life released pent-up forces. As in 1905, the Finnish system, under this external pressure, responded by extending its constitutional framework to embrace those who were allegedly threatening it. The obvious danger in the eyes of the traditionalists was that by doing this they might instead be promoting a 1917-1918 situation, a situation in which the newly-released political forces would obliterate the difference between Finland and Russia entirely. For the traditionalists, again faced with the inescapable Russian presence, the point was to maintain the difference and to find a way once more of at least coming to terms with this foreign executive.

A significant mitigating factor was that, when these changes were taking place, the West and the Soviet Union were allies and the changes occurred under the rubric of the "United Nations."[38] But once the United Nations, in spite of its designation, became more of a forum for disagreement than anything else, the old problem arose for the Finnish leaders in an accentuated form.[39] On the borders of

---

[36] The writer Hella Wuolijoki, a member of the SKDL and a friend of Bertolt Brecht, became head of the public radio corporation in 1945 but lost her post in 1949. The security police were under the control of the extreme left from May 1945 to December 1948. On the latter, see Reijo Ahtokari, *Punainen Valpo* (Helsinki, 1969), 41, 205-6.

[37] This was more an understanding of perceptive Finnish leaders than a direct command of the Russians. See Paasikivi, *Päiväkirjat 1944-1956*, 1:56, 62. The Soviet representatives were more concerned to point to the need to get the old forces out of commanding positions; see ibid., 107, 127.

[38] The preamble of the 1948 Finnish-Soviet treaty even refers to "the maintenance of international peace and security in accordance with the aims and principles of the United Nations Organization."

[39] As a result of the dissension of the Cold War, Finland's own application for UN membership was delayed until the end of 1955; see Klaus Törnudd, *Suomi ja Yhdistyneet kansakunnat* (Helsinki, 1967), 30-1. By 1950 Paasikivi was of the

Finland was a powerful, dynamic, anti-constitutionalist state, wedded increasingly to its global ambitions. The pressure of this state had helped to legitimize, through the requirements of the United Nations ethos written into the armistice agreement and peace treaty, potentially dangerous internal forces.[40] They were in parliament, the organ constitutionalists all over the world claimed to cherish. How much viability was there in the parliamentary system in Finland now?

II

If the United Nations had been the force it was intended to be, somewhere or other in the world would have been that helpful, even possibly manipulable, foreign executive the Finnish rulers had so often seemed to need. However, the United Nations was not originally a global constitutional structure but an alliance between very diverse states. The result of that alliance was that Finland was assigned to the Soviet sphere in the postwar world. Between September 1943, when he argued with his confidant that Finland had to be behind the Soviet frontier, and November-December 1943 at Teheran, when he argued for an independent Finland, Franklin Roosevelt had changed his mind on some rather important points.[41] What may well have happened is that in the period August-September 1943 Roosevelt lost hope of seeing Finland escape from the war, while, on the other hand, his concern to keep Russia in the war was overwhelming.[42] By November the Swedes again were attempting to help Finland extricate itself from its predicament.[43] Anyway, the Soviet Union did not appear to want to incorporate Finland and kept on trying to make peace on the basis of Finnish independence with its territories returned to the 1940 frontiers.[44] Whatever direction the settlement took, the western allies understood that Soviet considerations were the ultimate determinant.

---

opinion that UN membership was dangerous for Finland since it might draw the land into the Cold War; see Paasikivi, *Päiväkirjat 1944-1956*, 2:125, 151.

[40] Article 20 of the 1944 armistice agreement and article 7 of the 1947 peace treaty.

[41] Robert I. Gannon, *The Cardinal Spellman Story* (New York, 1962), 223; Polvinen, *Barbarossasta Teheraniin*, 290-2.

[42] Even the Finns were aware of alleged peace contacts between Germany and the Soviet Union in the late spring of 1943; see Paasikivi, *Jatkosodan päiväkirjat* (Porvoo, 1991), 284.

[43] R.M. Berry, *American Foreign Policy and the Finnish Exception* (Helsinki, 1987), 360.

[44] Polvinen, *Barbarossasta Teheraniin*, 286, 288.

Roosevelt also convinced himself that in a reconstructed postwar Europe the Russians had a chance of mellowing—"he hopes that in ten or twenty years the European influences would bring the Russians to be less barbarian"[45]—but this did not alter the basic fact of Soviet dominance over Finland. A belief in a degree of convergence only made Soviet dominance in certain areas more palatable to the hopefuls of the western world.

Convergence did not provide a framework for the Finns to live under, a fact well realized by the man who served as president from 1946 to 1956, J.K. Paasikivi. Furthermore, Paasikivi did not want to rely on the possibility of a hot war developing between the West and the Soviet Union. Unlike the victorious western countries, Finland had already had its hot wars with the Soviet Union, two of them, the latter of which followed by yet a war to expel the former German *Waffenbrüder* from Lapland. Silent cemeteries filled with the bodies of "young heroes" bore witness to the cost of all this warfare.

Paasikivi, in his political commitment before the First World War, had been an Old Finn of the Compliant school, which had sought, and ultimately failed to find, an accommodation with tsarist Russia.[46] Now Passikivi tried to find a parallel accommodation with the Soviet Union. He was not a lover of Russia. In 1918 he had pushed for a close economic and political relationship with Germany; between 1940 and 1942 he had looked forward to Nazi Germany wiping the Soviet Union out.[47] He doubted that Germany would invade the Soviet Union, but when it did, he hoped the Germans would win.[48] The nearest one can get to finding a broad line of consistency in his outlook is to dwell upon the thought that for him Finland could never afford to live in complete isolation. Finland had to lean upon Germany. Even as late as 1943 Paasikivi still hoped that Germany would serve Finland as a bulwark against Russia.[49] Alternatively,

---

[45] Gannon, *The Cardinal Spellman Story*, 222-4.

[46] The Compliants were that section of the Finnish elite who, in the period from 1899 to just before the First World War, felt that by making concessions to Russia the bulk of Finnish autonomy could be maintained. In the end they believed that they had failed.

[47] V. Assarsson, *Stalinin varjossa* (Porvoo, 1963), 45-7, 54-5, 64-5.

[48] Paasikivi, *Jatkosodan paiväkirjat*, 11-24, 31, 39, 64, 83, 172, 187.

[49] Ibid., 306-7.

Finland could enter a defense alliance with the Scandinavian states.[50] Or, if all else failed, it could seek a modus vivendi with Russia. The latter was now the only way. The evidence of this, from 1944 to 1947, was the Allied Control Commission, the silence of its British representative,[51] and the overriding power of Andrei Zhdanov. A complaining Agrarian Party delegation was laconically told by Paasikivi: "Zhdanov rules here."[52] This was not entirely true, but in saying it Paasikivi was implying something else: that he, Paasikivi, would handle things from the Finnish side, and with Zhdanov where necessary.

Paasikivi spoke to the Agrarians while still prime minister, over a year before he became president. The presidency was his natural position. It was the post from which to communicate with the foreign executive through its spokesman on the Control Commission, Andrei Zhdanov. The Finnish president began to mediate between the Finnish democracy and the external executive. This presidential policy affected parliament where two sets of dangerous forces were represented. On the one hand, there were the Communists[53] and their allies, ever inclined, thought Paasikivi, to have their own direct relationship with the Soviet Union.[54] On the other hand, there were strident voices in the patriotic parties, opposed to change and unable to envisage a successful working arrangement with the great neighboring power.[55] This taut situation imposed on Finland policies that were often less than representative of the will of the Finns, policies

---

[50] In the second half of the 1930s, Paasikivi had striven for a defense aliance of the Nordic states or one between Sweden and Finland; see Jakobson, *Paasikivi Tukholmassa* (Helsinki, 1978), 32-41. In December he was thinking of a Nordic Defense Alliance under German protection; see Assarsson, *Stalinin varjossa*, 54-5.

[51] Polvinen, *Beyond East and West* (Porvoo, 1986), 68-9, 108.

[52] Kyösti Skyttä, *Presidentin muotokuva* (Helsinki, 1969), 1:249; Paasikivi, *Päiväkirjat 1944-1956*, 1:96.

[53] The SKDL of the Finnish People's Democratic League was a coalition organization of the Finnish Communist Party and left Social Democrats who had broken with the SDP when it failed to join an electoral alliance with the Communists; see D.G. Kirby, *Finland in the Twentieth Century* (London, 1979), 160.

[54] Paasikivi, *Päiväkirjat 1944-1956*, 1:628, 676. In course of time, he somewhat modified his views; ibid., 700.

[55] These were the forces not merely of the right, but also of the patriotic Social Democrats under the old leader Väinö Tanner; see ibid., 45-6, 48, 62, 65.

that were pursued by selected political figures and forces.[56] The great selector was the president himself.

Yet in this situation there was a certain element that in its own negative way afforded the president a measure of support. In its previous policies Finland had been "wrong"; to the disgust of both the West and the Soviet Union Finland had collaborated with Nazi Germany. The ethos by which a large section of the educated class, for example the Academic Karelia Society, had lived was now outmoded.[57] Thus the Finns, as the Cold War began, were carrying a burden of guilt from their previous political involvements. Even when, as the relations between the West and the Soviet Union slumped with ever greater rapidity, and many Finns transmuted their guilt into *Schadenfreude*, they could do nothing but desist from provocation. Finland endeavored in its external policy not to get caught again. To avoid Russian suspicions of Finland, Paasikivi went along with the exclusion of the war leaders from power.[58] This was a suppression of ideas,[59] even when new ideas were at the same time coming forward from the left. It often seemed that full-dress debate had become dangerous, and this at the very period when parliament had been strengthened by an infusion of radicalism. Politics became personalized around the presidency.

Parliament was thus a potential source of embarrassment for Finland's foreign relations. In the summer of 1947 the peace treaty, though signed, had yet to be ratified, and to avoid any complications here, the Finnish government, backed by President Paasikivi, refused the invitation to the Marshall Plan conference. The Foreign Affairs

---

[56] Perhaps the most outstanding example here is that of Urho Kekkonen, who was distrusted by a large section of his own party (the Agrarian Union) and was known as "the weather-vane."

[57] See note 29. The historian of the Academic Karelia Society has even seen its later phase as Fascist; see Risto Alapuro, *Akateeminen Karjala-Seura* (Porvoo, 1973), 140-58.

[58] Paasikivi spoke directly to the former minister of finance, Tyko Reinikka, and told him to leave politics; Paasikivi, *Päiväkirjat 1944-1956*, 1:93.

[59] At the War Guilt Trials of the leaders who brought Finland into the war alongside Germany, the former president, Risto Ryti, was prevented from making the full defense he intended. This would have involved an important historical survey relating the Continuation War to the Winter War. See Kyösti Lallukka, ed., *Risto Rytin puolustus* (Helsinki, 1989), 10, 14-17.

Committee of parliament had actually voted acceptance of the invitation, but no debate was held on the floor of parliament.[60]

Another more complicated response to Soviet pressure emerged at the end of 1947 when a Finnish delegation to the Soviet Union was confronted with the disagreeable Soviet request for a security treaty. Paasikivi first vented his wrath upon the leader of the delegation, Mauno Pekkala, the prime minister,[61] and then, on receipt of a letter from Stalin, sought above all to bridle parliamentary opposition and produce the most limited version possible of the necessary treaty. To do this, Paasikivi hand-picked the members of the negotiating delegation, which was composed roughly of one person from each parliamentary group, although the Conservatives were not officially represented since they were not in the coalition government.[62] Some of its members were controversial figures in their own party, like Urho Kekkonen of the Agrarian Union or Yrjö Leino of the SKDL (the Finnish People's Democratic League). It should be noted that, with the exception of the latter and of the bourgeois Swedish People's Party, the parties in parliament initially wanted to shun all thought of negotiating a military agreement with the Soviet Union.[63] Parliament feared a loss of sovereignty for Finland should such a treaty be signed with the powerful neighbor. In fact, it was parliament that was to suffer the loss of sovereignty.

Parliament was simply used. Paasikivi, who pushed the treaty through in the face of parliamentary misgivings, contrasted the situation with that before the Winter war in autumn 1939. At that critical time, he believed, and Prime Minister Mauno Pekkala agreed, that parliament's opposition to making concessions to the Soviet Union was a factor justifying the government's refusal to allow the negotiators to make any compromise proposals of their own (the chief negotiator being Paasikivi himself).[64] Now eight members of the cabinet, a majority, opposed a military treaty with the Soviet Union.[65]

---

[60] Polvinen, *Between East and West*, 271.

[61] Toivo Heikkilä, *Paasikivi peräsimessä* (Helsinki, 1965), 304; Paasikivi, *Päiväkirjat 1944-1956*, 1:512-13, 518, 521, 552.

[62] Ibid., 572.

[63] J.O. Söderhjelm, *Kolme matkaa Moskovaan* (Tampere, 1970), 11-12, 116, 124-5, 131; Paasikivi, *Päiväkirjat 1944-1956*, 1:542, 587-8.

[64] Ibid., 565, 579.

[65] Ibid., 580.

The government's reluctance to conclude a treaty linked with parliament's reluctance. The government would, however, do as it was told by Paasikivi. But parliament's reluctance would be exploited by Paasikivi to get a treaty with the minimal possible scope.[66] This strategy so raised apprehensions among the Russians that even Molotov was worried lest the Finnish parliament refuse to ratify the treaty.[67] Such "parliamentarism" was token parliamentarism. Paasikivi and his partly hand-picked associates from the different parties bullied the treaty through.[68] It passed by 157 to 11. There was no initiative in parliament; the whole business was a much less genuine expression of the parliamentary will than had existed in 1939, however restricted in representation and outlook the 1939 parliament had been.[69]

After the Second World War the Russian impact on Finnish politics was contradictory. Parliament became more representative and so did the government of the day. The Communists formed a coalition of radical left groups under the rubric of the Finnish People's Democratic League.[70] Though the SKDL failed to attract the bulk of the Social Democrats, the latter with the SKDL and the Agrarian Union constituted a working coalition ("the Big Three") which made up the backbone of the Finnish governments from April 1945 until July 1948. This was parliamentary government based on a parliamentary majority, a not too common phenomenon in Finnish political life. In contrast, the constantly felt demands from Russia, even though it hardly planned to take the country over, produced strains that led to exalting presidential over parliamentary power.[71]

---

[66] Ibid., 578-9, 592.

[67] Söderhjelm, *Kolme matkaa Moskovaan*, 200.

[68] Paasikivi's view was that if it were not done this way, the Russians would only trust the Finnish Communists in the future; see Paasikivi, *Päiväkirjat 1944-1956*, 1:595.

[69] Both the Agrarian Union and the Social Democratic Party emphasized to their members the necessity of having a quiet vote of adoption of the 1948 treaty; ibid., 595-6.

[70] See note 54. The relations between these two political parties were more complicated than many imagined, being connected with the issue of how far the Communist Party was going to become a general party and how far it should remain a cadre party; see Hermann Beyer-Thoma, *Vasemmisto ja vaaran vuodet* (Helsinki, 1990), 46, 127-8.

[71] By 1949 Paasikivi seems to have become convinced that the Russians did not plan a take-over; see Paasikivi, *Päiväkirjat 1944-1956*, 1:700. The report made by

The Communist Party experienced these strains too. In spite of the fact that the "Big Three" made radical improvements in the Finnish social security system,[72] ordinary members and supporters of the Finnish Communist Party had expected much more. They had expected a fundamental transformation of Finnish society. In a situation in which Finland had to pay a large part of its domestic product to the Soviet Union in reparations, real wages were low, though employment was maintained. Paradoxically, the economic nexus with the Soviet Union led indirectly to exasperation in the workplace, an exasperation the anti-employer face of the Communist Party was compelled to exploit.

Nor was this all. Organizational activity, leading to strikes and other demonstrative actions, were recommended to the Finnish Communist Party by Andrei Zhdanov from the spring of 1947 onwards. Yrjo Leinö, the SKDL (and Communist) minister of the interior, was in an increasingly difficult position. His occupancy of this office, far from leading to a Communist infiltration of Finnish society, was an embarrassment to direct workplace action. Because he was also possibly feared as a potential Finnish Tito, Zhdanov told him to resign.[73] He promised to go, but he did not do so before, many months later, he had informed the Finnish military and Paasikivi of a possible coup d'état by the right, a coup intended either to oppose the treaty with the Soviet Union or to forestall a suspected Communist takeover.[74]

For Paasikivi's purposes it did not really matter. The crunch against the Communists was coming. To complete Leinö's sad tale, he was asked to resign after a parliamentary vote against him resulting from his action in deporting a group of Russian émigrés to the Soviet Union. This had occurred in 1945 with the official sanction of then foreign minister, Carl Enckell, and then prime minister, J.K.

Milovan Djilas of remarks passed at a Kremlin lunch in December 1947 is worth noting. There Zhdanov complained that Finland had not been taken over, but Molotov responded by stating that Finland "meant nothing at all"; quoted by Niels Jørgen Thögersen, "De finske-sovjetiske relationer" (licentiate dissertation, University of Aarhus, 1969), 93.

[72] On the transfer of income as a result of the introduction of a system of children's allowances, see Waris, *Suomalaisen yhteiskunnan sosiaalipolitiikka*, 224-5.

[73] Beyer-Thoma, *Vasemmisto ja vaaran vuodet*, 226-9.

[74] Yrjö Leino, *Kommunisti sisäministerinä* (Helsinki, 1991), 249-54.

Paasikivi.[75] Leino's subsequent attempt to publish his own story was thwarted by Finnish self-censorship. The work did not appear until 1991, thirty years after his death.[76]

These distressing personal events were but the fringes of an all too familiar political scenario. Increasingly Finland endured minority governments. From July 1948 until March 1950, Paasikivi ruled with a minority government of Social Democrats. One observer, Raimo Väyrynen, saw this as a crisis in Soviet-Finnish relations.[77] The SKDL remained excluded from power-sharing until 1966, ten years after Paasikivi's death.[78] Paasikivi used the treaty with the Soviet Union to keep things on an even keel.[79] Once again the Finnish executive and the foreign executive had made a deal, the key element being that the inner workings of Finnish society should not be disturbed.[80] Paasikivi had started off in the autumn of 1944 by recalling the old model of Finnish autonomy under Russia in the pre-1899 world.[81]

But Finland's inner workings were disturbed. Zhdanov had told a Finnish minister to leave office, and, whether or not known to Paasikivi, that was the sort of interference at the parliamentary and governmental level one might expect from the Soviet Union, using its influence in the Finnish Communist Party and the SKDL. Likewise, the ignoring of these groups by the Finnish establishment—in 1958 the SKDL, still without a share of power, became the largest single party with 50 seats in a 200 seat parliament—was reminiscent of the suppression of the radical left in prewar Finland.

These limitations on Finnish political life can easily be seen as features of the struggle to maintain Finnish traditionalism. In practice, the Soviet Union was either disinterested in or incapable of

---

[75] Beyer-Thoma, *Vasemmisto ja vaaran vuodet*, 96.

[76] The story of the original suppression of publication is told in Leino, *Kommunisti sisäministerinä*, i-viii.

[77] Raimo Väyrynen, *Conflicts in Finnish-Soviet Relations: Three Comparative Studies*, Acta Universitatis, ser. A, (Tampere, 1972), 47:96-9, 115-26.

[78] They were nonetheless offered posts in the new government led by K.A. Fagerholm, even though their parliamentary representation (SKDL) had fallen from 49 to 38. But Fagerholm and Paasikivi refused to give them the posts they themselves wanted. They went into isolation. On this, see Beyer-Thoma, *Vasemmisto ja vaaran vuodet*, 291-2.

[79] Paasikivi, *Päiväkirjat 1944-1956*, 1:597.

[80] Ibid., 631.

[81] Ibid., 69.

threatening this traditionalism.[82] It had, in spite of crises in Finnish-Soviet relations, worked with the traditionalist camp. It was driven to find bourgeois allies (part of the Soviet dilemma[83]) and to make use of the doctrine of peaceful coexistence. In turn, Finland, trading with the West through its great export industries, also concluded commercial agreements with the Soviet Union so that one of Finland's future presidents could thereby describe his country as being out of the Cold War.[84]

This man was Urho Kekkonen, and it was his party, the Agrarian Union, that began to occupy the place of the SKDL in Finnish relations with the mighty neighbor. Kekkonen won the presidency by the slimmest of margins in 1956, and thereafter presidential authority began to expand still further over parliament and the ruling governments. The latter tended to have a strong Agrarian character and were often minority governments. Somehow Paasikivi had seen what was going to come. Six years before Kekkonen became president, Paasikivi, in a discussion with the Agrarian politician Vihtori Vesterinen, had marked Kekkonen as the future president. But his prediction was accompanied by a caveat. The president of Finland was not, and ought not to be, simply a Russian governor.[85]

This, then, was the inevitable nexus with the foreign executive. Paasikivi, in the interest of upholding the nexus, had pushed unpopular policies upon the Finnish people, holding them necessary.[86] The problem for Kekkonen, as Paasikivi saw it, was the dangers inherent in making use of the Russian connection. The 1958 Night Frost Crisis and the 1961 Note Crisis with the Soviet Union, both in the early period of the Kekkonen presidency, confirmed presidential power in general and the power of the current president in particular.[87] As an alternative to Soviet interference in Finnish political

---

[82] It tended to take its stand from *within* the compass of the traditionalist forces, preferring Agrarians to Conservatives and Social Democrats.

[83] George Maude, *The Finnish Dilemma* (London, 1976), 51-8.

[84] Paasikivi, *Päiväkirjat 1944-1956*, 2:123, quoting a speech made by Urho Kekkonen.

[85] Ibid., 162.

[86] Paasikivi, *Päiväkirjat 1944-1956*, 1:565, 604.

[87] This Night Frost Crisis began to occur in the late summer of 1958 with the formation of the "pro-western" third Fagerholm government. A background factor was the formation in Western Europe of the EEC; the Night Frost Crisis also ran into

life, it became preferable to support the president of the day—and in the case of President Kekkonen that day from his inception was to last twenty-five years. Whatever their ultimate causes, the crises showed the key characteristics of the pattern of Finnish executive control in its relations with the foreign executive, namely the resignation of the government (the Night Frost Crisis) or the dissolution of parliament (the Note Crisis), after which minority governments ruled.

These governments were of a profoundly Agrarian cast. Since the Agrarian Union from its founding in 1906 had been a party committed to the defense of private property, the strong relationship between an Agrarian president and an Agrarian-dominated parliamentary and political scene, all bound up together in a security package intended to keep the Soviet Union at a distance, was there to ensure the preservation of "the Finnish way of life"—a point Kekkonen underlined.[88] How far this went hand-in-hand with a stultification of Finnish institutional life is a theme of some complexity.

III

The Finnish Note Crisis of 1961 is an explicit example of Soviet intent to involve Finland in Cold War politics and of the Finnish refusal to become so involved. The crisis arose when the Soviet Union, following the second Berlin crisis and the alleged threat of West German military and naval might on the stability of Northern Europe and the Baltic region, asked for military consultations with Finland under Article 2 of the 1948 treaty. The crisis was defused when the Soviet Union withdrew its request. Since Kekkonen played a key role in its defusion and, indeed, retained a brazen self-confidence throughout, the supposition has arisen that he may have rigged the whole thing in order to secure his re-election as president, namely as the one political leader who could manage relations with the Soviet Union and thus preserve the system.

It is not necessary to enter into the finer points of this unresolved question, a question that has recently come to the fore again in the

---

the second Berlin crisis as the autumn wore on. On this, see Väyrynen, *Conflicts in Finnish-Soviet Relations*, 83-6, 90-2, 99-101, 129-41.

[88] Tuomas Vilkuna, ed., *Neutrality: The Finnish Position. Speeches by Dr. Urho Kekkonen, President of Finland* (London, 1970), 83-6.

revelations of the historian Hannu Rautkallio.[89] It is important, however, to note the difference between the use of the treaty in the Note Crisis and its previous use.

The treaty, drafted and signed under the Paasikivi presidency, established the limits of Finnish involvement—no use of Finnish troops outside Finland and Soviet aid in repelling an attack from the West through Finland only to be given "where necessary." But Paasikivi was able to make use of the treaty, i.e., to extend its significance, by agreeing to renew it prematurely in 1955 for a period of twenty years, in the process getting back, prematurely, the Porkkala bases leased to the Soviet Union by the 1944 armistice agreement. It looked like a distinct *quid pro quo*, even if the Soviet Union, by virtue of changes in weapon technology, no longer needed these bases. These political maneuvers had nothing to do with a possible political future for the aged President Paasikivi. The treaty was simply an instrument, on this occasion, by which the presidential executive obtained a concession for the whole country from the foreign executive.

The tenor in the Note Crisis was different. The treaty was in this case the instrument of threat, the solution to which became personalized in the persistence in office of one man and only consequently in the exercise of the power of the office itself. The presidency, an institution used to protect Finnish internal politics from Soviet influence, had become a focal point for Soviet partiality in Finnish affairs. But lest we be unfair to the persona of Urho Kekkonen, it must be noted that Paasikivi too had at least become president because, unlike most of the rest of the traditional figures in Finnish politics at that time, he had not too badly compromised himself in Soviet eyes.

I have contended elsewhere that the Note Crisis might also be seen as a means of reminding Finland and Kekkonen of the importance of the Soviet connection.[90] In the period 1960-1961 Kekkonen made four trips to the West and was in the United States when the Soviet note was delivered to the Finnish embassy in Moscow. During this

---

[89] Hannu Rautkallio, *Novosibirskin lavastus. Noottikriisi 1961* (Helsinki, 1992), 136-42. Rautkallio has not proved that Kekkonen got the Russians to draft the note, but endeavors to show that Kekkonen accepted the drafting of a note as an aid to his presidential campaign. Rautkallio shows that the Kekkonen campaign fund received money from the Soviet Union; ibid., 102-3, 105, 263-4.

[90] Maude, *The Finnish Dilemma*, 21.

period, Finland was strengthening its economic links with the West and in 1961 the Finnish European Free Trade Agreement (FINEFTA) agreement was negotiated.

In the aftermath of the Note Crisis Kekkonen managed brilliantly to integrate to a considerable degree both the western and Soviet aspects of Finnish policy so that Finland became a great exception in the Cold War, a country with good relations on both sides and one which gradually began to make its own impact on European and even global policy. By the 1970s Finland emerged not merely to provide a suitable venue for U.S.-Soviet arms negotiations but also to promote an original Soviet démarche, the call for a European Security Conference. This was done in such a way that a whole contact process developed between the West and the Soviet Union and its allies under the Conference on Security and Cooperation in Europe (CSCE) rubric.

It seemed as if the close relations between the Finnish and the foreign executive was almost automatically bringing benefits to Finland. But behind the apparent success story strains in Finnish-Soviet relations continued to be felt. In prematurely renewing the security treaty in 1970, Kekkonen sought to get a joint communiqué specifically recognizing Finnish neutrality policy and even talked of resigning if this did not come to pass. It did come to pass,[91] but since Kekkonen considered the recognition of Finnish neutrality to be his life's work, he was clearly treading on thorny ground. [92]

These tensions in his relations with Leonid Brezhnev and others were not generally known in Finland at that time. The Soviet refusal to back Max Jakobson for the post of UN secretary general thus created deep astonishment in Finland and rancor in Kekkonen against his own advisers, knowledge of which filtered through to the public. [93] The truth was that the United States, then in its Kissinger-era contempt for the UN, had not held up on this question either, and it is easy to see Jakobson's failure as the failure of a small state that had overshot the mark in its dealings with all the great powers. [94]

---

[91] Jakobson, *38. kerros* (Helsinki, 1983), 264, 271-8. Undoubtedly, Kekkonen would have preferred a recognition of neutrality written into a revised treaty.

[92] *Ulkopoliittisia lausuntoja ja asiakirjoja 1961* (Helsinki, 1962), 38-43.

[93] Jakobson, *38. kerros*, 353.

[94] Ibid., 341, 355-6, 363-4; Sakari Määttänen, *Tapaus Jakobson* (Helsinki, 1973), 205.

The wider question of Finnish neutrality, however, takes us back to another aspect of the conclusion of the Note Crisis. Since it was believed that the Soviet army had been pressing for military consultations and that the civilians in the Soviet government had just gone along with this, it was easy for Finnish army leaders to argue that, had Finland had stronger armed forces, especially better weaponry, then there would have been less chance of a Soviet demand for military consultations and, by implication, no note.[95] Kekkonen was blamed for neglecting the armed forces. Therefore, as part of the solution to the problem of maintaining better relations with the Soviet Union, Finland began a policy of wriggling free from the prohibition on guided missiles in the peace treaty. It slowly started to procure guided missiles and improved its air force by purchasing MIGs from the Soviet Union.[96] Kekkonen did not seem to be very impressed by all this. He continued to lambast the Finnish army as "an amusement park," but wearily gave way to several of the military's demands. [97]

A convincing case of armed neutrality appeared to be born. Among other things, this led to a scholastic debate on the suitability of interpreting the military clause of the 1948 treaty by the doctrine of neutrality. The debate concerned the Soviet Union and assuredly did not improve Kekkonen's chances of getting the Soviet leaders to endorse Finnish neutrality in a basically political sense.

But the debate was also noticed by knowledgeable observers in the West who developed an admiration for the Finns, dwelling on their military institutions, the martial and independent spirit they fostered, linking it all to the David-versus-Goliath drama of the Winter War.[98] The fact that the developing Finnish conviction in armed neutrality also embraced the possibility of making a clear stand against a NATO intrusion did not seem to worry, or perhaps even strike the awareness of, western military pundits. It did not matter much so long as the Finns would be prepared to hold their own against a Soviet military thrust across Finland into Sweden or northern Norway.[99] One variant

---

[95] Sakari Simelius, *Jalkaväen kenraalin muistelmat* (Porvoo, 1983), 173.

[96] In fact, there seems to have been little sense of urgency—it took fifteen years for the Finnish anti-aircraft units to procure these missiles; ibid., 195.

[97] Ibid., 209.

[98] Actually Goliath won this time. But note the title of "Victory in Defeat" for the final chapter of Jakobson, *The Diplomacy of the Winter War*, 157-259.

[99] When in January 1983 the NATO commander-in-chief in Europe, General Bernard Rogers, cast doubt on this, a frenzied response was elicited from the Finnish military;

of the "ultimate scenario" envisaged war taking place everywhere else but in Finnish land and air space.[100] This western admiration culminated in the articles of Tomas Ries and in his book *Cold Will*, a work published after Kekkonen had died. [101] Such works are still being published and owe much to the sympathy and encouragement of the Finnish armed forces and Ministry of Defense.[102]

Within Finland too, armed neutrality was easily identifiable with independence and with freedom from the foreign executive, as a kind of image of last resort. In 1978, the pressure from a Soviet minister of defense, Dimitri Ustinov, for the inauguration of joint maneuvers between the Finnish and Soviet armies was repelled, thus showing that the usefulness of armed neutrality was not limited to an ultimate crisis scenario after all.[103]

But there was another side to the picture that few observers have cared to note. The Finnish army's "matching-up" process vis-à-vis the Soviet army, now no longer a mere "rib of the Red Army,"[104] created a self-confidence that was—as in the case of the Soviet army—based on authority and authoritarianism. A degree of camaraderie that emerged in relations between top officers of both armies—a smiling Marshal Grechko told the Finns to train tough soldiers[105]—was founded upon a semblance of similarity between the two institutions. In Finland, as in the Soviet Union, the army became an uncriticized element in society, the virtues of which all were expected to acknowledge. For Finland the army grew to be an embodiment of the

see George Maude, *The Finnish-Norwegian Tangle*, Studies on Political Science, no. 9/1987 (Turku, 1987), 59, 65.

[100] Everything would go by sea in the direction of the North Cape. On this originally Norwegian perception, see Simelius, *Jalkaväen kenraalin muistelmat*, 242.

[101] Tomas Ries, *Cold Will* (London, 1988), xiii, 372-5; Tomas Ries, "Finland's Armed Forces Isolated But Unbowed," *International Defense Review* 17 (1984): 266; Tomas Ries, "Defending the Far North," *International Defense Review*, 17 (1984): 880.

[102] H.M. Tillotson, *Finland at Peace and War* (Norwich, 1993). The author acknowledges that the idea of a book for the seventy-fifth anniversary of the Finnish defense forces came from General Aimo Pajunen, ix.

[103] Roy Allison, *Finland's Relations With the Soviet Union, 1944-1984* (London, 1985), 67-8.

[104] This view had been argued by Jouko Siipi, *Puna-Armeijan etuvartio?* (Hämeenlinna, 1968), 25.

[105] Maude, *The Finnish Dilemma*, 53.

favorite Finnish word of the moment, consensus, shaping an identity derived from the exercise of the will. Ries was very apt in the title of his book. Women, more than half of the Finnish community, were not shaped by military service, but shared in the sense of identity it brought, urging their men-folk to do this military service as an earnest manifestation of manhood and Finnishness.[106] The national consensus bred by such an outlook was symbolic of what the politics of the country should be aiming for.

All of which finally brings us to consider the changes in Finnish politics in the second half of the Cold War period which made consensus, if not the goal, at least the catchword and a *modus operandi* of the system. It has previously been noted that both Kekkonen and his predecessor Paasikivi were prepared to rule with minority governments, partly to avoid overly radical internal changes in Finnish society, and partly to prevent the emergence of an excessively assertive policy towards the Soviet Union. Kekkonen, in particular, after the 1958 Night Frost Crisis when Soviet pressure broke a majority government with a strong contingent in it of allegedly western-oriented Social Democrats,[107] avoided for years having Social Democrats in the governments. But by the mid-sixties the Social Democrats had gone to Canossa (read Moscow), made their peace, and thereby became, as the saying went, "acceptable to the court" ("hovikelpoinen"), meaning that Kekkonen would now have them in his governments.

Indeed, by the mid-sixties, Kekkonen had succeeded in reviving "the Big Three" of the Social Democrats, the Agrarians (since 1964 the Centre Party) and the SKDL, which now formed governments together. From then until the mid-seventies, a period of rather radical reform took place both through legislation and social movements in society. Trade unions, for example, were formed for conscripts and partially representative organs for the self-administration of universities replaced (outside the University of Helsinki) the *de jure* and, to some extent, the *de facto* dominance of the professoriate.

---

[106] As in Sweden, so in Finland women can now do military service. Few are expected to take advantage of this offer. For offer it is. Women who do not do military service will not be compelled into alternative service, the fate of men who refuse to bear arms.

[107] There was nonetheless something "un-parliamentary" about a majority government that did not include the party with the largest number of seats in parliament. That party was the SKDL with 50 out of 200 seats.

Nearly all these reforms represented a kind of western-style radicalism, and, with the exception of some changes in the structure of the educational curriculum (not content) and the educational system, in which the influence of East Germany could be seen,[108] little was learned or adopted from the Soviets and their client states.

Yet to say that the Soviet Union had no significance for the process of radicalization in Finland would be wrong. The Social Democrats changed their attitude toward the Soviet Union in part because of the feeling at the time that the Soviet Union would never go away and, indeed, had become a factor in world stability. The United States and the Soviet Union had become the two poles of a roughly-balanced world within which Finland had to live, but clearly, geographically Finland was a lot closer to the Soviet Union than to the United States. Within a few years other factors entered the picture not only for the Social Democrats, but for Finnish public opinion as a whole. Both the United States and the Soviet Union turned out to be, under certain circumstances, quite dangerous forces for small states. However, the Soviet invasion of Czechoslovakia in 1968 did not produce the horrible succession of TV film of barbarity after barbarity that the United States' involvement in Vietnam and Cambodia did. The overthrow of the Allende regime in Chile in 1973, a democracy that had chosen to be radical, also produced a revulsion against the United States among Finns. When it came to social radicalism, therefore, the Soviet Union, by force of contrast, got a gratuitous boost.

The change that permitted the emergence of the "Big Three," however, was also due to the Social Democrats' perception that coming to terms with the Soviet Union and coming to terms with Urho Kekkonen were one and the same thing as far as participation in Finnish governments was concerned. The intertwining of the top executive of Finland with the foreign executive had reached fulfillment, and the pace-setter was the Finnish president.[109] Paasikivi had urged Kekkonen not to become a president ruling solely as a Russian governor, but also to base his support in the minds of the

---

[108] Antti Lappalainen, *Suomi kouluttajana* (Porvoo, 1991), 190.

[109] And so, provided Kekkonen became president again in 1974 (and without re-election by the people), Finland could even enter into a Free Trade Agreement with the EEC. On this, see H.P. Krosby, *Kekkosen linja* (Helsinki, 1978), 281-2.

people.[110] In fact, assured of the confidence of the Soviet leaders, Kekkonen was able to take the Finnish people along with him. In reversing the order of Paasikivi's instructions, Kekhonen also sought to embody a degree of social radicalism that took a certain *cachet* from good relations with the neighboring power. But this link had to be ultimately forged, as far as Kekkonen was concerned, by executive will. Ever conscious of what was happening at the grassroots level, Kekkonen worked to prevent the Finnish Communists from establishing themselves as the main connection with the Soviet Union.[111] A Soviet ambassador, Alexei Belyakov, got his marching papers at Kekkonen's insistence for intriguing too ardently in the interests of the Stalinist wing of the Finnish Communist Party.[112] Kekkonen and his system established the definitions.

The system was one of "consensus," a word that took time to be introduced into the Finnish language.[113] Consensus politics was not necessarily all that broad-based, however. For one thing, the Conservatives were, in the narrowest of political terms, left out. They had dared to challenge Kekkonen in the presidential election of 1968 with the candidacy of the big banker, Matti Virkkunen. Although their leader, Juha Rihtniemi, tried to make a spiritual voyage to Canossa afterward, it did not work.[114] But outside the government, in the rest of Finnish institutional life—the army, the church, the universities, banking, even in some trade unions (AKAVA)[115]—the supporters of the Finnish Conservative Party (the National Coalition Party, as it is officially called) were entrenched. The radical reforms of the late sixties and early seventies had not touched the socio-economic

---

[110] See note 85.

[111] Jakobson, "Moskovan miehet mukana pelissä," review of *Presidentti. Urho Kekkonen 1962-1968*, by Juhani Suomi, *Helsingin Sanomat*, 19 October 1994, C6.

[112] Maude, *The Finnish Dilemma*, 54.

[113] The term "konsensus," now in the Finnish language, is not to be found in the great Finnish dictionary *Nykysuomen sanakirja*, 5th printing (Porvoo, 1963). Ten years later, at the time of CSCE beginnings, it was still found necessary to concoct the clumsy and less accurate term of "laaja suostumus" ("wide consent"), which perhaps said more about Finnish than CSCE politics.

[114] The year after Virkkunen's defeat Rihtniemi declared that the Conservatives would be prepared to enter a government with the SKDL. In fact, the Conservatives first entered a government in 1987, five years after the Koivisto presidency had commenced.

[115] AKAVA is the main professional union for university graduates and takes in civil servants, officers, teachers, doctors, and lawyers.

foundation of these institutions. Indeed, behind these important institutions a kind of consensus of its own developed, later officially manifest in the promotion of a state-led incomes policy.

Within the consensual framework, personified in an unbeatable president, the parties and interest groups lined up for their share, and more of their share, of power. Though he died at the end of 1969, the ruthless Agrarian Party organizer Arvo Korsimo was all too typical. Hitting people on the head with a constant assertion of the need for good relations with the Soviet Union (embodied in the policy of his own party), he cultivated the industrial bosses (in the financial interests of his party) by pointing out that internally, all that hindered the emergence of a socialist Finland was a strong Agrarian Party.[116] Deals were made and politics became devoid of ideas.

This was the real horror of the Cold War for Finland. Its very adaptability to the Cold War situation softened the contours of adversarial politics within the country. In the period after the Second World War a welfare state was built in Finland, a state whose characteristics put a nation like the United States to shame in respect to treatment of ordinary citizens. Nonetheless, the ease with which aspects of this welfare state have been dismantled in the free-market fanaticism of the 1990s is a tragic witness to the fact that the Finnish welfare state, in its creation and development, owed too little to the force of grass roots political striving and too much to the politics of a system which all too readily adapted itself to changes in international conjunctures.

The question that is begged here is that of the demands postulated by the shifting pattern of international relations (Finnish policymakers love to talk in terms of *force majeure*) and of how "readily" the response to them should come. Finnish high politics in the 1970s softened not merely the contours of internal politics but also the contours of international politics. Kekkonen and his helpers did this by furthering an original Soviet démarche that rapidly led to the creation of the permanent machinery of the CSCE, which also helped bring the United States into a dialogue with the Soviet Union on questions of wider import than simply arms negotiations. In this

---

[116]Korsimo claimed to embody a kind of leftism that would steal power from the radical left since the Social Democrats and Conservatives were either unable or unwilling to try such politics. See Sakari Virkkunen, *Korsimo. Kekkosen mies* (Helsinki, 1976), 169.

period in Finland there seemed to be a happy reflection of the internal Finnish political consensus in the consensual work that Finland was doing globally.[117] It would be foolish to denigrate the value of this Finnish input into policies aiming to reduce the tensions of the Cold War. But there is significance in the fact that when, in Eastern Europe and the Soviet Union, human rights groups emerged under the rubric of the Helsinki Committees to try to foster the implementation of the rights laid down in the CSCE Final Act, this tribute to the capital of Finland and the process in which the Finns had played so large a part went mainly unnoticed in Finland itself.[118] Was it not a question for politics at the grass roots?

Much of what Finland became after the Second World War, as a result of its relations with Russia, were summed up in the 1970s in the West in a theory called Finlandization. This theory assumed a creeping Sovietization of Finland and, potentially, of other "soft" Western European countries. Even if many of the individual allegations made about Finland in the name of this theory were true, I have always felt the theory to be an inadequate summary of the Finnish-Russian relation.[119] In the present essay I have attempted to show that the question of Finland in the Cold War can be seen in historical terms as part of a tradition by which a Finnish elite, especially those in or around the top executive of the country, have felt the need and utilized the need to cultivate a *modus vivendi et operandi* with a somewhat penetrative top executive of a foreign power. There is nothing extraordinary in this and examples can surely be found elsewhere in the world. We are postulating a kind of quasi-constitutionalism, the operations of a double-executive unknown to Montesquieu and hardly to be comprehended in his theory, in short, the quasi-constitutionalism of international relations. The most striking feature of all is the impingement of such a quasi-constitutionalism upon Finland's internal constitutionalism. In this way a control is exercised upon the natural development of the

---

[117] The candidature of Max Jakobson for the post of UN secretary-general (see notes 97 and 98) was part of this domestic and global outlook.

[118] When I raised the existence of these committees with students of the Faculty of Law of the University of Turku in the 1980s, no one had heard of them and few were interested to learn about them.

[119] Maude, "The Further Shores of Finlandization," *Cooperation and Conflict*, 17 (1982): 3-16.

internal political forces in the country. It is a control exercised *au fond* by the domestic executive.

This form of politics did not die with the demise of the Cold War. The Finnish political and business elite, almost across the board, has come out for a form of integration into Western Europe requiring full membership for Finland in the European Union. For this they received a 57% mandate from the people in the referendum on this issue on October 16, 1994.[120] In spite of the existence of an open campaign to argue the pros or cons of membership,[121] the familiar features of executive dominance were far from absent. Finland's newly-elected President, Matti Ahtisaari, came out openly for membership and immediately after the referendum results were known told parliament that they were "morally and politically" bound to follow the wishes of those in the majority in the referendum. This statement did not reflect the norms of the Finnish Constitution, according to paragraph 2 of which the Finnish people are *represented* by parliament. Further, referenda in Finland are by definition only advisory, in contrast to the determining role of referenda in Switzerland.

The haranguing of parliament by a foreign minister who did not have a seat in it was part of the same outlook. Returning from the Brussels negotiations on entry, the foreign minister, Heikki Haavisto, upbraided the parliamentarians *en masse* in the debate on Union membership of March 4, 1994. Their debate, he pointed out, was like a village brawl and they were not fit to be members of the Union. Since this man, the former head of the Finnish Agricultural Producers' and Forest Owners' Association, had argued the case for Finland in Brussels largely in terms of what his old interest group required, and since he was soon to speak of the "blackmailing" of Finland by Brussels,[122] his outburst was unfortunate. But it was not

---

[120] Apart from the 43% who voted against union membership, it is worth pointing out that 30% of the electorate did not vote.

[121] Unfortunately, much of the campaign revolved around the issue of agriculture, a sector of the economy left out of the hitherto prevailing EEA agreement between the EFTA countries (to which Finland belonged) and the European Community. Wider issues were fudged. In this connection, it was perhaps regrettable that one of the foremost opponents of union membership packed up and left for Arizona before the campaign was fully engaged.

[122] Haavisto, in an interview on TV1 channel (5 o'clock news) of August 27, 1992, was complaining of the tantalization of Union membership, the price for which, apparently, was a low threshold beyond which special payments for agriculture would

greatly so, for such "excrescences" on either side of the debate could be ignored. The fact was that in the meantime the bureaucrats in the Finnish ministries were working away, as they had done for years, "harmonizing" Finnish legislation with the norms of the Union.

Finnish pundits, with reference to the Brussels executive, were inclined to speak of a move away from a bilateral relation with a greater state to a move into multilateralism, a multilateralism in which Finland sat in a position of equality with other states.[123] Here Finland could have its influence. But anyone who knows something about Finnish history will be able to recall that the Finns had often had an influence on the foreign executive, whether Russian or German, and there are many in Finland who believe that the present bout of Western European multilateralism is but a cover for Germany, "the best boy in the class," as the Finnish president has fondly recalled.[124]

In any case, while the Finnish people have sometimes been stirred up by foreign events and ideas, in the end, it is the elite, through the traditional domestic executive, that deals with the foreigner, in the name of a defense of democracy, more particularly parliamentary democracy. In practice, the democratic deficit, as the phrase now runs, has frequently turned out to be a considerable one.

---

not be paid. (In contrast, Finnish agriculture has been subsidized by the Finnish state and taxpayer well above even the level of the Common Agricultural Policy of the European Community and Union.)

[123] Pertti Joenniemi, "Eurooppalaistumisen haaste; Suomi ulkopolitiikan jälkeen" (unpublished paper, The Tampere Peace Research Institute, September 1994). The fact that, structurally, the Union is a multilateral venue pleasantly recalls the endeavors of the later Kekkonen foreign policy to leaven the burden of the Moscow "executive" through the multilateralism of the CSCE. On the latter, see Maude, *The Finnish Dilemma*, 127-143.

[124] "Ahtisaari: Saksa ymmärtää käyttäytyä hienotunteisesti," *Helsingin Sanomat*, 26 November 1994, A7.

3

The Ideology & Politics of Midwifery in American-Finnish Relations, 1943-45[1]

R. Michael Berry

The Parameters of Finnish-American Relations

Between 1939 and 1948 Europe twice divided into hostile ideological and military blocs. Each time Finland developed a special relationship with the principal American enemy in Europe, but continued to retain an unusually good relationship with the United States. The 1940s also brought new departures in the foreign policies of the United States and Finland. Both countries developed foreign policies that they believed would best defend their traditional values—foreign policies that had the potential to place them, but did not, in hostile camps.

Perhaps the most intriguing aspect of Finnish-American relations is the link between Finland's symbolic association in the American mind with principles of economic and political liberalism and American efforts during the Second World War and the early postwar period to encourage Finnish acceptance of accommodation with the Soviet Union. In short, the Roosevelt administration pondered ways to resolve the conflict between Soviet security concerns and the continuation of Finnish independence in large part because Finland represented in the American mind a symbol of political democracy and liberal capitalism.

If we read history through the prism of the traditional Finnish dualistic world view of power politics or through the Cold War-tinted prism of the NATO West, this link appears to be a paradox. If,

---

[1] This essay is a revised version of a paper presented at the Fourth Soviet-American Symposium on World War II, Rutgers University at Brunswick, October 16-18, 1990. I would like to thank George Maude, Keith Olson and Olli Vehvilainen for their helpful suggestions in writing this paper.

however, we read history forward through the prism of American ideological preferences for a multilateral world in the years before the Cold War, the logic becomes apparent. The paradox is in the mind of the historian who attempts to impose inappropriate logic to explain the Finnish "exception." Reference to a paradox is explanation of an exception via a skewed perception of reality.

American policy towards Finland and the symbolic role of Finland in American foreign policy can best be understood within the context of a "liberal world order paradigm" that has dominated twentieth century American foreign policy. Prior to the Second World War American policymakers advocated an informal international order based on principles of political and economic liberalism—a world in which nations would turn their backs on the economics of mercantilism and balance-of-power politics and learn to benefit from the free flow of goods, capital, and ideas. In the 1930s the image of "Honest Little Finland" that paid its debts when the European powers defaulted became a symbol of the "positive" community-building element in this paradigm, which assumed that an international sense of community could be achieved by countries that share similar values and goals. The liberal world order paradigm also contained a subordinate, security-community element of opposition to countries with closed economies—the Axis countries and later the Soviet-led Communist bloc. During the Second World War and Cold War the "negative" side of the paradigm often took the foreground over the "positive" side.

The image of "Valiant Little Finland" defending the ramparts of civilization during the Winter War reflects this negative side of the paradigm. This is not to suggest that the Winter War image lacked a positive element. It was "positive" insofar as it rested on defense of common values, but "negative" insofar as the sense of community was defined by reference to a shared enemy. This distinction between the positive and negative sides of liberalism is essential to explaining important aspects of American policy toward Finland during the 1940s when American policy shifted from policies of Soviet-American ideological conflict, to policies of Soviet-American wartime cooperation, to the politics of containment. In contrast to the prewar liberal world order paradigm, dominated by a "positive," voluntary community-building element symbolized by debt payment, the postwar containment paradigm was dominated by a "negative," security-community aspect symbolized by the Winter War.

Consequently, good relations between Finland and the United States depended on the extent to which the "positive" rather than the "negative" thrust in the liberal world order paradigm continued to affect American-Finnish relations, even if only as a subordinate consideration.

The Politics of Allied Coalitions

In the Second World War Great Britain, the Soviet Union, and the United States pursued competing strategies while cooperating to defeat Germany. The British and Soviet spheres of influence approach stood in contrast to the American preference for an open multilateral world order. These competing foreign policies spawned a two-tier alliance system. The United Nations alliance, symbolized by the Declaration of Europe, constituted the umbrella alliance.

The Anglo-Soviet alliance, epitomized by the percentage agreements of May and October 1944, and the Anglo-American relationship, exemplified by the Atlantic Charter, often worked at cross purposes within the UN alliance. The Anglo-Soviet-American world views, as they were played out and modified during the course of the war by military developments, set the limits within which Soviet neighbors could promote their national interests. The chemistry of the domestic regimes in the countries along the Soviet border determined the capacity of those countries to maneuver within the great-power-imposed framework. The limits, as well as the chemistry of the domestic regimes, differed from country to country, in part because they differed from region to region. These Soviet neighbors also fell within the sphere of different Allied coalitions. The Balkans was primarily an Anglo-Soviet affair. Czechoslovakia and Poland became a UN, i.e., an Anglo-Soviet-American, issue. Finland belonged primarily to the realm of Soviet-American diplomacy.

The British, with a greater interest than the Americans in continental affairs and conditioned by their tradition of empire building and spheres of influence, advocated an Anglo-American invasion of the Balkans to protect their position in Greece. Had this strategy worked, the British would have established a presence in the region as liberators/conquerors with a strong negotiating position in the region vis-à-vis the Soviet Union. British strategy was frustrated, however, by American insistence on a second front in France. Having failed to achieve a military solution in the Balkans within the framework of an Anglo-American understanding of the UN alliance, the British were thrown back on the Anglo-Soviet alliance. As the Soviet Union advanced into the Balkans in 1944, the British gave up hope for a favorable military solution in that region and began to seek a political modus vivendi which culminated in the Anglo-Soviet percentage agreements of May and October 1944.[2]

Finland never meant much to the British. In December 1941 the Soviets expressed an understanding of British rights to bases in Norway, and the British wrote off Finland, assuming their position was secured in Scandinavia. The Finnish question, having been resolved early in the war, fell outside the scope of the percentage agreements. Unlike countries in Eastern and Southeastern Europe, Finland somehow belonged more to the domain of Soviet-American diplomacy than to UN or Anglo-Soviet diplomacy—a role expressed by the American decision to maintain wartime relations with Finland.

At the formal level Finland was an element in Anglo-Soviet relations: Britain declared war on Finland in December 1941 as a result of Soviet pressure, and the British were observers on the postwar Allied Control Commission (ACC) in Finland. But the British preferred to leave the initiative on Finland to the Soviet Union and the United States. A reading of State Department documents for 1943-1944 suggests that American policy toward Finland, as in the case of Czechoslovakia and Poland, often reflected a preoccupation with the postwar era. In contrast, American interest in Rumania, Bulgaria, and Hungary reveals preoccupation with winning the war.

In 1943-1944 the United States formulated policy as if it were above spheres of influence politics. Finland had to come to terms with the Soviet Union, but the context of that accommodation was postwar UN cooperation that would lend itself to a multilateral world order. This essay examines how Allied policy determined the framework within which Finland could operate and how the nature of the Finnish domestic regime enabled Finland to maneuver within that framework.

Wartime Finnish-American Relations

American wartime policy towards Finland was influenced by the positive images of *Honest* and *Valiant* Finland, but the rationale for maintaining diplomatic relations was premised on the hope that those

---

[2] For these negotiations, see Joseph M. Siracusa, "Frankin D. Roosevelt & the Night Stalin and Churchill Divided Europe," in his *In The Dark House: American Diplomacy & the Ideological Origins of the Cold War* (Claremont, CA., 1998), 1-30, 160-179.

relations could provide the United States leverage in Helsinki. In 1941-1942 American policy influenced the Finnish decision to remain on the front established in December 1941 in Soviet Karelia. After Stalingrad, Finnish policymakers premised their attempts to exit from the war on the hope that any arrangement with the Soviet Union would entail some kind of American guarantee. The State Department believed that maintenance of diplomatic relations would contribute to easing Finland out of the war. These Finnish and American perceptions, while essential to maintaining the wartime relationship, were flawed. The Soviet Union wanted to settle the Finnish question on a bilateral basis. Finland, wary of Soviet intentions and mindful of a possible two-front war against Germany and the Soviet Union, feared a leap into the dark; and the gulf between the Finnish insistence on the pre-Winter War borders and the Soviet demand for the post-Winter War borders could not be bridged. These problems became painfully clear to Washington in March 1943 when the State Department attempted to mediate a separate peace between Helsinki and Moscow.[3]

The failure of the American attempt to bring Finland and the Soviet Union to the peace table in spring 1943 prompted the United States to decide to sever diplomatic relations. This decision was reversed at the last moment, however, because the break would have coincided with the Polish-Soviet conflict over the Katyn controversy.[4] Thereafter, the State Department pursued a cautious policy, encouraged by the emergence of a group of Finnish peace activists representing a broad spectrum of Finnish opinion[5] and by concrete official Finnish peace feelers.[6]

Between Stalingrad and Teheran the Roosevelt administration's concept of a "friendly-democratic" solution for Soviet neighbors began to take shape. Leading figures in the administration, the State Department, and the internationalist-oriented press began to distinguish between the details of the Atlantic Charter (insistence on specific borders) and the spirit of the Charter (national self-

---

[3] For the unrealized peace hopes of February and March 1943, see R. Michael Berry, *American Foreign Policy and the Finnish Exception: Ideological Preferences and Wartime Realities* (Helsinki, 1988), 264-74 and sources.

[4] Ibid., 285-6 and sources.

[5] Ibid., 253-64, 274-9, and sources.

[6] Ibid., 319-21 and sources.

determination). There was no inherent contradiction between international cooperation and spheres of influence arrangements, as long as those spheres were "open." This concept of open spheres, better known as the notion of friendly and democratic Soviet neighbors, was spelled out in September 1943 in a Policy Group memorandum, written in part by Charles Bohlen, which assumed Soviet predominance in Eastern Europe but held out hope for self-determination of Soviet neighbors.[7]

On October 6 Laurin Zilliacus, the primary link between Finnish peace activists and the American legation in Helsinki, gave American chargé Robert McClintock a lengthy memorandum to be transmitted to the Soviet Union before the Moscow Conference. Dealing first with the general problem of weakening Axis unity in Europe, Zilliacus outlined the attitudes of three different groups in countries along the Soviet border: those who saw salvation through revolution; those who had looked to Germany but were now looking to the West to counter Soviet influence; and those who believed that only postwar Allied cooperation held out hope for postwar peace. Zilliacus, who identified with the third group, hoped that the Allies would act to bring those in the second group around to the position of the third group.

Using language similar to the wartime writings of Walter Lippmann, Zilliacus suggested that the basis for a Soviet-Finnish settlement could be a "good neighbor policy."[8] Finland should recognize Soviet security concerns around Leningrad, but the Soviet Union should understand the advantages of having friendly and secure small neighbors rather than annexed territory and apprehensive neighbors. Zilliacus called for an open Allied commitment to postwar Finnish independence to strengthen the position of the Finnish peace activists.[9] He was typical of the non-Communist left that hoped for postwar Allied cooperation.

Three days later an exchange between the Finnish desk officer Randolph Higgs and Assistant Secretary of State Adolf Berle placed the Finnish question squarely within the context of the pre-Moscow

---

[7] Edward Marks, "Charles E. Bohlen and the Acceptable Limits of Soviet Hegemony in Eastern Europe: A Memorandum of 18 October 1945," *Diplomatic History* 3 (Spring, 1979): 204.

[8] For Lippmann, see Berry, *American Foreign Policy and the Finnish Exception*, 337 and sources.

[9] McClintock to SD, 6 October 1943, State Department Records (hereafter SD), RG 59, 740.00119 EW 1939/1911, National Archives (hereafter NA).

memorandum that Bohlen helped to draft and that Zilliacus gave the American legation in Helsinki. Ironically, however, the Higgs memorandum was written, not in response to the Zilliacus memorandum, but to a Finnish aide-memoire of October 6. Higgs complained to Berle about the Finnish inability to see the larger picture. Finland was not at fault morally and could not have remained neutral in the European conflict, but "nations like Finland cannot afford to guess wrong." Despite Higgs' pessimism about Finland being "between the upper and the nether millstone," his memorandum contained an element of hope: "UN victory may save Finland—what is relevant today is whether all nations can bury the past well enough that the security of all great powers (especially Russia) will allow the existence of small nations like Finland."

Finland had been on the wrong side and, therefore, "must prove that it can give this security. This proof is all that Finland can give under existing circumstances." Higgs added that "these facts of life are beyond the control of Finland and the United States. It might be helpful," he concluded, "if it were put to Finland in these terms." Berle replied, "this is almost the way I see it. But these are still some millions of *people* who ought to be able to live in peace."[10] The memoranda by the Policy Group and Higgs represented the *realpolitik* that was emerging at different levels in the State Department as policymakers shifted from a paradigm of Soviet-American conflict to Soviet-American cooperation: Finland's fate would rest on finding a balance between Soviet security requirements and Finnish self-determination. Berle's reaction revealed acceptance of Higgs' logic, but skepticism about Soviet intentions. From autumn 1943 into the post-Yalta period, the views expressed by Bohlen, Zilliacus, Higgs, and Berle continued to set the parameters of American policy towards Finland.

When Roosevelt left for Teheran in November 1943 he hoped to persuade the Soviets to be magnanimous towards their neighbors, so that he could try to convince Soviet neighbors that it was in their interests to cooperate with the Soviet Union. A Finnish-Soviet accord

---

[10] Higgs memorandum to Berle, 9 October 1943, ibid., FW760d.61/1683. A year later Berle wrote a strong statement in favor of American support for a Soviet good neighbor policy in Eastern Europe; Policy Committee Document A-B/1, "Principal Problems in Europe," by Adolf Berle, 16 September 1944, cited in Martin Weil, *A Pretty Good Club: The Founding Fathers of the U.S. Foreign Service* (New York, 1978), 190-1.

would contribute to this policy.[11] Roosevelt raised the Finnish issue at Teheran, if only cautiously. Hull was even more cautious. When Harriman reported from the Soviet Union Swedish interest in a peace settlement and the American position,[12] Hull warned against initiating discussions about Finland with Soviet officials. Past efforts had "been barren of result," and the American "status as an ally of the Soviet Union" made its position in the matter "somewhat delicate." Consequently, the United States looked to Sweden, which had "an equally vital interest in getting Finland out of the war as soon as possible."[13]

Finland eventually learned of the Soviet conditions in February 1944, but only after their contents had been communicated to the United States and Great Britain. President Roosevelt expressed appreciation for being kept informed, but did not wish to comment on the Soviet terms. From that point until the signing of the Finnish-Soviet armistice in September 1944 the Soviet Union communicated its exchanges with Finland to the United States, and the State Department refrained from commenting on specific terms. Unwilling to cede the territory lost during the Winter War and won back in 1941 and wary of possible German retaliation, the Finnish parliament rejected Soviet terms in April 1944. The Finnish government continued a policy of wait and see, hoping that it could sit out the rest of the war and have its fate decided at a general peace conference, i.e., within a UN rather than a Soviet-Finnish framework.[14]

A top-level American intelligence analysis of Finland in February 1944 lent credence to the Finnish confidence in its short-term defensive position: "If Finland elects to remain in the war, and if the Soviet Union decides to attack her, only an overwhelming Soviet ground force with considerable armor supported by a much greater amount of strategic bombing of military objects than the Soviets have exhibited in the past could defeat organized Finnish resistance." Prospects of a Finnish exit from the war were not yet very good.

---

[11] For Roosevelt's views on Finland at Teheran, see Berry, *American Foreign Policy and the Finnish Exception*, 360-2 and sources.

[12] Harriman to SD, 12 December 1944, SD, RG 59, 740.0011 EW 1939/32330 1/4 and 1/2, NA.

[13] Hull to Harriman, 17 December 1943, ibid., 740.0011 EW 1939/32330 1/2.

[14] For the failure to reach a Finnish accord in spring 1944, see Berry, *American Foreign Policy and the Finnish Exception*, 386-96 and sources.

Finland would opt for peace only if given a western guarantee or if forced by military defeat. The analysis was ambivalent about Soviet postwar intentions: "No tangible evidence exists for Soviet preparations of a Communist or a 'Free Finland' movement; the Soviets recall the failure of such efforts in 1939." Nevertheless, gradual infiltration and Finnish intransigence "might well mean the end of even nominal Finnish independence."[15] A Finn could not have written a better rationale for Finnish policy in spring 1944.

In April 1944 John Scott of *Time* and *Life* magazines (and the Office of Strategic Services) interviewed J.K. Paasikivi, the conservative long-time advocate of good Soviet-Finnish relations, after his return from the negotiations in Moscow. Paasikivi understood that the United States could not make any commitments to Finland "because in the last analysis you [the United States] would need four million soldiers to back them up." Scott's account continued: "One of the most impressive speeches I remember hearing was made by Paasikivi. Repeating to me what he had probably told Molotov—a description of what the results would be if Russia overran Finland— Paasikivi stood up, shook a bony freckled forefinger in the air and said, 'We will shoot from behind every stone and tree, we will go on shooting for fifty years. We are not Czechs. We are not Dutchmen. We will fight tooth and nail behind every rock and over the ice of every lake. I will not fight for long. I am old, but others will fight.'"[16] This interview throws light on Paasikivi's concept of *realpolitik*. He recognized the necessity of adjusting to Soviet security requirements, but there were limits to how far he would go. *Realpolitik* also required recognition and defense of legitimate domestic requirements. Good Finnish-Soviet relations would have no meaningful content if achieved at the expense of Finnish self-determination.

Discouraged by the failure of the Soviet-Finnish talks in April, the State Department decided to break relations with Finland. Yet even as Hull proposed a break, which Roosevelt refused to act on,[17] the State

---

[15] Joint Intelligence Staff, Finnish Situation, J:I:S:24/M, 8 February 1944, CCS 387 Finland (2-22-44), NA; Memorandum by Cumming, 26 February 1944, *Foreign Relations of the United States, 1944* (hereafter *FRUS* followed by year and volume), 3:565-6.

[16] John Scott, "Report on a Fortnight in Finland," 21 April 1944, OSS Document 76824.

[17] Berry, *American Foreign Policy and the Finnish Exception*, 397-400 and sources.

Department saw a ray of hope in the Finnish situation. In a memorandum drawn up for Hull's discussion of the Finnish case with Roosevelt, Hugh Cumming of the Division of Northern European Affairs noted that Soviet terms would leave Finland at the mercy of the Soviet Union militarily, economically, and thus potentially politically; but the Soviet conditions left Finland independent internally and the British, despite apprehension about their economic interests in Finland, considered the Soviet terms reasonable.[18] Cumming's hope that the peace activists would eventually rise to leadership positions in the postwar era implied a Finnish ability to develop a foreign policy acceptable to the Soviet Union. His memorandum can be read together with the high-level intelligence analysis of February and Scott's interview with Paasikivi in April to suggest that the Soviet Union would have to pay a high price to occupy a well-defended and united Finland but could obtain a friendly neighbor if a Paasikivi-led peace opposition came to power. This perception proved to be well founded during the difficult period between the Finnish-Soviet armistice of September 1944 and Yalta in February 1945.

The Allied Offensives in the Summer of 1944

The landings in Normandy and the massive Soviet offensive on the Karelian Isthmus set the stage for a rapid decline in Finnish-American relations. When the Soviet offensive began on the eastern front, Finland was the first target. No longer could Finland hope to keep a low profile on the periphery and to have its fate determined at a general peace conference.[19] In Moscow, Stalin told Harriman that the main Soviet offensive had been delayed two weeks because of logistical difficulties. He then explained the two-fold objective of present military action on the Finnish front: to protect Leningrad and to convince the Finns of the "stupidity of their continuing the war." When Harriman indicated that Roosevelt would consider any suggestion Stalin might have regarding American policy towards

---

[18] Memorandum by Hugh Cumming to Hull, 6 May 1944, SD, RG 59, 760d.61/5-644, NA.

[19] For unofficial Finnish responses to the allied offenses, see Berry, *American Foreign Policy and the Finnish Exception*, 407-8; Touko Perko, *Aseveljen kuva. Suhtautuminen Saksaan jatkosodan Suomessa, 1941-1944* (Porvoo, 1971), 201-21; Olli-Pekka Nyberg, "Sotaa maihinnousun varjossa," (M.A. thesis, University of Turku, 1987), 96-126.

Finland, Stalin mentioned the possibility of a break in diplomatic relations but agreed that it was not desirable for the present. Despite earlier Soviet-American differences over American policy towards Finland, the two governments agreed even at this late date on the value of the United States maintaining diplomatic relations with Finland. Moreover, Stalin reaffirmed his commitment to an independent Finland under new leadership.[20]

The Finnish government immediately asked the Swedish secretary, Erik Boheman, to establish contact with the Soviet minister in Stockholm, Alexandra Kollontay.[21] The Soviets replied that talks could begin only after Helsinki issued a statement that it was ready to "capitulate." The German counter to the Soviet offensive was the arrival of German Foreign Minister Joachim von Ribbentrop promising German support in return for a Finnish pledge to remain in the war. Unaware of von Ribbentrop's presence in Finland, but aware of the Finnish interest in peace and Swedish concern about the term "capitulate," the State Department authorized Harriman to approach Molotov and tell him that Finland had decided to break with Germany.[22] On June 27 Harriman discussed the problem with Stalin, who replied that there was nothing the United States could do for the moment. The Finnish government had not yet responded to the latest Soviet communique. Stalin considered the talk of a new cabinet "only rumors," and he did not believe a statement respecting Finnish independence would be of any value. The United States should decide its own course of action towards Finland, Stalin added, but it could informally mention to the Finns that the Soviet Union had no designs on that country.[23]

Meanwhile, von Ribbentrop obtained a written promise from President Ryti that he would not initiate peace negotiations without

---

[20] Harriman to the President, 11 and 12 June 1944, Map Room, Box 11, Harriman Messages, State Department, Franklin D. Roosevelt Presidential Library (hereafter FDRL).

[21] Georg A. Gripenberg, *Finland and the Great Powers* (Lincoln, NB, 1965), 322-3; Johnson (Stockholm) to SD, 22 June 1944, SD, RG 59, 860d.01/194, NA; Tuomo Polvinen, *Suomi Kansainvälisessa politiikassa. II Teheranista Jaltaan* (Juva, 1980), 69-70.

[22] Hull to Harriman, 24 June 1944, SD, RG 59, 860d/6-2444, NA.

[23] Harriman to SD, 27 June 1944, *FRUS, 1944*, 3:603-4.

German approval.[24] The United States immediately broke relations with Finland.[25] The United States now stood clearly on the sidelines, even more removed than the disinterested British who, nevertheless, had to take a stand on the Soviet terms offered to Finland. A memorandum prepared by Foreign Minister Eden and presented to the War Cabinet on August 9, 1944, summarized British policy. Eden expected the Soviet Union to pursue a moderate policy in Eastern and Southeastern Europe: "Although we shall no doubt hope that Finland will be left some real degree of at least cultural and commercial independence and a parliamentary regime, Russian influence will in any event be predominant in Finland and we shall not be able, nor would it serve any important British interests, to contest that influence."[26]

Ryti's decision to act without parliamentary approval caused considerable unrest among Social Democrats and representatives of the Swedish Peoples' Party in parliament, but, as so often during the war, their representatives in the government remained unwilling to threaten national unity. After suffering heavy losses the Finnish army stabilized the front. On July 12 the Soviet Union suspended offensive operations and informed Finland via Stockholm of its readiness to begin negotiations. Finland would have to take the initiative, however, and be represented by a new government. Ryti resigned, and parliament elected Marshal Mannerheim president by a unanimous vote, thus freeing Finland of the burden of Ryti's personal pledge to Hitler.[27]

---

[24] For Ryti's leadership in general as well as the immediate pressure on Ryti on from Germany and the Finnish military political leadership, see Olli Vehvilainen, *Kuilunyli*, vol. 3 in Silvo Hietanen, ed., *Kansakunta Sodassa,* I-III (Helsinki, 1992). See also, Gripenberg, *Finland and the Great Powers*, 331-2; Polvinen, *Suomi kansainvalisessa politiikassa*, 70-8.

[25] Berry, *American Foreign Policy and the Finnish Exception*, 412-14, 416-17, and sources.

[26] This memorandum was written prior to the massive Soviet breakthrough in Rumania which frightened Churchill but probably had little impact on British policy toward the Nordic countries. For Anglo-Finnish and Anglo-Soviet relations, see Peter Ludlow, "Britain and Northern Europe, 1940-1945," *Scandinavian Journal of History* 4 (1979): passim and 154-5 for the Eden quote.

[27] Polvinen, *Suomi kansainvalisessa politiikassa*, 82; Olli Vehvilainen, "Finland's Withdrawal from the Second World War," in Ilkka Seppinen, ed., *Aspects of Security: The Case of Independent Finland* (Vaasa, 1983), 203; Väinö Voionmaa, *Kuriiripostia 1941-1946* (Helsinki, 1971), 369-72.

Antti Hackzell, a former foreign minister and envoy to Moscow who was a conservative member of parliament, became the new prime minister. The new government included representatives from all the political parties except the small neo-fascist Patriotic Peoples' Movement that had been excluded from the government since early 1943. The Soviets, who had previously refused to support the formation of a government-in-exile because they considered the peace opposition powerless against the financial and industrial support given the wartime government, were pleased with the composition of the new government.[28]

Mindful of Hungary's fate,[29] Mannerheim remained cautious about breaking relations with Germany. A consensus gradually emerged, however, among the wartime and the current leadership about the necessity of a break with Germany and an armistice with the Soviet Union. The final decision was made on August 24, just after the massive Soviet offensive on its southern front led to a ceasefire in Rumania. The following day the Finnish minister in Stockholm proposed negotiations to Kollontay. Molotov consulted the British ambassador in Moscow and also brought Harriman up to date on the Finnish situation. The British approved of Soviet terms; the United States refrained from comment.[30] The Soviet reply arrived in Helsinki on August 29: Finland had to break relations with Germany immediately and to demand the withdrawal of German troops within fifteen days, after which German troops were to be interned.

Mannerheim accepted the Soviet preconditions after consulting the military chief of general staff and representative members of Finland's wartime leadership. In Stockholm Kollontay worked hard to keep the channel of communication open between Helsinki and Moscow, perhaps exaggerating the Finnish willingness to disarm German troops and explaining to the Finns that details about disarming German troops could be negotiated in Moscow.

Taking the bull by the horns, Mannerheim sent a telegram directly to Stalin on September 1 proposing a ceasefire on September 3 so that Finnish troops could be released for action against German troops.

---

[28] Gripenberg, *Finland and the Great Powers*, 332-8; Polvinen, *Suomi kansainvalisessa politiikassa*, 82-3.

[29] Germany occupied Hungary in March 1944 when it attempted to exit the war.

[30] For the Soviet terms, see Harriman to Secretary of State, 26 August and 4 September 1944, *FRUS, 1944*, 3:611-12, 615.

Withdrawal to the 1940 frontier would be carried out by September 20. In this way Mannerheim expressed a willingness to withdraw troops prior to the commencement of negotiations. This could serve to improve the atmosphere for negotiations and to deny the Soviets a pretext for launching another offensive.

The ceasefire began on September 5. Two days later the Finnish delegation, led by the prime minister, the minister of defense, and the chief of general staff, arrived in Moscow where they had to wait the outcome of the Soviet negotiations with Rumania. The delegation had extensive experience in Russian affairs and represented the establishment in prewar and wartime Finnish society. Looming in the background was Finnish reluctance to begin yet another war. But fear of Soviet intentions made Finland even more reluctant to provide Soviet troops a pretext for entering Finland.[31]

Negotiations in Moscow

On September 6, the day after British Ambassador Archibald Clark Kerr reminded Molotov that he had not yet been informed about the armistice terms for Finland, Molotov gave the British and American ambassadors a draft of peace terms, based, as Molotov told Clark Kerr, on the Rumanian armistice draft, and invited them to meet that evening to discuss details with members of the Soviet delegation. Harriman agreed to attend on the understanding that he would be present only as an observer.[32]

That evening the British and American ambassadors met with the entire Soviet negotiating team. Harriman noted the similarity between the Finnish peace and the Rumanian armistice terms. The Soviet Union planned to operate the Allied Control Commission in Finland until the termination of the war in Europe and to exchange diplomatic representatives with Finland after the war. Harriman concluded that the Soviet Union would object to political representatives from other countries, but would probably permit the establishment of consulates.

Harriman requested the Department's reaction to the Soviet terms and to a Soviet proposal that the Finnish government compensate American interests for losses in the nickel-rich Petsamo area. He was

---

[31] Tuomo Polvinen, *Between East and West: Finland in International Politics, 1944-1947* (Helsinki, 1986), 17-23; Vehvilainen, "Finland's Withdrawal from the Second World War," 203-6.

[32] Harriman to SD, 6 September 1944, *FRUS, 1944*, 3:617-18. The Finnish case was never discussed in the European Advisory Commission, ibid., 3:608-9.

particularly interested in the Department's views on American political and military representation in Finland.[33] The following day, the Department instructed him to refrain from commenting on the Soviet terms. The Department hoped, however, to be informed of future developments and to keep the possibility of an American consulate in Helsinki open.[34]

The draft treaty contained limited modifications of the treaty presented Finland in spring 1944: Finland could permit German troops two weeks to leave the country before beginning to intern them, but the Soviets now demanded the right to lease a naval base at Porkkala. When Clark Kerr noted that Helsinki fell within the range of the guns at Porkkala, Molotov responded that the days of armed conflict between Finland and the Soviet Union were over. The Soviet navy needed, however, a "new Gibraltar" to control the Gulf of Finland. Airfields in southern Finland would be available to the Allied (Soviet) military command to use in the Baltic region. The Allied Control Commission (ACC) would have unlimited access to all offices and institutions and the right to obtain any information considered necessary to perform their duties. The treaty also called for the elimination of all fascist organizations and propaganda.[35]

The British proposed three formal changes in the Soviet terms: the exclusion of long-term peace arrangements from the armistice agreement; provision for direct contact between British representatives on the Allied Control Commission and Finnish authorities; and compensation for foreign property interests in the Petsamo district.[36] The Soviets rejected the second proposal, but accepted the other two.

The British wanted the Soviet Union, not Finland, to be responsible for compensation in the Petsamo district. They did not want to establish a precedent of having the ceding party pay compensation. Moreover, they doubted Finland's ability to meet both the reparation and the compensation demands. Harriman urged the State Department to intervene in the Petsamo question, lest the Soviet Union interpret American silence as approval of terms that were "not in accord with

---

[33] Harriman to SD, 6 September 1944, ibid., 3:618-19.

[34] Hull to Harriman, 7 September 1944, SD, RG 59, 740.00119 EW 1939/9-644, NA.

[35] Polvinen, *Between East and West*, 24, 58.

[36] Winant (London) to SD, 14 September 1944, *FRUS, 1944*, 3:621.

our basic principles."[37] American silence reigned, however. The
Soviets eventually agreed to pay compensation for property in
Petsamo out of the reparations Finland would pay the Soviet Union.[38]
In this way the principle of compensation was met, but agreement was
never reached on the sum of the reparation. Even though the
reparation demand had been reduced from 600 million dollars in the
spring to 300 million, both the British and American governments
considered the sum excessive. In the end, Clark Kerr agreed to sign
the armistice on the condition that he could write a separate protest.
The perplexed Molotov finally agreed to the formula that combined
British acceptance of the armistice with the right to voice a dissenting
opinion.

The Soviet decision to offer Finland a peace treaty rather than an
armistice remains one of the intriguing unanswered questions in
Finnish-Allied relations. Perhaps the Soviet Union hoped to finalize
the Finnish-Soviet relationship immediately while Anglo-American
troops were still on the periphery of the continent and/or to
demonstrate the limits of Soviet goals. Although plausible, this
explanation, which the Finnish historian Tuomo Polvinen has
advanced,[39] raises still another question: why a peace treaty for
Finland and an armistice treaty for Rumania? When combined with
other evidence the difference suggests that Moscow required in
Rumania's case more confirmation that it would have a friendly
postwar neighbor in a more stable region and access to southern
waters.

Whatever the Soviet motives for a peace treaty, the British objected.
The Northern Division of the Foreign Office argued that the need to
consult the United States and the Dominions and to obtain
parliamentary approval made a peace treaty unrealistic. It was also
unwise to establish unacceptable precedents, such as compensation for
property by the ceding nation and a final decision on reparation sums
and territorial questions before the end of the war. The Soviets
initially accepted the British suggestion to sign an armistice and a

---

[37] Harriman to SD, 10 September 1944, ibid., 3:619-20.

[38] Winant (London) to SD, 14 September 1944, SD, RG 59, 740.00119 EW
1939/9-1444, NA. The agreement was included in a separate Anglo-Soviet protocol;
Winant to SD, 14-15 September 1944, ibid., 740.00119 EW 1939/9-1444; *FRUS,
1944*, 3:621-2.

[39] Polvinen, *Between East and West*, 24.

preliminary peace treaty, but decided at the last minute to present Finland an armistice treaty.

The Finnish-Soviet talks got off to a bad start. The chairman of the Finnish delegation suffered a stroke several hours before the delegations met, and the Finnish minister of defense and the chief of general staff were unable to provide precise information on the location of German troops. Clark Kerr reported that he was uncertain whether the Finnish "helplessness" was real or feigned. "Molotov showed most surprising patience and in the confusion of conversation which followed seemed to me to treat Mr. Walden [the minister of defense who served as the Finnish chairman] as a good-natured nurse would treat a very backward child."[40]

The atmosphere improved somewhat the following day after Finnish troops repelled a German attack on Suursaari, a strategically located island in the Gulf of Finland. German troops were withdrawing from southern Finland, but the Finnish delegation had not yet produced any evidence of disarming German troops in northern Finland. Although the Soviet desire to keep casualties to a minimum probably explains Soviet insistence that Finland disarm German troops, the Finnish chief of general staff also detected a pedagogical element in Soviet policy. The Finns must learn their lesson. The better the job they did in the process, he concluded, the sounder the basis of future Soviet-Finnish relations.[41]

Finland's gamble on German power, which had been rooted in fear of Soviet intentions, left Finnish wartime policy bankrupt. A ray of hope for Finnish self-determination existed, however, even against this backdrop of Finnish despair. From the time when Soviet troops confronted a united and determined Finland in the Winter War, the

---

[40] One possible explanation for the Soviet turnabout was the long shadow of the Dumbarton Oaks controversy over the structure of membership of the future United Nations organization. Molotov told Clark Kerr that representatives of the Soviet eastern republics would sign a peace treaty with Finland if representatives of the dominions also signed. Given British reluctance to accept this formula and Soviet unwillingness to delay the issue any longer, the Soviets decided to offer an armistice; Polvinen, *Between East and West*, 32-3.

[41] Erik Heinrichs, *Mannerheim-gestalten* (Helsinki, 1959), 413. It is impossible to tell whether Heinrichs' observation reflected his perception at the time or in the 1950s, but a study of Heinrichs demonstrates that the Finnish chief of general staff was pursuing already in September 1944 a strategy of cooperation with the Soviet Union so that Finland could maintain a postwar army; Martti Turtola, *Erik Heinrichs, Mannerheimin ja Paasikiven kenraali* (Helsinki, 1988), 216-21, 234-47.

Soviet Union had exhibited a degree of respect for Finnish independence. All issues related to Finnish independence were negotiable. The Finnish decision not to advance beyond the line established in December 1941 demonstrated Finnish interest in promoting Finnish, as opposed to German, interests. During the war the Soviet Union made more attempts to open peace talks with Finland than with any other neighbor in the Axis camp. With Germany in retreat and the United States unwilling to become a counterbalance to the Soviet Union, Finland had no choice but to act on possible Soviet respect for Finnish independence.

Reaching a Modus vivendi with the ACC
(Who will drive out the Germans?)

The chairman of the Allied Control Commission arrived on October 5, 1944. The ACC acted, as in Italy and Rumania, on behalf of the allied military command. In the case of Finland the term "allied" was followed by the word "Soviet" in brackets, lest there be any question about the role of the ACC. The choice of General Andrey Zhdanov revealed the importance the Soviet Union placed on the ACC. The political section was headed by Pavel Orlov who had served as the Soviet minister to Finland between the two Russo-Finnish Wars.[42]

The expulsion of German troops was the top ACC priority, but this priority was complicated, from the Finnish perspective, by the Soviet demand for demobilization to prewar status within two and one half months. Resolution of these two problems created considerable tension in the early stage of the ACC.[43] The German 20th Mountain Army in Lapland consisted of nine divisions. It was, in the words of Hitler, "the best army which I have at my disposal. It consists almost entirely of mountain troops. They are thoroughly hardened and trained in battle."[44]

The German military command had begun, however, to draw up contingency plans in autumn 1943 for a possible Finnish exit from the war. By April 1944 the two most southern army corps had been

---

[42] Polvinen, *Between East and West*, 58.

[43] Ibid., 62-3; Aulis Blinnikka, *Valvontakomission aika (Porvoo, 1969)*, 17-18.

[44] The quote from Hitler's description of the Mountain Army in Lapland when it was handed over to General Rendulic in June 1944; Polvinen, *Between East and West*, 37.

withdrawn to protect the Petsamo nickel mines. Once Finland actually began to withdraw from the war, Hitler approved a plan to encourage pro-German Finns to join the German ranks, only to be informed by the German minister in Helsinki, Wipert von Blucher, that Mannerheim had the backing of the entire Finnish population.[45]

Having achieved a stable front and prospects of an armistice with the Soviet Union, Mannerheim began to transfer troops from the Karelian front even before the ceasefire came into force on September 5. The armistice terms permitted German troops access to Finnish railroads until September 15. As the deadline approached, a tacit Finnish-German modus vivendi permitted Finnish occupation of Oulu on that date. For the remainder of the month the Finnish military cooperated as German troops continued their retreat, and German troops permitted evacuation of the civilian population in the North.[46]

Molotov's demand for immediate and forceful Finnish military action in the North threatened to undo the tacit Finnish-German understanding. Worried about the possible failure of negotiations in Moscow, Mannerheim was initially willing to begin the offensive, but the Finnish military high command, determined to follow on the tail of the German retreat, pursued a strategy of barking from a distance to give the impression of military advancement.[47] Mannerheim permitted the tactic of German retreat and Finnish advance until the end of September. Meanwhile the civilian population of Lapland was evacuated; the German military command resisted pressure from Berlin to destroy all immovable property; and the Finnish military command resisted Soviet pressure to begin an offensive against German troops. Had the Soviet commander on the Karelian front had his way, he would have attacked the German Mountain Army—a move which would have upset the Finnish strategy—but Stalin intervened, threatening to relieve him of command and arguing that the Finns should perform their duty.

With the arrival of the ACC in late September, Mannerheim's inclination to act before being compelled to do so became the basis of Finnish military policy—a policy made somewhat easier by the

---

[45] Ibid., 39-40.

[46] Ibid., 42-3.

[47] P. Vuolento, *Suomalais-Saksalaiset sotilaalliset neuvottelut syksyllä 1944* (Helsinki 1973), 40-3; U.S. Haahti, "Varjosota: Lapin Sodan 1944-1945 alkuvaihe," *Sotilasaikakauslehti* 10:701-4.

German decision to abandon northern Finland in order to secure a strong position in Norway. As the Germans retreated, Finland requested Soviet assistance to capture the two crossroads in Lapland essential to the German retreat. Stalin apparently considered the proposal because he asked Churchill, who was in Moscow at the time, about a joint Anglo-Soviet offensive.

The Anglo-Soviet leaders, who were drawing up the percentage agreements for the Balkans, were willing to consider military cooperation in Finland. And Finland, reluctant to permit Soviet troops on Finnish territory, was willing to risk Soviet intervention in northern Finland. Churchill offered, however, only naval assistance, and Stalin rejected the Finnish request. Had he approved, Soviet troops would have carried the brunt of the battle. Stalin's refusal to commit Soviet troops also suggests recognition of the secondary nature of and acceptance of the slow pace of the Finnish advance.[48] The German troops retreating into Norway, unlike German troops in Central Europe, were not blocking the Soviet advance to Berlin.

American Political Representation in Finland

The Soviet Union insisted on the leading ACC role in Finland and Rumania—a role that the United States and Britain acknowledged without fully realizing the degree of subordination that the Soviet Union envisioned. Stymied in their efforts to gain Soviet acceptance of a dual role for their representatives on the ACC, as subordinate members of the ACC but also as independent political representatives in Rumania and Finland, the British appointed separate political representatives to those countries.

On October 3, the British sent representatives to Rumania, Bulgaria, and Finland. They requested that the United States follow suit in the case of the two Balkan countries, but made no mention of Finland.[49] The State Department still hoped to resolve the problem of political representation in Rumania within the framework of the ACC,[50] but

---

[48] Polvinen, *Between East and West*, 468,504,54.

[49] Winant to SD, 3 October 1944, SD, RG 59, 740.00119 Control (Finland) 10-344, NA; *FRUS, 1944*, 4:245.

[50] On October 4 Hull sent a message to several American representatives stating that "an Allied Control Commission is being established in Rumania. It is expected that the only official relations between the Rumanian and United States governments will be conducted through that channel until such time as diplomatic relations are resumed"; Hull to Certain Diplomatic and Consular Officers (Ankara, Istanbul, Bern, Lisbon, Rome, Stockholm and Madrid), 4 October 1944, *FRUS, 1944*, 4:246.

soon decided to follow the British example. On October 12 Hull directed Harriman to notify the Soviet government of the American intention to appoint a political representative to Rumania.[51] The following day the State Department began to move cautiously on representation in Finland, asking Harriman his views on possible Soviet reaction to an American representative who would act as an intermediary between the American government and the ACC.[52] Harriman recommended the appointment of a consul; an intermediary would not have direct access to Finnish officials.[53] The American legation in Stockholm went a step beyond Harriman, suggesting a representative with a rank equivalent to that of the British representative in Finland.[54] In early November George Kennan, first secretary in the American embassy in Moscow, objected to American reliance on Swiss representation of American interest in Finland and suggested that the Soviet Union might be perplexed by the American failure to follow the British example in Finland.[55]

The Soviet acceptance in late October of an American political representative in Rumania[56] and mutually reinforcing advice from American representatives in Moscow and Stockholm prompted the State Department to nominate a political representative to Finland. On November 11 President Roosevelt appointed Maxwell M. Hamilton "the representative of the United States in Finland." The State Department expected Hamilton to have freedom of movement and access to Finnish officials and to represent American interests in Finland just as the American political representative outside the ACC in Rumania and Bulgaria were representing American interests in those countries. Randolph Higgs, the second secretary of the American legation in Stockholm, was to be transferred to Helsinki

---

[51] Secretary of State to Harriman, 12 October 1944, ibid., 4:250-1. The Soviets responded favorably two weeks later to the American proposal; Kennan to SD, 28 October 1944, ibid., 4:252.

[52] Hull to Harriman, 13 October 1944, ibid., 3:624-5.

[53] Harriman to SD, 16 October 1944, ibid., 3:625.

[54] Johnson to SD, 25 October 1944, SD, RG 59, 124.60d/10-2544, NA.

[55] Kennan to SD, 1 November 1944, *FRUS, 1944*, 3:625-6. The Stockholm legation repeated in early November its call for American representation in Finland; Johnson to SD, 3 November 1944, SD, RG 59, 711.60d/11/334, and 7 November 1944, 711.60d/11-744, NA.

[56] Kennan to SD, 28 October 1944, *FRUS, 1944*, 4:252.

without delay and to represent American interests until Hamilton's arrival.[57]

Soviet officials immediately objected when Kennan informed them of the American intention to send a representative to Finland, arguing that the situation in Finland was not analogous to that in Rumania and Bulgaria. Kennan suggested that the Finnish case could be discussed on its own merits and informed Washington that there should not be any difficulty once the issue reached the attention of higher officials.[58] On December 5 the State Department directed Higgs to proceed to Helsinki, but not before Soviet officials in Finland were aware of his appointment. Meanwhile, Higgs should avoid contact with the Finnish legation in Stockholm and should rely on Soviet rather than Finnish officials to provide the necessary visas for his staff. The Department reminded Higgs that diplomatic relations with Finland had been severed and that Finland was "still in a technical state of war with our Soviet and British allies."[59]

When Kennan requested that arrangements be made for Higgs, he was confronted by questions raised in Helsinki by Zhdanov about the implications of the term "mission" and reference to American political representation in Rumania and Bulgaria. Kennan once again repeated that Finland could be discussed on its own merits. The term "mission" had been chosen to avoid any suggestion of a regular diplomatic accreditation to Finland.[60] Kennan's explanation failed to satisfy Soviet officials. The formal Soviet reply to the American note of mid-November concerning Hamilton's appointment rejected a comparison between Finland and Rumania and Bulgaria. The United States had not been at war with Finland and had not taken part in the armistice talks. Harriman replied, as Kennan had during earlier exchanges, that there was no analogy between Hamilton's proposed functions and those of the American representatives on the ACC in Rumania and Bulgaria. The comparison had been made with political representatives outside the ACC, but since the parallel had not served to clarify the issue, the American ambassador suggested that the pertinent section of Kennan's letter of November 16 be considered

---

[57] Stettinius to Kennan, 14 November 1944, ibid., 3:626-7.

[58] Kennan to SD, 17 November 1944, ibid., 3:627-8.

[59] SD to Stockholm, 5 December 1944, ibid., 3:628-30.

[60] Harriman to SD, 8 December 1944, ibid., 3:630-1.

withdrawn.[61] Two weeks later, on January 4, 1945, Soviet officials informed the American embassy that the Soviet Union had no objection to Hamilton's appointment, which the Soviet government understood did not represent the reestablishment of American diplomatic or consular relations with Finland.[62]

American Economic Policy Towards Finland

When J.K. Paasikivi, the strong-willed conservative advocate of good Finnish-Soviet relations, became prime minister in November, he had two priorities: creation of a domestic regime acceptable to the Soviet Union and the reestablishment of economic relations with the West. The interdependent nature of these two goals can be seen in the Finnish strategy to solve the reparations problem.[63]

On December 8, 1944, the American minister in Stockholm reported a Finnish inquiry about the possibilities of obtaining American credits to meet reparation demands. The State Department directed the legation to assume "a discouraging attitude with regard to the possibility of any substantial assistance by the United States."[64] A memorandum to President Roosevelt spelled out the larger policy considerations. The United States should strive to keep allied reparation demands as low as possible. Accordingly, it should refrain from loans or assistance to a country paying reparations because any loan or assistance would encourage other allied powers to make large reparations demands. The United States could consider direct aid,

---

[61] Harriman to SD, 17 December 1944, ibid., 3:632-3.

[62] Harriman to SD, 5 January 1944, ibid., 3:633. Soviet anxiety over Hamilton's role in Finland might date back to the American ambivalence about the role its representative would play in Bulgaria. On November 11, the same day that Roosevelt approved the appointment of Hamilton, the State Department proposed that Maynard Barnes be appointed the American representative in Bulgaria: "In view of the functions he will perform, either as head of the American delegation on the Control Commission...or as American political representative with a separate establishment, or acting concurrently in both capacities," the Department proposed that Barnes be appointed with the personal rank of minister; secretary of state to President Roosevelt, 11 October 1944, ibid., 3:446-7.

[63] For the linkage of these two issues, see Higgs to SD, 25 January 1945, *FRUS, 1945,* 4:598-600.

[64] SD to Johnson, 19 December 1944, ibid., 4:633-4. For the reparations question in general, see Hannu Heikkilä, *Liittoutuneet ja kysymys Suomen sotakorvauksista 1943-1947* (Helsinki, 1983).

however, if it wished to aid a reparation recipient.[65] In other words, after the dust had settled the United States might make an exception for Finland. This memorandum is significant at two levels. The Soviet Union had, in fact, encouraged Finland to turn to the United States to obtain credits. Yet Soviet recognition of Finnish dependence on American credits to meet reparation demands also required Soviet acceptance of postwar Finnish integration into the postwar capitalist system.

The day before Higgs' arrival in Finland the Finnish minister of commerce and industry, Åke Gartz, informally told a member of the American legation in Stockholm that the highest Finnish priority in its relations with the United States was credits during the next two years.[66] In Finland, Finnish Foreign Minister Carl Enckell told Higgs that American assistance would enable Finland to import products necessary to produce reparation materials.[67] Prime Minister J.K. Paasikivi was even more explicit. Finland faced two principal problems: the "internal" question related to the treatment of war culprits (those responsible for Finland's involvement in the war) and the "international" question of obtaining necessary materials from abroad to fulfill reparation requirements. The Finns could solve the internal question, which involved Soviet political demands to remove wartime leaders from positions of political responsibility, but financial and economic agreements with the United States and other western countries were necessary to solve the international problem.[68] At this critical stage in Finland's efforts to reestablish its prewar international

---

[65] Memorandum from FMA for the president, "Financial Assistance to Finland in Meeting its Reparation Obligations to the USSR," 29 December 1944, SD, RG 59, 860d.51/12-2944, NA.

[66] Johnson to SD, no. 196, 16 January 1945, SD, RG 59, 740.00119 Control (Finland)/1-1645, NA.

[67] Higgs to SD, 20 January 1944, *FRUS, 1944*, 4:625-6.

[68] Higgs to SD, 25 January 1945, *FRUS, 1945*, 4:598-600. This conversation is an explicit expression of the postwar Finnish policy of organizing Finnish society so that political groupings considered hostile by the Soviet Union could not hold positions of political power, and, at the same time, organizing Finnish society so that Finnish products could be competitive on foreign markets. For the geopolitical imperative of never upsetting the Soviet sense of security and the economic imperative of being competitive in western markets, see Klaus Törnudd, "Finland and Economic Integration in Europe," *Cooperation and Conflict*, 4 (1969): 63-72; and Michael Berry, "The Limits of Community: Finland as a Symbol of Frontier-infused Liberalism," in Michael Berry, George Maude, and Jerry Schuchalter, *Frontiers of American Political Experience* (Turku, 1990), 97-9.

status, it turned to the United States to obtain help, not against the Soviet Union, but to enable Finland to travel the rocky eastern route to a postwar western destination.[69]

The Internal Finnish Situation
(Who Will Guarantee a Friendly Regime?)

Finland had two short-term governments prior to the Paasikivi government. The leading figures in the wartime leadership moved to the sidelines, but the first postwar government represented more the prewar and wartime power structure of Finnish society than the views of the wartime peace opposition. After the signing of the armistice, Urho Castrén, president of the Supreme Administrative Court, formed a new government with few changes in composition. The Castrén government failed to address the issues of integrating the radical left back into Finnish society and of providing active leadership for creation of better relations with the Soviet Union. It collapsed from within when the opposition-wing Social Democratic ministers resigned.

The time was ripe for the rise to power of J.K. Paasikivi. Paasikivi knew what he wanted. Unlike the previous governments that had signed the armistice and overseen the transition from war to the armistice, Paasikivi was looking beyond the end of the war towards a new postwar Finnish-Soviet relationship. The task ahead was difficult at best. But he could build on a Finnish tradition of public support for a strong Finnish state which had been legitimized by a prewar and wartime adherence to constitutional and parliamentary norms. This tradition continued into the postwar period as political elites inside and outside the government generally strove for consensus.[70]

If the Castrén government represented the transition from war to initial implementation of the armistice terms, the Paasikivi government began the long process of building the basis for a new relationship with the Soviet Union. Paasikivi moved on three fronts. On one front,

---

[69] For this approach to postwar Finnish policy, see Urho Kekkonen, *Tässä sitä ollaan* (Helsinki, 1944).

[70] This is not to say that there were no disagreements among Finnish elites. The Social Democratic leader Väinö Tanner openly resisted Paasikivi's policy in the early armistice period but he eventually pulled in his horns. Unlike Paasikivi who hoped to build his policy within a context of allied cooperation, Tanner assumed Soviet-American conflict and argued that Finland should resist Soviet demands until such time that the United States was ready to intervene on Finland's behalf. See for example, Paasikivi, *Päiväkirjat, 1944-1956* [diaries], passim, especially 45, 62.

his government included representatives of the Communist party and the Peoples' Democratic Union, a league of Communists and opposition social democrats who had left the Social Democratic party.[71] The Finnish Communists were thus integrated into the constitutional, parliamentary system, but kept in subordinate positions.[72] The Communist party dominated the Democratic Union, but most of the Union's ministerial positions went to opposition-wing social democrats who had joined the Union with a view to building a unified socialist party. This approach enabled Paasikivi to manipulate a system in which the main political division in Finland ran between the Communist party and the non-Communist socialists within the Democratic Union.

On a second front, he began to develop a postwar relationship with the Soviet Union that contained elements of *realpolitik* at two levels: Finnish respect for Soviet security concerns and Finnish insistence on Soviet respect for Finnish self-determination. At the official level he had parliamentary support. At the unofficial level he had the support of the Finnish-Soviet Friendship Society, which had been organized under bourgeois leadership. The non-socialist architects of good relations with the Soviet Union cooperated with Social Democrats to ensure that the Communist party would play only a subordinate role within the government and within the Finnish-Soviet Friendship Society.

On a third front, Paasikivi turned to the United States for economic support to rebuild the Finnish economy and to meet Soviet reparation demands. The road ahead was full of uncertainty both in terms of what the Finnish public would accept and the Soviet Union would demand, but there is little evidence of Finnish efforts to play the United States off against the Soviet Union in the early armistice period or of Soviet displeasure with American representatives in Finland after their arrival in January 1945.

---

[71] K.A. Fagerholm, *Puhemiehen ääni* (Helsinki, 1977), 184-205; Lauri Hyvämäki, *Valtioneuvosto toisen maailmansodan jälkeen vuoteen 1957* (Helsinki, 1977), 248-251; Edvin Linkomies, *Vaikea aika: Suomen pääministerinä sotavuosina, 1943-1944* (Helsinki, 1970), 408-9; Väinö Voionmaa, *Kuriiripostia 1941-1946* (Helsinki, 1971), 288-9.

[72] Paasikivi considered the extreme left more dangerous outside than inside the government because the government could not resort to police force to control them; Diaries, 52, 85.

The one unresolved issue in Finnish-Soviet relations at the end of 1944 and the beginning of 1945 was Finnish reluctance to remove influential wartime leaders from positions of power in Finnish society. This problem was resolved in part by an element of cooperation, albeit in Paasikivi's case under duress, between Paasikivi, the Soviet-led ACC and the State Department. In making the distinction mentioned above between the "internal" and "international" problems facing Finland, Paasikivi acknowledged to Higgs that the war culprits posed a difficult challenge. He considered repudiation at the polls during the forthcoming election the only constitutional means of dealing with political leaders who had been elected democratically. Paasikivi understood, however, that more was at stake than legal considerations. The extreme left was agitating for removal of wartime leaders from office; but when Higgs asked about foreign influence on the extreme left, Paasikivi replied that the ACC had promised not to interfere in internal matters. Higgs reported to Washington that Paasikivi had a "clear though perhaps unspoken idea of the realistic factors for Finland involved in the present situation."[73]

Trapped between Soviet expectations, agitation by the Finnish extreme left, and possible strong public reaction to any move against the wartime leaders, Paasikivi planted in the conservative Swedish *Svenska Dagsbladet* an article on the danger of reelecting wartime leaders, and he approached Higgs informally through intermediaries to request American assistance (to get wartime leaders to withdraw from the campaign). By obtaining Swedish and American support, Paasikivi hoped to gain his objective without direct Soviet intervention.[74]

After two weeks in Helsinki, Higgs summarized his impressions for Washington. He considered the domestic political conflict over the candidacy of wartime leaders a continuation of the conflict between the wartime government and the wartime peace activists, with the peace activists now rallying around Paasikivi in an attempt to keep wartime leadership out of the parliament. The "Paasikivi group" was motivated by a desire to establish good relations with the Soviet Union rather than by personal political ambition. Given Paasikivi's objectives

---

[73] Higgs to SD, 25 January 1945, *FRUS, 1945*, 4:598-600.

[74] Michael Berry, "The Limits of Community: American Foreign Policy and Finland, 1941-1945," (Ph.D. dissertation, University of Wisconsin-Madison, 1975), 312

and the widespread Finnish hope to reestablish relations with the United States, Higgs suggested that an American statement of solidarity with the USSR on this issue would help Paasikivi lay the basis for good Finnish-Soviet relations.[75]

The State Department was unwilling to intervene publicly in a matter that fell within the purview of the ACC.[76] This did not mean, however, that the Department wanted Higgs to remain silent. John Morgan, the assistant chief of the Division of Northern European Affairs, who drafted the telegram sent to Higgs, also addressed a memorandum to Assistant Secretary of State James C. Dunn noting that Higgs would "probably find the opportunity in such informal conversation as he may have with Finnish officials to indicate our general views concerning the 'war politicians' without directly involving the Mission."[77]

Paasikivi's attempt to gain his political objective without reference to direct Soviet pressure failed. On February 4, the ACC handed the Finnish government a list of war politicians who should not stand for election. The following day the prominent candidates on the list withdrew their candidacy. Nevertheless, as Higgs put it, the ice had "been broken for the widespread removal of 'war culprits' from position and influence."[78] Significantly, on the eve of Yalta the United States and the Soviet Union shared a common concept of a democratic and friendly neighbor in the case of Finland (or at least the convergence of perceptions outweighed the divergence). Under Paasikivi's leadership, Finland had begun to meet Soviet expectations in a manner acceptable to the western allies.

As early as December 1944 Eero Wuori, a wartime peace activist and head of the Finnish Association of Labor Unions, who served as minister of labor in Paasikivi's government, had inquired at the American legation in Stockholm about the possibility of obtaining American credits to meet reparation demands. The summary of the

---

[75] Higgs to DS, 30 January 1945, *FRUS, 1945*, 4:601-2.

[76] DS to Higgs, 3 February 1945, ibid., 4:602-3.

[77] Memorandum by John Morgan to James Dunn, 1 February 1945, SD, RG 59, 860d.00/1-245, NA.

[78] Higgs to DS, 5 February 1945, *FRUS, 1945*, 4:603-4. In 1945 Paasikivi gave in to Soviet pressure to bring the war culprits to trial. The alternative would have been a Soviet trial; Jukka Tarkka, *13. artikla* (Porvoo, 1977), 184-7, 242-57.

American minister's report sums up the convergence of Finnish, Soviet, and American policy:

> There is not the slightest evidence of Russian desire to gain control of the internal government of Finland, although those inclined to interpret all Russian actions at their worst can regard various measures as easing the way for future interference. Wuori does not take this pessimistic view but he does think Moscow will ruthlessly press all demands with the two-fold object of squeezing every possible material gain out of Finland and making sure that a "reliable" Finnish regime will arise and really hold power.[79]

Essential to the convergence of Finnish, Soviet, and American views was the Soviet policy of defining what constituted an unfriendly government, but permitting Finland to determine the composition of a friendly government. This was all the United States wanted and more than the British expected.

Asking the Right Questions

The ability of nations and of political groupings to read correctly the writing on the wall, i.e., to predict future great-power-imposed parameters within which they would have to operate, and to act accordingly, is basically a function of the extent to which ideological predispositions conditioned by history make possible detection of what they wanted to see, or at least were willing to see, while others tended to remain incapable of recognizing what they preferred not to believe. Seen from this perspective, brilliant and incompetent leadership often derive from the appropriate or inappropriate link between deep-rooted world views and new exigencies. In a dynamic situation the farsighted of today easily become victims of myopia tomorrow.[80]

The insights provided by the paradigm of Soviet-American cooperation, which included recognition of legitimate Soviet security requirements and self-determination in the borderland as well as an American preference for a liberal world order and Soviet "associate

---

[79] Johnson to SD, 8 December 1944, SD, RG 59, 760d.61/12-844, NA.

[80] With hindsight the historian can argue that the right question for leaders of countries along the Soviet border to have asked after Stalingrad was not whether to pursue a Western, Eastern, or Central European policy, but how to carve out an area of autonomy within a new Europe divided between East and West. Berry, *American Foreign Policy and the Finnish Exception*, 431-453. For a perceptive analysis along these lines of the Czechoslovakian situation, see Erazim Kohák, "Making and Writing History (Eduard Benes, 1943-18)," in Norman Stone and Eduard Strouhal, eds., *Czechoslovakia: Crossroads and Crises, 1918-88* (London, 1989), 183-203.

membership" in that order, suggested to American policymakers the feasibility of attempting to stabilize Finland's position on the interface periphery of Europe (within the Soviet geopolitical sphere but open to the western economy).[81]

In 1941 Finland forgot the message of the Finnish philosopher J.V. Snellman who had warned in 1863 against taking advantage of Russian weakness—not for Russia's sake but for Finland's sake; for Russia would always be a great power and a neighbor of Finland.[82] In 1944 the Snellman in Paasikivi advocated a policy with one basic message: recognize limits and carve out as much autonomy within the Soviet sphere as possible. In practice, this meant a return to the foreign policy insights of the period of nineteenth century autonomy in the Russian empire while retaining all the domestic gains of the period of independence.

American observers understood Paasikivi's policy while not necessarily appreciating the historical and philosophical basis of his insight. In June 1944 Walter Lippmann, perhaps the leading American foreign policy commentator, observed that "a true settlement with Finland [could] be had only by the adoption in Helsinki and in Moscow of the Good Neighbor principle." Lippmann argued that no other settlement could work because no other took into account the realities and the vital interests at stake. The influential journalist outlined the path that Finland should follow in order to remain independent. The foremost problem facing the Finns and the Russians, he wrote, was the disposing of Finnish wartime leaders. If Stalin allowed the Finns to do the job themselves rather than rely on the Red army and a puppet regime, the Soviet leader would earn "handsome dividends in all matters that are vital to the Soviet Union. For it [would] not only disarm Finland more thoroughly than any physical disarmament; it [would] be the foundation for a wholly different relation."

Lippmann then added a key ingredient in American thinking to his analysis: "It would be idle to say this if democracy in Finland were not a genuine thing. But there can be no real doubt that it is and, that being the case, the great objective of settlement with Finland must

---

[81] For a discussion of Finland's position on the interface periphery of Europe, see Berry, *American Foreign Policy and the Finnish Exception*, 44-7 and sources.

[82] J.V. Snellman, "Sota tai rauha Suomelle," in J. V. Snellmanin *Kootut Teokset*, VII Tutkielmia ja kirjoitelmia (Porvoo, 1930), 239-51.

be to strengthen its position against the oligarchs and conspirators who subverted it." Hoping that a solution to the Finnish question would have a positive impact elsewhere, Lippmann placed his discussion in a larger context and suggested that "though the circumstances and the issues are very different, the same conception of their power and their real interest ought to reign in the relations of America, Britain, and Russia."[83]

Lippman affirmed the State Department hope that Soviet adherence to the peace terms would eventually allow the wartime peace opposition to gain political control of Finland and establish a foundation for good relations with the Soviet Union. The result would be a pro-Soviet, but non-Communist, Finland. Finnish acceptance of Soviet terms and Soviet abstention from interference in internal Finnish affairs would suggest that there was no reason for the United States to assume that Soviet policy towards Finland was indicative of a Soviet world policy in conflict with American foreign policy.[84] Indeed, it would suggest just the opposite.

John Scott of *Time* and *Life* magazines, who interviewed leading Finns in April and November, echoed Lippmann's assessment and that of the State Department. Representatives of the extreme left indicated that a new political party would be founded, but none of the leaders of this potential "people's party" with whom he talked "believed that the United States is coming in to save little Finland from the clutches of the Bolshevik bear." Moreover, Scott believed that the appearance in Helsinki of an American diplomat would not "create any false hopes in the minds of these men that America was making common cause with them against the Russians."

Scott further concluded that "Finland's people have made up their minds to a future Finland within the general geographic and cultural orbit of the Soviet Union. They are buckling down to Finland's two immediate cardinal tasks: fulfillment of armistice terms (most important and most difficult, interning Germans); and reorganizing Finland's economic life in such a way as to avoid unemployment." Optimistically, he continued, "the overwhelming majority of Finns believe that if the armistice terms are fulfilled Finland will retain its territory, integrity and independence. They are

---

[83] Walter Lippmann, "Finland," *Washington Post*, 24 June 1944.

[84] Memorandum by Hugh Cumming for Hull, 6 May 1944, SD, RG 59, 760d.615-644, NA.

also convinced that, if postwar unemployment in Finland can be avoided, Communist influence in the country will remain relatively small, and therefore relatively moderate."[85] As Scott suggested in his assessment of Finnish "optimistic fatalism," the external and internal prerequisites for a friendly and democratic solution to Soviet-Finnish relations were present.[86] Significantly, American foreign policy still operated from the assumptions of Soviet-American cooperation. By the time this cooperation paradigm gave way to one of Soviet-American confrontation after Yalta, the foundations of the Paaasikivi Line of good Soviet-Finnish relations proved firm enough to weather the Cold War. Finnish-American relations had endured the crisis of the Second World War much better than the logic of power politics suggests. These relations suggest how subtle that logic is.

Part of the explanation was American needs and Finnish deeds. Finland's wartime cooperation with Germany almost tarnished a positive prewar image beyond salvation, but the United States needed a "friendly-democratic" solution to the emerging conflict between Soviet security requirements and American expectations of national self-determination in Eastern Europe. Otherwise there would be no international order based on principles of economic and political liberalism. Given hope by the peace opposition, the American administration and the internationalist press linked Finland's prewar reputation for democracy with the expectations of—and hope for—a solution to the postwar "Russian problem."

These views in the summer of 1944 were an extension of the prewar liberal world order paradigm and included "associate membership" for the Soviet Union in a postwar liberal order. Finland's symbolic role in this liberal vision was no longer as important as it had been in the 1930s, and American internationalists understood the necessity of making adjustments to insure Soviet cooperation. Nevertheless, they hoped that Finland would find its proper place within this context and perhaps even contribute to the developments that the Roosevelt administration was fostering.

---

[85] John Scott, "Finland's Peace Prospects," 9 November 1944, OSS file 118490.

[86] Optimistic fatalism is my term. Much of Finnish mentality during and after the Second World War can be explained by a conviction that Finland's options were severely restricted but somehow everything would work out. For wartime morale reports see Eino Jutikkala, *Valtioneuvoston Tiedoituslaitoksen historia* (Helsinki, 1945) and Berry, *American Foreign Policy and the Finnish Exception*, passim.

More was at stake, however, than Soviet-American relations in the borderland. American views were global. On June 24, 1944, a *New York Times* editorial drew a parallel between recent Soviet military success in Finland and a Senate resolution to proclaim Philippine independence once the United States expelled Japanese forces from those islands. Both Finland and the Philippines were small countries. They could not be independent if the world returned to the unstable power politics of the late 1930s. According to the *Times* the United States intended to retain bases in the southwest Pacific, and those bases would "always give us the power to prevent the Philippines from doing anything we consider harmful to our interests."

Finland, for its part, was independent between the two world wars only because Russia and Germany saw nothing to gain in interfering with its independence. When this situation changed, the *Times* recounted, Finland "was attacked by Russia, and threw herself into the arms of Germany....Even though the Finnish Government has been aiding our enemies, we ought to be sufficiently magnanimous to spare a little sympathy for the harassed Finnish people."

After this review of the logic of Finnish conduct during the war and of American wartime sympathy for Finland, the *Times* hammered home its point about the lessons of history: Small nations can survive "only in a worldwide system committed to nonaggression. Finland can live and maintain her own culture under such a system and so can the Philippines. The alternative is a system of rival imperialism, with a balance of power which inevitably will end in other wars." In short, only a world with open spheres of influence which defend the "legitimate" security interests of great powers and permit international economic and cultural exchange would insure postwar peace for small and great powers. As the *New York Times* often wrote during the second Russo-Finnish War, Finland was a "test case" for the ultimate success of the wartime and postwar alliance between the United States and other members of the United Nations.[87]

Conclusion

Finland's peripheral location next to stable Scandinavia was perhaps the primary consideration in postwar Soviet policy towards that country. Yet Finland's ability to adjust to external exigencies was

---

[87] *New York Times* editorials, 11 August 1943; 2 March 1943; 16 March 1944; 24 June 1944; and 30 June 1944.

also important. Finland demonstrated its will and ability to fight, and it survived the war unoccupied with its traditional institutional arrangements intact. Finland also resettled ten percent of its population while expelling German troops and establishing new governments acceptable to the Allied Control Commission. This capacity to recognize limits and to maximize options within those limits enabled Finland to make the best of a difficult situation.

Throughout the dramatic events of 1944 the United States remained on the sideline pursuing a policy supportive of Finland within the context of UN cooperation if only Finland and the Soviet Union had the will and the capacity to achieve a modus vivendi. In autumn 1945 Charles Bohlen stated the fading American hope for allied cooperation in the borderland along the Soviet Union. Concerned about Soviet expansion in Eastern Europe directed towards the establishment of complete Soviet domination, Bohlen wrote: "The one exception to this pattern has been Finland and it is worth noting in this connection that Finnish-Soviet relations are on a sounder footing for the future even from the Soviet point of view than the relations with other bordering countries where the same restraint has not been shown."[88]

American policy toward Finland proved successful in the 1940s largely because success did not require extensive American political or economic commitments. Finland carried its own weight. In the end the United States did little concrete to aid Finland. Viewed within the context of the Cold War, one could argue that the United States gave Finland limited aid because it could, so to speak, get Finland "for free." But to leave it at that is to underestimate the extent to which Finland itself determined its own future and to misunderstand the ideological preference of the United States: to maximize opportunities while minimizing obligations within an informal, liberal international regime. Put another way, the United States acted as a mid-wife in the birth of the Paasikivi Line. Finnish postwar policy was conceived and nurtured by Finnish parents. The Allied powers divided over the fate of Eastern Europe and the Finnish test case became the only success story along the Soviet border.

---

[88] Bohlen memorandum, 18 October 1945, Bohlen Records, Box 4, NA, cited in Eduard Mark, "Charles E. Bohlen and the Acceptable Limits of Soviet Hegemony in Eastern Europe: A Memorandum of 18 October 1945," *Diplomatic History* 3 (Spring 1979): 207.

4

"We Are Not Czechs": Finland and the "Spring Crisis" of 1948 in Comparative Perspective[1]

Jussi M. Hanhimäki

> We now learn that Finland is next in line to feel the blow of the hammer and the sweep of the sickle.[2]
> —Rep. Charles Vursell, March 5, 1948

> "The [FCMA] treaty is not dangerous, but rather very satisfying for us...Our affair should not be confused with the anti-Soviet propaganda war being waged inside the United States."[3]
> —J.K. Paasikivi, April 19, 1948

> "[This treaty is] a convincing example of the lack of aggressiveness in Soviet foreign policy."[4]
> —V. Molotov, May 4, 1948

For a brief moment in the spring of 1948 Finland caught the world's attention. As the Finns and the Soviets negotiated their Treaty of Friendship, Cooperation and Mutual Assistance (FCMA), many outside observers were ready to brand Finland as the latest addition to the Soviet empire. But as events unfolded, as the FCMA Treaty differed significantly from Soviet Union's treaties with its Eastern

---

[1] This essay is a modified version of the second chapter in my study *Containing Coexistence: America, Russia, and the "Finnish Solution," 1945-1956* (Kent, OH, 1997).

[2] U.S., Congress, House, *Congressional Record*, 80th Cong., 2nd Sess., 1948, vol. 94, part 2, 223.

[3] Paasikivi's diary entry, 19 April 1948, *Paasikiven päiväkirjat, 1944-1956* [The diaries of Paasikivi] (Helsinki, 1985), 1:598.

[4] From a conversation between Molotov and Walter Bedell Smith, the American ambassador to the Soviet Union. Quoted in Roy Allison, *Finland's Relations with the Soviet Union, 1944-1984* (New York, 1985), 30.

European allies, as the domestic scene in Finland did not indicate a shift towards a "people's republic," and as the USSR did not intervene in Finland's domestic affairs, there was little doubt that something extraordinary, something that did not quite fit into the popularly accepted view of limitless Soviet-Communist aggression, was occurring. Consequently, the American reaction to the 1948 events in Finland was ambiguous. On the one hand, American and other western observers fitted the Finnish Solution into a simplistic Cold War framework: as Finland did not get included into the Soviet bloc, it must have been a victory for the West, a symbol of containment. On the other hand, the fears of Finland falling prey to an aggressive USSR that characterized the early reactions to the FCMA Treaty and subsided somewhat during the summer of 1948, were never lost. Rather, in Finland the Soviets could be seen as using a new strategy, a more gradual approach that would sooner or later bring that problem child into the Kremlin's arms.[5]

This last point is further illuminated when the Finnish case is placed into the larger context of the Cold War by contrasting it with two equally significant milestones: the Communist coup d'état in Czechoslovakia in February 1948 and the Tito-Stalin split of 1948-49. While the Prague coup invited protest and outrage, the American foreign policy establishment in a sense welcomed it as further proof of limitless Soviet expansionism. Finland and Yugoslavia in contrast represented two rather perplexing cases that might be used as vehicles for combating that expansionism, but had a high potential for backfiring. Comparing American policy towards these three countries will therefore provide significant insight into the changing dynamics, persistent paradigms and inherent problems of American foreign policy in Eastern Europe during the shaping of the Soviet-American confrontation.

---

[5] The only study focusing solely on American reactions to the FCMA Treaty is Jukka Nevakivi's factually accurate, but uninsightful, "American Reactions to the Finnish-Soviet Friendship Treaty of 1948," *Scandinavian Journal of History* 13 (1989): 279-91. For an extremely thoughtful analysis, see Kevin Devlin, "Finland in 1948: The Lessons of a Crisis," in *The Anatomy of Communist Takeovers*, ed. Thomas T. Hammond (New Haven, 1975), 433-47. Although Devlin is very good on arguing about Soviet motives in dealing with Finland the way they did, his article hardly touches on the reaction in the West. See also Jukka Nevakivi, *Zdanov Suomessa* [Zdanov in Finland] (Helsinki, 1994), and the essays in Nevakivi, ed., *Finnish-Soviet Relations, 1944-1948* (Helsinki, 1994).

A "Friendly Invitation"

Finland's spring crisis began when Stalin invited President Juho K. Paasikivi in late February 1948 to come to Moscow for "friendly" talks with the Soviet leaders. The summons came as no surprise. As early as 1944-45 the Soviets had suggested a defensive pact for the Finns, but the then Prime Minister Paasikivi had averted a treaty by referring to the Moscow Armistice which forbade Finland from joining any military alliances before the official final peace treaty was signed.[6] The 1947 Paris Peace Treaty, however, had removed that block. The Finns had also anxiously followed two sets of military consultations that had an impact on their position: the series of defensive pacts between the USSR and its other European neighbors—Hungary, Bulgaria and Rumania—that had been signed in late 1947, and the rumors of an upcoming Scandinavian military pact which were also circulating in 1946-47. Furthermore, during a series of meetings between the Finnish and Soviet leaders in Moscow in early November 1947, the Soviets had indicated their desire to negotiate a defensive treaty with Finland. According to the British minister to Helsinki, Oswald Scott, Finnish Prime Minister Mauno Pekkala at that time indicated to the Soviets that the Finnish government was ready to enter such a pact. Thus, on January 3, 1948, Scott cabled to London, maintaining that a "[Finno-Soviet] military pact is getting very near a reality now." That Foreign Minister Enckell denied the existence of any Soviet pressure on January 10 did nothing to calm Scott's concern.[7]

---

[6] On the 1944-45 Soviet approaches see an OSS memorandum on Finland by G. Edward Buxton, 9 June 1945, Record Group 59 (hereafter RG 59), State Department (SD), 760d.6111/6-945, National Archives, Washington D.C. (hereafter NA); and Maxim Korobachkin, "The USSR and the Treaty of Friendship, Cooperation and Mutual Assistance with Finland," in Nevakivi, ed., *Soviet-Finnish Relations,* 171-3. On the impact of the Scandinavian talks, see Jukka Nevakivi, "Scandinavian Talks on Military Cooperation in 1946-1947: A Prelude to the Decisions of 1948-1949," *Cooperation and Conflict,* 19 (1984): 165-75.

[7] From these meetings on, the possibility of a formal proposal by the Soviets was constantly on the minds of the Finnish leaders. See Paasikivi's diary entries: 4, 10, 11, 12, 15, 16 November 1947, *Paasikiven päiväkirjat,* 1: 502-6. In November 1947 the wildest rumors went as far as saying that a military alliance between Finland and the USSR had been concluded secretly and that Finnish forces would be integrated into the Russian army; Secretary of State to Hamilton, 10 November 1947, SD, RG 84, Helsinki, Secret File, 711.9, Box 2, Washington National Records Center, Suitland, Maryland (hereafter WNRC). Oswald Scott (British Minister to Finland) to Foreign Office, 23 December 1947; Scott to Bevin, 3 January 1948; Scott to Bevin, 10

In addition, the declining popularity of the Finnish Communist Party (SKP) may have affected the Soviet desire to push for a treaty with Finland in early 1948. In the October 1947 trade union elections and the November municipal elections, the People's Democratic League (SKDL)—the coalition of the SKP and left-wing Social Democrats created at the end of war—had suffered severe losses. During 1947 the SKP's membership had suddenly begun to decline, another indication that Communist popularity had peaked during the early postwar years. To an astute American observer the decline of the Red Star did not necessarily seem encouraging, but rather doomed the Finns to a fate similar to the East Europeans. The director of the State Department Policy Planning Staff, George Kennan, argued that Moscow would not tolerate this kind of "conservatism," but would retaliate. In early 1948 the author of "Soviet Conduct" predicted a Kremlin-directed "tactical maneuver" by the Finnish Communists, which would threaten Finland's delicate position between East and West and, if successful, add that country to the USSR's East European empire.[8]

Reports that the Soviets were moving towards a negotiated pact with Finland began to appear in American newspapers for the first time in late January 1948. The *New York Times* reported a "stiffening" Russian attitude towards the Finns, citing as evidence a withdrawal of transit permits to the Porkkala base from the Finns, as well as an alleged shift in Soviet support from the local Finnish Communists (the SKP) to those Communists that were still in (self-imposed) exile in Finland.[9]

January 1948; all in Foreign Office Records (hereafter FO) 371/71405, Public Record Office, Kew, Surrey, England (hereafter PRO).

[8] Hannu Rautkallio, *Suomen suunta, 1945-1948* (Helsinki, 1979), 132-6; Raymond Ylitalo, *Salasanomia Helsingistä Washingtoniin: Muistelmia ja dokumentteja vuosilta 1946-1948* [Secret Messages from Helsinki to Washington: Memoirs and documents from years 1946-1948] (Helsinki, 1978), 160-4; Robert W. Matson, "The Helsinki Axioms: U.S. Finnish Relations and the Origins of the Cold War" (Ph.D. dissertation, University of Oregon, 1981), 204. In early 1948 Kennan was quite convinced that the Soviets would be furthering their aims not by military conquest, but "from within, by stooge political elements." Kennan to Secretary of State, 6 January 1948, RG 59, Policy Planning Staff (PPS), Country and Area Files, Europe, 1947-1948, Box 27, NA. See also George F. Kennan, *Memoirs, 1925-1950* (Boston, 1967), 403; and Bennett Kovrig, *Of Walls and Bridges: The United States and Eastern Europe* (New York, 1991), 29-30.

[9] *New York Times*, 26 January 1948, 12. The most famous of the "exiled" Communists was Otto W. Kuusinen, who in 1939 was the head of the so-called

Such alarmist stories intensified after January 17, 1948, when a new Soviet minister to Finland, General Grigori M. Savonenkov, arrived in Helsinki. A former member of the Allied Control Commission in Finland, Savonenkov was known to Finns as an uncompromising hardliner who they feared had been sent to Finland to do some "dirty work." The Finns' concern proved accurate. On January 23, 1948—less than a week after his arrival in Helsinki—Savonenkov had a hour and a half discussion with President Paasikivi. The Soviet minister alleged that Finno-Soviet relations had seriously deteriorated due to Finnish violations of the 1947 Paris Peace Treaty. To improve this unfortunate trend, Savonenkov added, Paasikivi should make a trip to Moscow to meet with the Soviet leaders. Five days later Paasikivi, after extensive consultations with his advisors, turned down the Soviet minister's informal invitation, referring to his old age and to the negative effect a president's trip abroad (and especially to the Soviet Union) would have on the Finnish public. Paasikivi also stressed that the Finnish government's foreign policy would remain unchanged, regardless of internal political struggles.[10]

This was the first time during the spring of 1948 that Paasikivi used a stalling tactic in his dealings with the USSR. Throughout the upcoming months the Finnish president delayed his answers to various Soviet initiatives in a manner which speaks for his extremely coolheaded manner while negotiating with the Soviets. On the other hand, it makes one wonder if Paasikivi postponed his answers for another reason: in order to "let the word out" and give the West, especially the United States, a chance to react. To be sure, he did not at any point expect a direct intervention by the West, nor deem petitioning for an open show of support worthwhile. What is equally sure, however, is that Paasikivi received increasing moral support from

---

Terijoki government, a group of exiled Finnish Communists who were selected by Stalin as the "true" Finnish government.

[10] Juho K. Paasikivi's collection (hereafter JKPK), 5:18, "Savonenkov, 28/1/48," Valtion arkisto (State Archives), Helsinki, Finland (hereafter VA). Savonenkov referred to, for example, the arms caches affair (the alleged hiding of large quantities of arms and ammunitions by Finnish officers afraid of a coming Communist coup) and what he considered the Finnish press' negativism towards the USSR. See also Paasikivi's diary entries: 22, 23, 28 January 1948, *Paasikiven päiväkirjat*, 1:543-5, 550-1. Archibald Randolph of the American legation and Oswald Scott of the British legation saw Savonenkov's invitation as a likely prelude to a military pact. Randolph to Secretary of State, 15 January 1948, SD, RG 59: 760d.61/1-1548, NA; Scott to Robin M. Hankey (FO), 31 January 1948, FO 371/71405, PRO.

the West. At the same time the Soviets, especially after the way the Czechoslovakian events were perceived in the West and the parallels between Finland and Czechoslovakia drawn publicly and privately, were locked in a situation in which unrelenting pressure on the Finns would have been counterproductive.[11]

While Paasikivi stalled for time he was also getting ready for the inevitability of negotiations with the USSR. In late January and throughout February the president collected long and detailed memoranda about different friendship treaties around the world. Still in mid-February, however, Paasikivi was hoping that he could postpone the negotiations past the July 1948 Diet elections and argued to Foreign Minister Carl Enckell that the Finnish people were "not ready" for a treaty with the Soviets.[12]

All this changed on February 23, 1948, when Savonenkov handed Paasikivi a letter from Stalin. In it the Soviet dictator called for open negotiations between Finland and the Soviet Union that would lead to a defensive treaty similar to those the USSR had concluded with Hungary and Rumania in 1947. At this time even Paasikivi lost his cool for a moment. The two people he told about the letter that evening—Enckell and Urho Kekkonen, the Speaker of the Diet—both remember the president as being very upset, and Enckell even mentioned that Paasikivi was ready to resign. He soon recovered his composure, however, and sought advice during a series of consultations and meetings Paasikivi had during the next two days with K.J. Ståhlberg (specialist in international law and the president of Finland, 1919-1925), Erik Hornborg (an author and a historian), Reinhold Svento (deputy foreign minister), and Karl August Fagerholm (the Social Democratic Party's strongman). These meetings only confirmed the obvious: with Stalin's personal prestige on the line, the USSR was not about to take any more stalling from the Finns. The question was no longer whether Finns could avoid negotiations or signing some kind of a security pact with the Soviet

---

[11] 'Top Secret" memoranda by Paasikivi: 18, 19, 21 February 1948, JKPK, 5:18, "erittäin salainen," VA. Paasikivi made several points about how to stall with the Soviets: refer to parliamentary procedures, to the fact that the treaty is totally unprepared, and that "time is not right" for such a treaty.

[12] Paasikivi to Enckell, 10 February 1948, JKPK, 5:18, VA. On the different studies, see for example, Kaarlo G. Idman's (Professor of International law at Helsinki University) 23 January 1948, memorandum in Carl Enckell's collection (hereafter CEK), 106, VA.

Union, but how to respond properly and limit the treaty's impact on Finland's sovereignty. With that question in mind, Paasikivi called the members of his government together on February 26, 1948, to inform them about Stalin's letter.[13]

In the meeting Paasikivi first read Stalin's letter and then brought up his reservations about a treaty. He recognized the severity of the matter and informed those present that he would follow constitutional procedures: he would do nothing without consulting the members of the Diet. Paasikivi also refused to go to Moscow himself, arguing that the less authority to make decisions the members of the Finnish delegation had the better. As the rounds of consultations with Diet group leaders began, Paasikivi simply acknowledged Stalin's letter with a brief note he sent to the Soviet leader on February 27, 1948. Meanwhile, a meticulous examination of the different possibilities regarding a potential treaty, place of negotiations, the substance of the negotiations, as well as the composition of the delegation began in Helsinki.[14]

At the same time, however, the Finno-Soviet exchanges had become an integral part of the larger context of the Cold War. Given the Czechoslovakian events in late February, it seemed quite clear to many observers that Finland would be the next target. Like Finland's ambassador to Sweden, Georg A. Gripenberg, they asked themselves: "Finis Czechoslovakia! One asks oneself when it will be Finland's turn. Perhaps before the [July 1948 Diet] elections."[15]

The Next Target?

While the Finns agonized over the proper response to Stalin's invitation in late February and early March 1948, Americans and

---

[13] Enckell's memoranda, 23-24 February 1948, CEK, 106, "muistiinpanoja 2," VA; Juhani Suomi, *Vonkamies: Urho Kekkonen 1944-1950* ["Vonkamies" cannot be translated, but means, roughly, "a man who struggled against the winds"] (Helsinki, 1988), 30-45, 316-19. See also the diaries of Georg A. Gripenberg (Finland's ambassador to Sweden), entries 23-26 February 1948, G.A.Gripenbergin collection (hereafter GAGK), VAY 3458 (Microfilm), VA. Stalin's letter is reprinted (in Finnish) in *Suomen ja Neuvostoliiton suhteet 1948-1983. Asiakirjoja ja aineistoa* [Finno-Soviet relations 1948-1983. Documents and material] (Helsinki, 1983), 13-14; McCagg, *Stalin Embattled*, 301; Ulam, *Rivals*, 119-20.

[14] JKPK, 5:18, "Paasikiven muistiinpanoja helmimaaliskuulta 1948," VA; Paasikivi's diary entries: 24-28 February, 1-8 March 1948, *Paasikiven päiväkirjat*, 1:559-71; Suomi, *Vonkamies*, 316-19.

[15] Gripenberg's diary entry on 24 February 1948, GAGK, VAY 3458, VA.

other westerners pondered the meaning of the latest Soviet move. They had to deal with two, somewhat conflicting, points of view. While the Finns themselves were belittling the rumors about an upcoming Finno-Soviet defense treaty and denied the potential of a military pact to interested western observers, the story emanating from Sweden was quite different. For example, the American legation in Stockholm, basing its information on discussions between legation members and officials at the Swedish foreign ministry, warned Washington of an upcoming Finno-Soviet military pact that would soon be followed by the complete inclusion of Finland into the Soviet orbit. As the secretary general of the Swedish Foreign Ministry, Hans Gustaf Beck-Friis, put it, the Swedes were seriously afraid that the "Soviet regime may follow its Balkan pattern in Finland."[16]

Why were the Swedes so pessimistic about Finland, while the Finns themselves were trying to calm down any overreaction? The answer probably lies in the two countries' interpretation of the acceleration of the Cold War in early 1948 and its impact on the the possibilities and preconditions the leaders of these countries considered as optimal for safeguarding their national security. The Swedes realized that Finland's remaining outside the East-West conflict was very much a prerequisite for the continuance of their neutrality; if Finland was drawn closer to the USSR the Swedes would probably be pressured by the West to abandon their "alliance free" position. Exaggerating the Soviet threat to Finland might produce western pressure on the USSR and thus reduce the possibility of a "takeover." On the other hand, the Finns had little desire to become a battleground for the Soviet-American confrontation. For them denying Soviet pressure was, therefore, an attempt to keep the potential negotiations with the Soviets from exploding into an international crisis that might make Finland into a test case of the Cold War. Initially, western observers were rather easily persuaded into adopting the Swedish interpretation. The French, the British and the Americans believed that Finland's

---

[16]Matthews to Secretary of State, 26 January 1948, RG 59, (SD) 760d.61/1-2648, NA. Contrary reports from Helsinki are, for example, Warren to Secretary of State, 13 February 1948, U.S., Department of State, *Foreign Relations of the United States, 1948* (hereafter *FRUS* followed by dates and volume), 4:760. Finnish minister to the U.S., Kauko Jutila, also did his share to try and calm the rumors when he met with the director of the State Department's Northern European section, Benjamin Hulley, on 16 February 1948; Memorandum of Conversation, RG 59, (SD) 760d.61/2-1648, NA.

days as a western democracy were about to end in the spring of 1948, especially after Stalin had put his personal prestige on the line.

The French were perhaps the most panicky and all but accused the Americans of appeasement. On February 18, in his meeting with the French minister to Finland, François Coulet, Finland's Foreign Minister Carl Enckell had given the impression that Finland was under severe Soviet pressure. Coulet was quick to characterize this meeting to his American counterpart Avra M. Warren as the "Finnish SOS." As the events in Czechoslovakia then unfolded during the following week, the French got increasingly worried about Finland. French Foreign Minister Georges Bidault soon accused the Americans of failing to recognize Russian expansion and insisted that American inaction, first in Czechoslovakia and now in Finland, allowed it. In a passionate plea to the American ambassador, Bidault tried to awaken the ghost of Hitler in the actions of Stalin: "This may sound extravagant, but we are sitting here under the guns and your people are on the other side of the ocean." Bidault and Coulet thus implied that if nothing was done, Finland would quickly follow the route of Czechoslovakia. To them, it was Munich all over again.[17]

The British agreed. In the House of Lords, Lord Pakenham was quick to arouse the anti-Soviet sentiments of the British public on March 3, 1948, pronouncing that: "Now the unhappy government of Finland [is] being embraced with the kiss of death and...being invited to visit Bluebeard's [ie., Stalin's] mansion." According to the British chargé d'affaires to Finland, Oswald Scott, Foreign Minister Enckell was "slipping in determination [and] has no fight left." On the other hand, the Foreign Office was somewhat less pessimistic than its French counterpart. While they expected the Finns to follow the Czech road,

---

[17] Matthews to Marshall and Warren to Marshall, 20 February 1948, *FRUS, 1948*, 4:761-4; Caffrey to Marshall, 4 March 1948, ibid., 3:629. A similar reaction was reported in Italy, where Count Sforza likened the Soviet actions to those of Hitler. See Dunn to Secretary of State, 1 March 1948, ibid., 3:835. Also in a State Department Brief on March 1, 1948, Truman's naval aide pointed out that "the French are considerably shaken by the Soviet action in Czechoslovakia and Finland," Papers of Harry S. Truman, Naval Aide Files (NAF), State Department Briefs, Box 21, Harry S. Truman Library (hereafter HSTL), Independence, Missouri. On the "Finnish SOS," see also J. Raymond Ylitalo, *Salasanomia Helsingistä Washingtoniin*, 187-8, 190-1. For more on the Western Europeans' fears, see Melvyn P. Leffler, *A Preponderance of Power: National Security, the Truman Administration, and the Cold War* (Stanford, 1992), 206ff.; Geir Lundestad, "'Empire by Invitation?' The United States and Western Europe, 1945-1952," *Journal of Peace Research* 23 (1986): 263-77.

the British were convinced that strong Finnish resistance might "moderate Soviet demands." Despite his alarm Scott, for example, was certain that the Finns were not bound to appease the Soviets by simply agreeing to all of their demands. Thus, while the French wanted a strong western show of support, the British favored encouraging the Finns to take a strong stand against the Soviets on their own.[18]

The Americans subscribed to the general sentiments expressed by the British and the French. However, the diplomat closest to the events, Avra M. Warren, did not find the situation as urgent as many of his West European counterparts. The U.S. chargé d'affaires in Helsinki had doubts about the seriousness of the situation that may have originated from two sources. On the one hand, the Finnish press was relatively quiet about the recent developments in Finno-Soviet relations. On the other hand, Warren's meeting with K. A. Fagerholm, the Finnish Social Democratic Party's leader (*Suomen Sosialidemokraattinen Puolue*, hereafter SDP), may have raised some doubts in the American's mind. While expressing his concerns about Stalin's letter, Fagerholm at the same time attempted to profit from the situation by appealing to the U.S. for economic aid. This, Fagerholm argued, would be the best thing the Americans could do in order to help Finland "in stalling off the Soviets." Perhaps because of this somewhat callous attitude as well as the seeming self-confidence of President Paasikivi, who gave no indications of being intimidated by the USSR, Warren concluded that the Finns did not generally seem too alarmed by the situation, but might even postpone negotiations with the Soviets until the summer.[19] Warren's opinion was, however, the exception to the rule.

---

[18] From Warren's notes about his discussion with Scott. Warren to Marshall, 27 February 1948, *FRUS, 1948*, 4:765; Scott to Bevin, 28 February 1948, FO 371/71405, PRO; Douglas (London) to Secretary of State, 2 March 1948, SD, RG 59, 760d.61/3-248, Box 4010, NA; Douglas to Secretary of State, 4 March 1948, SD, RG 59, 860d.00/3-448, NA. For a slightly different interpretation of the British view see, Jukka Nevakivi, "Miten Suomen ja Neuvostoliiton välinen YYAsopimus otettiin vastaan Englannin ulkoministeriössä helmimaaliskuussa 1948" [The reception of the Finno-Soviet Treaty of Friendship and Mutual Assistance at the British foreign ministry in February-March 1948], *Historiallinen arkisto* 84 (1984): 137-53.

[19] Warren to Secretary of State, 20 February 20, 1948, *FRUS, 1948*, 4:761-4; Warren to Secretary of State 27 February 27 1948, SD, RG 59, 760d.6111/2-2748, Box 4010, NA. Fagerholm himself remembered how Warren had said that Finland should not make a treaty and that the U.S. would help Finland. But, as Fagerholm adds in his memoirs, the American minister "would not tell how" the U.S. would help

American diplomats in Moscow and Stockholm expressed grave concern over Finland. For example, Ambassador Walter Bedell Smith, from his post in Moscow, urged Washington to take immediate action on behalf of Finland. "With firm backing from the U.S. and other western powers, Finnish Parliament might...turn down [Stalin's] request," Smith argued, adding that, "we should assure Finns that we and other western democracies [are] prepared to back them in *anything short of war*." The ambassador concluded that the western powers "have to face up to them [the Soviets] as a body rather than allow them continue to pick off one country after another." To Smith and his counterpart in Stockholm, H. Freeman Matthews, Finland seemed like a test case of American resolve.[20]

In the United States, pessimism was also growing. The Joint Chiefs of Staff (JCS) had by early March come to believe that Finland was the next Soviet target. Moreover, there appeared to be little, perhaps nothing short of war, that the West could do to help Finland. As a Central Intelligence Group memorandum of March 2, 1948, stated: "Stalin's letter [was] the first overt step in a long range campaign to reduce Finland from semi-independence to total subservience [and the] USSR will probably demand the integration of the Finnish defense system with its own." Unlike Smith and Matthews, however, the JCS could see no way, save outright war, in which the United States could help Finland, because the Soviets would quickly retaliate if the Finns were either to refuse a pact, force the Communists out of the government, or seek closer ties with the West.[21]

At the same time, pressure on the Truman administration to do something was slowly building in the American press and on Capitol Hill. In its first report on Stalin's letter on February 28, 1948, the *New York Times* joined those who speculated that the invitation was the

---

Finland. See K.A. Fagerholm, *Puhemiehen ääni* [The voice of the speaker] (Helsinki, 1977), 230-2.

[20] Smith also suggested using Iran as an example of how American support had prevented Communist expansion, and using the Baltic states as proof of what the Soviets were all about; Smith to Secretary of State, 1 March 1948, *FRUS, 1948*, 4:766; Matthews to Marshall, 20 February 1948, ibid., 4:761-2. Also see Ylitalo, *Salasanomia Helsingistä Washingtoniin*, 211-12, 219-20; William Taubman, *Stalin's American Policy: From Entente to Détente to Cold War* (New York, 1982), 180.

[21] Central Intelligence Group memorandum to the President, 2 March 1948, Records of the Joint Chiefs of Staff (RG 218), Chairman's File, Admiral Leahy, 1942-1948, Box 19, Folder 122, NA.

"first step of a long plan for the seizure of power by Finnish Communists."[22] In the House, Representative Charles Vursell mirrored this opinion, describing Finland as "teetering on the brink of communism." The problem, however, was that no one seemed to have conclusive advice on what to do regarding the situation, or if, indeed, there was anything the U.S. could do. As Senator Kenneth Wherry of Nebraska asked his Senate colleagues with some frustration: "now, without any aid from us...Finland is going to be taken over by the Russian sphere of influence...I wonder if there is anything in the world we could do...unless we were to have an outright break with Russia...What is our responsibility?"[23]

The problem was that, although everyone agreed that the Finns seemed to be in trouble, the Finns themselves had done nothing to indicate that they wanted outsiders to step in and help them to stand up against Soviet pressure. The Truman administration was, therefore, in a rather awkward situation: it was under pressure to take action from almost everyone except from those who were supposed to be in grave danger. Secretary of State Marshall could hardly take action in support of Finland by giving the Soviets some sort of an ultimatum without the Finns themselves requesting that. Instead, he ordered Minister Warren to "make quite informal or casual inquiry" about Finnish willingness to take their case to the United Nations, where the U.S. would support Finland in the face of Russian demands.[24]

Although Enckell's eyes were reportedly "filled with tears," when Warren made his promise of support in the UN, President Paasikivi was not impressed. "The U.S. cannot help us," he wrote in his diaries on March 2, 1948.[25] Instead of jumping after western support, the president continued to postpone his reply to Stalin's letter.

---

[22] *New York Times*, 28 February 1948, 1; see also ibid., 29 February 1948, 4.

[23] U.S., Congress, House, *Congressional Record*, 80th Cong., 2nd Sess., 1948, vol. 94, part 2, p. 2223; Senate, p. 1969. In addition, some Finnish immigrants were extremely wary about the possibility of Finland's falling into Soviet hands. For example, in his letter to Truman on March 1, 1948, B. Jay Knight (of Winnebago, Illinois) expressed the concerns of his Finnish-American community and asked the president to do something "to help Finland in what appears to be a final stand for that country." President's Official File (POF), Miscellaneous Files (MF), Box 1286, HSTL.

[24] Marshall to Warren, 1 March 1948, *FRUS, 1948*, 4:767-8.

[25] Paasikivi's diary entries: 2-4 March 1948, *Paasikiven päiväkirjat*, 1:564-6; Warren to Marshall, 2 March 1948, and 6 March 1948, *FRUS, 1948*, 4:768-71. It must be noted that the "tears" story is from Warren, whereas Enckell's notes from

The true irony of the situation was that the American move, which was calculated to steer the Finns away from signing a pact with the Kremlin, in fact pushed them closer towards it once the Soviets— through their well-established intelligence network in Helsinki— became aware of the Warren-Enckell talks. On March 4, the Soviet press attaché, Valeri Istomin, accused Enckell of conspiring with the "western imperialists" and making secret treaties with the Americans and the British, a threat which made even Paasikivi nervous. At the same time the Finnish minister to Great Britain, Eero A. Wuori, informed the Finnish Foreign Ministry that "he could not avoid getting the impression that the U.K. had washed its hands of Finland," and that the events in Czechoslovakia and Finland were only being used "to mold public opinion."[26]

With the Americans making vague promises, the British less than committed to take a strong stand, and the Soviets putting on additional pressure, Paasikivi finally blinked. On March 9, he agreed to proposed Finno-Soviet negotiations in Moscow. These were later scheduled to begin on March 23, 1948.[27]

Paasikivi's decision to accept Stalin's invitation, while perhaps the "safest" thing to do from Finland's standpoint, was to cause an even further wave of pessimism with respect to Finland among the western observers. At the same time, however, it seemed to hasten the chances for a consolidation of pro-western and anti-Soviet sentiments among the Norwegians and the Swedes, and was seen as a measure to be used in the alliance-building of 1948-49. While a CIA "Review of World Situation" of March 10, 1948, recognized the events in Finland as

---

March 2, 1948, do not display any great enthusiasm for Warren's "offer." In fact, he complains about Warren accusing the Finnish police of being Communist-controlled, a charge which Enckell strongly denied. Enckell's memorandum, 2 March 1948, CEK, 106, "muistiinpanoja 2," VA.

[26] Wuori to Helsinki, 5 March 1948 (nr. 6/1948), 5 C7: "Lontoo 1948," Ulkoministeriön arkisto [Finnish Foreign Ministry Archives] Helsinki, Finland (hereafter cited as UMA).

[27] Paasikivi's diary entries: 8-13 March 1948, *Paasikiven päiväkirjat*, 1:571-4. Warren to Secretary of State, 6 March 1948, SD, RG 59, 760d.6111/3-648, NA. See also Matson, "The Helsinki Axioms," 208. It must be added that although his public actions created a picture of a cool-headed real-politician, Paasikivi was less secure in private. For example, on March 4, after meeting with Istomin he wrote in his diaries: "This is horrible! With these kind of people [referring to the Soviets] we have to deal with; now—and always in the future. How will this all end?" Paasikivi's diary entry, 4 March 1948, *Paasikiven päiväkirjat*, 1:566.

part of a "Soviet intention to consolidate Communist control in the border states," it at the same time asserted that Soviet behavior had "quickened the pro-western trend in Norway and strengthened the conviction of high military officers in Sweden that their country's foreign policy [ie. neutrality] is unrealistic."[28] The Finnish minister to Sweden, Georg A. Gripenberg, had noticed a similar increase in anti-Communist activity in Sweden stemming from the events in Czechoslovakia and Finland. As he wrote to Helsinki on March 8, 1948, "Swedish society has begun a furious campaign against communism...[and this] movement will most definitely expand and intensify in the future."[29]

As a result, in the coming months the development of Finno-Soviet relations had a crucial impact on the strategic considerations regarding the entire Scandinavian peninsula. One might even argue that the Soviet pressure on Finland assured Norway's participation in the Atlantic Pact owing to a sense of increased vulnerability to potential Soviet aggression. Rumors that the Soviets would soon invite the Norwegians to sign a similar pact as they were designing with Finland certainly pushed the leaders in Oslo closer towards the West. At the same time, the mild nature of the FCMA Treaty allowed the Swedes to remain neutral despite American pressure to the contrary. In effect, what had begun as a bilateral affair helped to shape the northerns frontiers of the East-West struggle for years to come.[30]

In no other time was this internationalization of the Finno-Soviet development more evident than when President Truman delivered his St. Patrick's Day speech in New York on March 17. Himself the

---

[28] CIA "Review of the World Situation As It Relates to the Security of the United States," 10 March 1948, Minutes of the Meetings of the National Security Council, 1947-1977; UPA Microfilms, Reel 1. Rumors of a similar Soviet proposal to Norway as to Finland circulated widely among western diplomats in early March and may have had an effect on the Norwegian stand. For example, Bay (Oslo) to Warren (Helsinki), 8 March 1948 and 11 March 1948, SD, RG 84, Helsinki Top Secret File, 1947-1955, 320, Norway-USSR, Box 1, WNRC; State Department Brief on March 8, 1948, Truman Papers, Naval Aide Files, Box 21, HSTL.

[29] Gripenberg to Helsinki, 8 March 1948 (nr. 4/1948), 5 C2, "Tukholma 1948," UMA.

[30] On the Scandinavian countries in midst of the alliance building see, Geir Lundestad, *America, Scandinavia and the Cold War, 1945-1949* (New York, 1980), esp. 167ff. In fact, Norwegians inquired on March 11 what kind of support they might expect from the West in case the Soviets did put pressure on them. From London to Secretary of State, 11 March 1948, PPS: Country and Area Files, Europe, 1947-1948, Box 27, NA.

embodiment of a Cold Warrior, Truman had earlier in the day spoken to a joint session of Congress about "The Threat to the Freedom of Europe." In New York he outlined the same call for Americans to rise against Soviet aggression before it was too late. As Truman put it,

> One nation has obstructed cooperative effort...steadily expanded the control over its neighbors. It is a tragic record. Latvia, Lithuania, Estonia. Poland, Rumania, Bulgaria. Yugoslavia, Albania, Hungary. And now Czechoslovakia...Nor is this the whole story. *For that nation is now pressing its demands upon Finland.* Its [Russia's] foreign agents are fighting in Greece and working hard to undermine the freedom of Italy.[31]

Finland was, at least in public speeches, simply another example of Soviet expansionism. Being put into the same category with Greece and Italy, however, would have suggested a massive aid effort for Finland. But the U.S. and its allies did not "take the gloves off" with respect to Finland as they did in 1948 by intervening in Italy's elections and had done for some time by sending military aid to Greece. The policy towards Finland did not become "interventionist." This suggests that, despite the strong call for uniform resistance in the West against anything that seemed to spell the advance of communism, there was room for a less rigid policy in such select countries as Finland.[32]

Still, a clear American policy towards Finland was yet to be designed. The negotiations in Moscow between March 22 and April 5 coincided with the severest wave of pessimism concerning the Finno-Soviet situation. That Finland was en route to becoming the latest addition to the Soviet empire characterized reporting between American officials in Washington and abroad who seemed to conclude, especially after the treaty was ratified in late April by the

---

[31] U.S. President, *Public Papers of the Presidents: Harry S. Truman, 1948* (Washington, D.C., 1948), 188. Italics added. Paasikivi's reaction to Truman's mention of Finland was generally positive; he even told Enckell that the speech may influence the Soviet position on Finland in the upcoming negotiations. "Maybe they don't want to blackmail us now," Paasikivi wrote in his diaries. Paasikivi's diary entry, 19 March 1948, *Paasikiven päiväkirjat*, 1:580.

[32] On American policies in Italy and Greece, see James E. Miller, "Taking off the Gloves: The United States and the Italian Elections of 1948," *Diplomatic History* 7 (1983): 35-55; James E. Miller, *The United States and Italy: The Politics and Diplomacy of Stabilization* (Chapel Hill, 1986); E. Timothy Smith, *The United States, Italy and NATO, 1947-1952* (New York, 1992); Lawrence S. Wittner, *American Intervention in Greece, 1943-1949* (New York, 1982); Howard Jones, *"A New Kind of War": America's Global Strategy and the Truman Doctrine in Greece* (New York, 1989).

Finnish Diet, that Finland was "lost." And yet the American policy towards Finland speaks of a seeming ambiguity, a lack of a full understanding or concern, with reference to that country. On the one hand, the Americans sent a strong message that a military pact would be viewed as an act that *de facto* committed Finland to the Soviet side. On the other hand, the United States also listened and understood the Finns—if only to the extent that they could be helpful in the struggle against the main enemy: "Soviet directed world communism."

A Curious Treaty

The Finnish delegation left for Moscow on March 20, 1948. The group included Prime Minister Mauno Pekkala, Foreign Minister Enckell, Minister of Interior Yrjö Leino, Minister of Social Works Onni Peltonen, and, as Paasikivi's personal "trustees," Urho Kekkonen and J.O. Söderhjelm, a member of the Swedish People's Party's (RKP) parliamentary group. Paasikivi gave the delegation strict orders about limiting the commitments included in a treaty, instructed them not to agree on anything without consulting him, and stayed in constant contact with the group. On April 2, Söderhjelm and Kekkonen even flew back to Helsinki to receive further directions from the president. Paasikivi's instructions had been laid down on March 17, 1948, and stressed Finland's "special circumstances," the need to limit the treaty to cover only Finland's territory and the necessity to underline only Germany as the potential aggressor. In other words, the delegation was not to enter into a general military pact that the Soviets could use to demand Finnish participation in, say, a possible border conflict between the Soviet Union and Turkey, or if the western allies suddenly invaded the USSR through Southeastern Europe.[33]

Although Sir Robin Hankey of the British Foreign Office was sure that the Soviets were "out for bigger game" than that, the end result was close to what Paasikivi had wanted. The Finno-Soviet FCMA Treaty that was signed on April 5, 1948, was not a military alliance similar to the treaties between the USSR and its East European satellites. It did obligate Finland to help the USSR if a military conflict broke out, say, somewhere in Kazakhstan. In addition, it specifically

---

[33] Paasikivi's diary entries: 7-22 and 29-31 March, 1-3 April 1948, *Paasikiven päiväkirjat*, 1:570-81; 584-91; Suomi, *Vonkamies*, 344-51. Paasikivi's instructions in JKPK, 5:19, "neuvottelumateriaalia," VA. See also J.O. Söderhjelm, *Kolme matkaa Moskovaan* [Three trips to Moscow] (Helsinki, 1970), 95-214.

guaranteed Soviet noninterference in Finland's internal affairs and recognized Finland's desire to remain outside of the great power conflicts. The Soviets had accepted most Finnish proposals, while insisting on a clause (Article One) that committed Finland to defending her territory against an invasion by "Germany or any country allied with Germany."[34]

To be sure, the Finns did not welcome the FCMA Treaty with open arms. From their viewpoint, the most troubling clause dealt with potential Finno-Soviet consultations if a threat from Germany seemed imminent. Although the pact did not obligate Finland to accept Soviet military assistance if such a threat was on the horizon, there was the possibility that the Soviets might "manufacture" a threat and demand consultations, perhaps even military bases in Finland. For example, if West Germany rearmed, the Soviets might use such an occurrence as a basis for suggesting military talks between themselves and Finland. As political scientist George Maude put it, however, the FCMA Treaty did not make Finland a "full member" of the Soviet security system in Eastern Europe. In fact, the pact paradoxically served to strengthen Finnish neutrality in the long run. Article 4 of the treaty prohibited either party "from participating in alliances directed against the other party." This clause later served to enhance Finland's efforts to remain outside the East-West conflict, while the pact in general became one of the cornerstones of postwar Finnish foreign policy and something President Paasikivi and his successor, Urho K. Kekkonen, would repeatedly refer to when explaining Finland's position vis-à-vis the USSR and the Cold War. In short, for the most part the FCMA Treaty merely confirmed the status quo of postwar Finno-Soviet relations: that Finland's neutrality was a modified one, and that the Soviets were the main concern of, and exercised relatively strong influence over, Finland's foreign policy without interfering in its domestic affairs.[35]

[34] About the instructions and negotiations, see JKPK, 5:18, "JKP:n esityslista" and "Paasikiven muistiinpanoja," VA; K.G. Idman's memorandum of 11 March 1948, JKPK, 5:19, "eräitä Suomen puolueettomuutta koskevia huomautuksia," VA; CEK, 105: "Moskovan maalishuhtikuu 1948 muistiinpanoja"; CEK, 106: "sähkevaihtoa Moskova-Helsinki," [telegrams Moscow-Helsinki] VA. Suomi, *Vonkamies*, 322-31. For a full text of the treaty, see *United Nations Treaty Series*, 48 (1948), 150-61.

[35] Matson, "The Helsinki Axioms," 213-14. See also Kalevi J. Holsti, "Strategy and Techniques of Influence in Soviet-Finnish Relations," *Western Political Quarterly* 17 (March 1964): 68-9; Hakovirta, *East-West Conflict*, 101, 118-21; Kevin Devlin, "Finland in 1948: The Lesson of a Crisis," 439; and Efraim Karsh, "Finland: Adaptation and Conflict," *International Affairs* 62 (Spring 1986): 265-78.

Why were the Soviets so "soft" on Finland? One explanation
based on recently opened Soviet archival materials suggests that
Paasikivi's toughness and the prolongation of the treaty negotiations
had convinced the Soviets that the Finns would not blink and make
far-reaching concessions, and that even the Finnish Communists who
were in the cabinet had little power to change that. As Maxim L.
Korobochkin put it, Stalin and Molotov, even if somewhat reluctantly,
had come to the conclusion that in this case they would have to
compromise and they "were ready to go rather far to meet the
Finnish point of view, provided that their strategic aim had been
achieved." The apparent western interest in Finland's position also
served to moderate Soviet pressure on the Finns. As Korobochkin
adds, the Soviet leaders "preferred to accept Finland's 'semineutral'
position on the Soviet border, [rather] than risk the breakdown of
negotiations and a conflict potentially involving their Western
opponents."[36] In other words, it seems that the Soviet Union's
demand for security had overcome any expansionist dreams the
Kremlin may have had earlier concerning Finland.

From the Soviet point of view, the FCMA Treaty was a defensive
one that reflected first and foremost Soviet fears of a revitalized
Germany that might ally itself with anti-Soviet western powers. While
the treaties completed between the Soviet Union and its East European
satellites previously had been virtual preambles of growing Soviet
hegemony in Eastern Europe, the Finno-Soviet pact recognized the
limits of Soviet influence. Its main concern was to avoid the possibility
that Finland might be used as a springboard for an attack against the
USSR. This seems to support the argument present in a large body of
literature that suggests that the guiding principle in the Soviet Union's
postwar foreign policy was not so much an effort to expand
communism, but rather a concern, conditioned by the experiences of
World War II, about the USSR's national security. Given the memories
of World War II, such concern naturally focused on doing everything
to prevent a renewed attack from the West, especially from
Germany.[37] In such a context Finland was not a similar strategic "hot

---

[36] Maxim L. Korobochkin, "USSR and the Treaty of Friendship, Cooperation and
Mutual Assistance with Finland," 186.

[37] Examples of such views include the following: Fernando Claudin, *The
Communist Movement: From Comintern to Cominform*, trans. Brian Pearce and
Francis MacDonaugh (Middlesex, England, 1975); William Taubman, *Stalin's
American Policy: From Entente to Détente to Cold War* (New York, 1982); Vojtech

spot" as were many Central European states, because it did not lie directly between Germany and the Soviet Union.

Thus, the FCMA Treaty satisfied Soviet security in Finland in a way that a similar treaty with Poland or Czechoslovakia could not. Nor did Finland lie directly between the USSR and its Cold War adversaries. Neutral Sweden, which was much more likely to stay neutral if Finland was not forced into a military alliance, was an added bulwark between the USSR and the West. Accordingly, as the Cold War progressed and the division between East and West solidified, Finland and Sweden often found their neutral aspirations closely tied. In sum, the Finno-Soviet FCMA Treaty seems to indicate that, dictated by their larger security interests in Europe, the Soviets had limited aims in Finland.[38]

Moreover, the Soviets may have hoped that the "lenient" treatment of Finland would be seen as a clear demonstration that they were not "red Nazis" swallowing one country after another. The Czechoslovakian events had, after all, produced a host of negative outbursts in the western world.[39] The cordiality of Finno-Soviet relations might reduce some of that criticism and strengthen the Soviet argument that they were hardly such expansionist monsters as western propaganda portrayed them to be. Indeed, the British were relieved over the terms of the treaty and, in the words of Oswald Scott, believed that the Finns had concluded a pact with the "best terms they could

---

Mastny, *Russia's Road to the Cold War* (New York, 1979); and Vojtech Mastny, "Stalin and the Militarization of the Cold War," *International Security* 9 (Winter 1984-85): 109-29. See also Leffler, *A Preponderance of Power*, 511-15.

[38] This interpretation is essentially the same as in Devlin, "Finland in 1948: The Lesson of a Crisis," 439-42. For a somewhat different view see Adam B. Ulam, *Expansion and Coexistence: The History of Soviet Foreign Policy* (New York, 1978), 420-1. For interpretations stressing the importance of Finland's geographic location, see Hans Peter Krosby, "The Communist Power Bid in Finland in 1948," *Political Science Quarterly* 75 (June 1960): 229-43; and particularly Efraim Karsh, "Geographical Determinism: Finnish Neutrality Revisited," *Cooperation and Conflict* 21 (1986): 43-57; and Risto E.J. Penttilä, *Finland's Search for Security through Defence, 1944-1989* (London, 1991), 29-34. On the significance of Czechoslovakia's geographic location to the Soviet Union's strategy, see Josef Kalvoda, *Czechoslovakia's Role in Soviet Strategy* (Washington, D.C., 1978).

[39] For a discussion of the way Soviet communism and German fascism were linked in the American mind after World War II, see Les K. Adler and Thomas G. Paterson, "Red Fascism: The Merger of Nazi Germany and Soviet Russia in the American Image of Totalitarianism, 1930's-1950's," *American Historical Review* 70 (1970): 1046-64.

hope for" and that "nothing in the treaty as published need[s to] weaken Finland's position as regards to the USSR." During an April 8, 1948, cabinet meeting Ernest Bevin even maintained that the Kremlin had treated Finland "rather as a neutral buffer state than as a Soviet satellite," and that the Finns had "at least been given a breathing space." The British credited this to Finnish "toughness," particularly to the firm grip of President Paasikivi.[40]

In contrast, the initial American reaction to the FCMA Treaty was extremely negative. It reflected an unwillingness to accept and openly recognize the basic differences between the Finnish treaty and the ones between the USSR and other Eastern European countries. In a sense this was quite logical. The National Security Council had earlier identified Finland as one of the countries under "an immediate threat" from Soviet communism. Thus, it was no wonder that immediately after the text of the FCMA Treaty was released, Americans suspected a "cover-up." In their respective analyses both Smith from Moscow and Douglass from London raised the possibility of secret clauses. At a cocktail party on April 17, 1948, Smith even told Jorma Vanamo, a member of the Finnish legation in Moscow, that the treaty was only the first step in a long-term Soviet plan to subordinate Finland.[41]

Some Finns who shared this strong suspicion about anything the Soviets did and who had been sidelined at the end of World War II fed American suspicions. Hjalmar Procopee, former minister of foreign affairs and Finland's minister to Washington during the war, is a case in point. After serving as the defense attorney for former President Risto Ryti in the "war guilt" trials of 1946, Procopee had left Finland in disgust and moved to Sweden. While there, he kept a constant interest in Finland's affairs, as well as close contact with his American friends that included several newspaper men and State Department officials. Procopee's anti-Soviet attitudes and his pessimism about

---

[40] Scott to Foreign Office, 8 April 1948, and "Cabinet Conclusion Regarding the Finno-Soviet Treaty," (same date) FO 371/71407, PRO.

[41] NSC 7: "The Position of the United States with Respect to Soviet Directed World Communism," 30 March 1948, *FRUS, 1948*, 1:546-50; Smith to Secretary of State, 7 April 1948, and Douglas to Secretary of State, 7 April 1948, SD, RG 59, 760d.6111/4-748, NA; Lovett to Warren, 9 April 1948, SD RG 59, 760d.6111/4-948, NA. Vanamo to Helsinki, 19 April 1948, JKPK, 5:35, "Kirjeitä Moskovasta," VA. Compare also with Hannu Rautkallio, *Paasikivi vai Kekkonen: Suomi lännestä nähtynä 1945-1956* (Helsinki, 1990), 91-3.

Finland's future, while they did not represent the official Finnish point of view, must have reinforced the negative views of those he contacted in Washington. On March 25, 1948, for example, Procopee wrote to Sumner Welles that, although Stalin might be willing to make some concessions to the Finns, "a military treaty is always a military treaty, integrating Finland in the Russian Military bloc and it ought therefore be avoided....World opinion should not be fooled...and it should always be remembered that it [a treaty] is made against the free will of the Finnish people."[42]

More significant, however, was the information from within the Finnish government. On April 12, Supply Minister Taavi N. Vilhula told an official in the American legation that there indeed were a number of "unpublished protocols" included in the FCMA Treaty that dictated the integration of Finnish forces into the Red Army in the event of a crisis. Vilhula, a strong opponent of any treaty with the USSR, may have hoped that this kind of information would result in strong pressure from the U.S. against ratification of the pact. Reports that "large numbers of trained Communists have infiltrated into Finland" also added to the growing sense within the U.S. delegation in Helsinki that "apparently the Soviets plan to initiate action after the ratification of the USSR-Finnish agreement and before campaigning for the July elections gets under way." [43]

As a result, despite numerous Finnish assertions to the contrary, the rumors of the hidden clauses remained alive well into May as American pressure against ratification strengthened.[44] On April 9 Avra Warren told Finnish minister-designate to the U.S., Karl Imanuel, that the American people would "consider Finland formally inducted [into the] Soviet orbit with [the] ratification [of the] pact." In addition, the U.S. exerted some economic and political pressure on the Finnish government in trying to prevent the ratification of the FCMA Treaty. The Commerce Department, for example, had withheld export licenses to Finland already in late March, and although the Finns were repeatedly assured that this was only due to "technical

---

[42] Procopee to Sumner Wells, 25 March 1948, Hjalmar Procopeen kokoelma (Hereafter HPK), 22: "kirjekonseptit," VA.

[43] Warren to Secretary of State, 13 April 1948, SD, RG 59, 760d.6111/4-1348, NA. See also Warren to Secretary of State, 13 April and 16 April 1948, and Lovett to Warren, 21 April 1948, *FRUS, 1948*, 4:778-9; State Department Brief, 12 April 1948, NAF, Box 21, HSTL.

[44] Jutila's letter to the Secretary of State, 10 May 1948, *FRUS, 1948*, 4:781-2.

difficulties" (the overflow of export license applications at the time), its timing makes one suspect something more. Given that Warren told Foreign Minister Enckell on April 19 that, if the Finnish Parliament ratified the FCMA treaty, the U.S. would not give "one dollar" to Finland indicates the existence of some American economic pressure on the Finns.[45]

While President Paasikivi considered the American attitude unfortunate, he did not take these warnings too seriously. "Tell Warren," Paasikivi told Enckell, "that he should look at things objectively and not combine our affair with the anti-Soviet propaganda waged in the United States." It was not that Paasikivi had some kind of blind trust in Stalin, but the Soviet Union, not the United States, was his major geopolitical concern and the major subject of his foreign policy. Everything else was secondary. As Paasikivi noted, "the U.S. cannot help us in any way if we get into a conflict with the USSR, because we cannot defend ourselves with dollars....It would be unfortunate if the U.S. didn't give us the little credit we need, but in that case we would just have to get by without it."[46] Paasikivi understood full well that, while American aid was beneficial, it was not a necessity and while the FCMA Treaty was not something he viewed as desirable, it did not change Finland's position vis-à-vis the USSR that much. Convincing the U.S. that Finland was not about to turn Communist was hardly worth creating added friction with the Soviet Union.

---

[45] Paasikivi's diary entry, 19 April 1948, *Paasikiven päiväkirjat*, 1:598; Warren to Secretary of State, SD, RG 59, 760d.6111/4-748, NA. In a conversation on April 7 some Finnish legation members in Washington charged that the export licenses were being handled on a "purely political basis" and hoped for a "thaw" in American practices with Finland; Memorandum of conversation, SD, RG 59, 660d.119/4-748, NA. The British Embassy in Washington also pointed out the American economic pressure on Finland in April; Chancery at Washington to Foreign Office, 21 April 1948, FO 371/71426, PRO. See also Hannu Heikkilä, "The United States and the Question of Export Licenses to Finland, 1947-1948," *Scandinavian Journal of History*, 8 (1983): 250-4 and the sources cited. Many Americans, especially in the military, did consider Finland as a "lost cause" by this time; General Lucius Clay even told General Bradley, Army Chief of Staff on April 10 that "We have *lost* Finland" (emphasis added); see Daniel Yergin, *Shattered Peace: The Origins of the Cold War and the National Security State* (Boston, 1977), 376.

[46] Paasikivi's diary entry, 19 April 1948, *Paasikiven päiväkirjat*, 1:598. It should be noted that in his outstanding study on American relations with Sweden, Norway and Denmark during the early Cold War years, Geir Lundestad argues that the U.S. did not exert any pressure on Finland in 1948. This, as the above has shown, is not quite true; Lundestad, *America, Scandinavia and the Cold War*, 209.

Therefore, despite some pressure from abroad, and notwithstanding the existence of a large anti-ratification faction within the Finnish government, the Diet, and general public, Paasikivi did not change his mind about the pact. With influential domestic allies—including the Social Democratic and Agrarian Parties' strong men, K.A. Fagerholm and Urho K. Kekkonen—Paasikivi pushed the Diet into ratifying the pact. At the same time, however, some American newspapers and magazines criticized him for trying to betray the Finnish public about the real meaning of the FCMA. *Time*, for example, said that Paasikivi was trying to "sugarcoat the news [about the treaty] in order to minimize anti-Russian feeling among Finns."[47]

By the time the Finnish Diet finally ratified the FCMA Treaty on April 28, 1948, the alarm had been sounded. The U.S. seemed quite determined to make Finland pay for its pact with the USSR by canceling the special postwar Finnish-American relationship—relatively extensive economic aid outside the Marshall Plan—as a punishment. Despite the Finns' claims that the pact did not include secret protocols, and despite the fact that the FCMA Treaty differed fundamentally from agreements between the USSR and its Eastern European allies, its ratification was initially viewed as a clear expansion of the Soviet sphere. The common belief was that the FCMA Treaty was only the first step that would soon be followed by a Communist takeover. As Ambassador Matthews from Stockholm argued: "Finland must go the way of the other satellites for the simple reason that the Soviet Union will not tolerate or understand any relationship which does not give it complete domination...within its sphere."[48]

From the American viewpoint, it was expansion and not coexistence, hegemony and not security, that the Soviets were ultimately after in Finland. In late April of 1948 the FCMA Treaty was, therefore, interpreted as an initial step in the Kremlin's

---

[47] *Time*, 19 April 1948, 30. See also *Time*, 12 April 1948, 35; *New York Times Magazine*, 11 April 1948, 10 ff.; *New York Times*, 17 April 1948, 2. Cf. Juhani Paasivirta, *Suomen kuva Yhdysvalloissa 1800-luvun lopulta 1960-luvulle* [The American view of Finland from the late 19th century to the 1960's] (Porvoo, 1962), 147-9, 157-8. On Paasikivi's maneuvers to get the treaty ratified, see Paasikivi's diary entries 7 to 28 April 1948, *Paasikiven päiväkirjat*, 1:593-604; Suomi, *Vonkamies*, 354-8. Only the SKDL was wholeheartedly for the treaty, other parties were either convinced by their leaders—most of the Agrarians by Kekkonen, most Social Democrats by Fagerholm—to vote for ratification or refrain from voting at all.

[48] Matthews to Secretary of State, 5 May 1948, *FRUS, 1948*, 3:112-13.

conspiracy against Finland's independence. What would be the next step? Invasion did not seem likely, but an internal coup à la Czechoslovakia was a possibility. As that coup never took place and as Finland's internal politics started moving into an entirely different direction as envisioned, American policy towards Finland made a remarkable turnaround.

A Cold War "Victory" and Dilemma

A coup orchestrated by the SKP had for many years seemed a strong possibility in Finland. During the immediate postwar years, the Communist press had relentlessly attacked Paasikivi for his supposed conspiring with "western imperialists." In addition, left-wing propaganda had charged the Finnish economic system with being unfair to the labor force and advocated a move towards a people's republic. The Communist losses in the 1947 local elections, however, had sent the party into an internal debate about future courses of action. Specifically, SKP leaders differed over the extent to which they should advocate the establishment of a "Finnish People's Republic." This debate caused severe friction even within the "first family" of the SKP. While Interior Minister Yrjö Leino thought that the party had no future if it embraced an extremely radical line, his wife, Hertta Kuusinen (daughter of Otto W. Kuusinen, later a member of the Soviet Politburo), believed that the party was losing some of its mass support because it had moved too far to the right. In fact, Leino was dismissed from the SKP leadership prior to Stalin's February 22 letter and retained his post as the minister of interior only because no potential Communist successor was in sight. Yet the more "radical" line that the party was apparently embarking upon at this point met a severe blow when SKP's application for membership in the Cominform was postponed on the eve of Stalin's invitation.[49]

Despite the Kremlin's apparent lack of confidence in their abilities, the radical wing of the SKP continued to advocate its revolutionary line during the FCMA negotiations. On March 25, 1948, Hertta Kuusinen even suggested during a speech that the Finnish Communists should follow the "Czech example." Coming only a month after the Communist coup in Czechoslovakia, Kuusinen's comment propelled the already existing rumors and fears

---

[49] Kimmo Rentola, "Soviet Leadership and Finnish Communism, 1944-1948," in Nevakivi, ed., *Finnish-Soviet Relations,* 235-8.

in Finland and even led to the creation of a counter-revolutionary council by conservative Finnish politicians. More importantly, the rumors gave the Finnish government justification to take measures to prevent such a coup, which in turn helped put the Communists on the defensive in Finnish domestic politics. This contributed significantly to their electoral defeat in July 1948.[50]

President Paasikivi himself was apprehensive about the potential for a coup and took several steps to prevent matters from getting out of hand. In late April he ordered a general alert of the armed forces and doubled the security precautions in Helsinki. He also studied closely the Communist strategy used in the Czechoslovakian coup d'état, which indicates that—despite what some authors have argued— Paasikivi was seriously troubled by the fate of Eduard Benes. Perhaps because of such deliberations he became extremely distrustful of Leino, who also served as the head of the Finnish Security Police, *Valtion Poliisi* (VALPO). On one occasion, Paasikivi admonished Leino and Mauno Pekkala, the moderate socialist prime minister with the words: "We are not Czechs."[51]

At the same time, the SKDL/SKP's public image in Finland was being successfully tarnished. While the rumors of an upcoming coup attempt did their part, even more dramatic was Yrjö Leino's sudden dismissal from the cabinet. On May 19, 1948, the conservative *Kokoomus* [Coalition] party's parliamentary group launched a no-confidence vote against Yrjö Leino. Charging that he had violated the Finnish Constitution by returning some Estonian refugees to the USSR shortly after coming into office in 1945, Leino's opponents won the vote by 81 to 61 on May 20, 1948. Leino, in an unprecedented and clearly unconstitutional act, refused to resign.

---

[50] On the Kuusinen speech, the Communist propaganda and the rightist opposition, see Anthony F. Upton, *Communism in Scandinavia and Finland* (New York, 1973), 28-56; Rautkallio, *Suomen suunta*, 248-9; Lauri Haataja, *Demokratian opissa: SKP, vaaran vuodet ja Neuvostoliitto* [Learning democracy: SKP, the dangerous years and the Soviet Union] (Helsinki, 1988), passim.; Suomi, *Vonkamies*, 359-64.

[51] 'Czechs" in Paasikivi's diary entry of 20 April 1948, *Paasikiven päiväkirjat*, 1:598-9; Raymond Ylitalo to Secretary of State, 11 May 1948, SD, RG 84, Helsinki Confidential File, 1948: 800, Box 12. The study of Czechoslovakia from 3 May 1948 in JKPK, 5:20, "Tsekkoslovakian kommunistien vallankaappausstrategia," VA. The most blatant (and poorly supported) argument identifying Paasikivi as the primus motor of a large-scale framing of Finnish Communists as revolutionaries and traitors is in Rautkallio, *Paasikivi vai Kekkonen*, 79-89.

Only two days later, in another unprecedented event, President Paasikivi dismissed Leino at the end of a heated cabinet meeting.[52]

Although Leino had lost his position within the SKP—something that was not a known fact outside the leadership of the party—his sudden dismissal seemed to provide an opportune moment for a popular uprising. In May 1948 a number of Communist-controlled labor unions went on strike protesting Paasikivi's actions. This was another politically disastrous move by the extreme left. From Hertta Kuusinen's speech and the persistent (if most likely false) coup rumors, to Leino's resistance to following constitutional procedure and the labor movement's immediate attempt to pressure the president, the SKP had received so much negative publicity in Finland during 1948 that its lack of success in the upcoming July elections was predictable. The non-Communist parties' eagerness to accuse the SKP of illegal actions was becoming an effective tool of this Finnish-style "redbaiting."[53]

This was something that, while ignored among the radical SKP leaders who had anxiously waited for their moment, could not be overlooked in Moscow. Only a few days into the strike the SKP received orders from the Kremlin to retreat and followed it "with an aching heart," as Hertta Kuusinen put it in a letter to his father Otto W. Kuusinen on May 28, 1948.[54] In the end, the Finnish Communists were, therefore, clearly subservient to the Communist "motherland" and not willing to act on their own without Moscow's blessings. That such an endorsement did not arrive, despite the SKP's apparent belief that it would, seems to indicate that the Soviets had little trust in the ability of the SKP to succeed in its bid for power. They certainly had

---

[52]Rautkallio, *Suomen Suunta*, 252-4; Upton, *Communism*, 294. See also Warren to Marshall, 23 May 1948, *FRUS, 1948*, 4:782-3; Paasikvi's diary entries, 12-23 May 1948, *Paasikiven päiväkirjat*, 1:610-15. Paasikivi's comment on Leino's refusal to resign was: "This is unheard of behavior from a cabinet member. It's a challenge to the constitution, to law and order. It reveals how the Communists really feel about things [like that]"; ibid., 615. Leino's view of his actions as the minister of interior was very different; in fact, Leino virtually portrayed himself as the "savior" of the country; Yrjö Leino, *Kommunisti sisäministerinä* [Communist as the minister of interior] (Helsinki, 1991; first ed. 1958), passim.

[53] Upton, 29-45. Although there was no united anti-Communist campaign, all other parties, especially the Social Democrats, the Agrarians and the Conservatives used the SKDL and SKP as the major target of their campaigning. See Haataja, *Demokratian opissa*, passim; and Suomi, *Vonkamies*, 364-74.

[54]Rentola, "Soviet Leadership and Finnish Communism," 240.

no interest in taking the risks that an intervention on behalf of the SKP potentially held. Thus Stalin pulled the rug from underneath the May movement and opted for the security and stability that the conclusion of the FCMA Treaty and the continuation of the Paasikivi Line provided. Although there was no overt Communist coup attempt, the events of the spring of 1948 had disastrous effects on the SKP/SKDL. In 1945 this coalition gained 23.5% of the vote; three years later, they gathered less than 20%. More importantly, the result of the heated and prolonged government negotiations in July led to the creation of a new government without any Communists or more moderate People's Democrats. Fagerholm's Social Democratic minority government was, in fact, the least likely to pay lip-service to the Russians. The extreme left would have to wait until the mid-1960s before its members would appear in the Finnish cabinet.[55]

What has puzzled historians much more than the activities of the Finnish Communist Party in 1948 is the inactivity of the USSR. Why did the Soviets not send in armies or overtly intervene on behalf of the SKDL/SKP? Indeed, the only thing that may be interpreted as an attempt to boost the Communist campaign before the July elections was the Soviet cancellation of half of Finland's war reparations in early June. While a Finnish Communist delegation in Moscow claimed credit for the Soviet decision, most Finns, including President Paasikivi, viewed it as a rather callous move to boost the SKP/SKDL's campaign. What made the argument even more persuasive was the fact that the Soviets announced that the starting date of the reduction would be July 1, 1948, immediately before the Diet elections were held.[56] The apparent Soviet inaction is partly explained by looking at the possible consequences of a Communist uprising in Finland. Even

---

[55] Upton, 297-8; Hodgson, 225. About the government negotiations, see Suomi, *Vonkamies*, 374-85, and Raymond Ylitalo, *Vaaran vuosilta viistkytluvulle: Muistelmia ja dokumentteja vuosilta 1948-1950* [From the dangerous years to the fifties: Memoirs and documents from the years 1948-1950] (Keuruu, 1979), 16-27. The biggest winners were the *Maalaisliitto* (Agrarian Party) which increased its seats from 49 to 56; *Kokoomus* (Coalition) from 28 to 33; and the Social Democrats from 50 to 54. The new government consisted purely of Social Democrats and one "nonpolitical" minister; Carl Enckell continued as the minister of foreign affairs.

[56] Matson, "The Helsinki Axioms," 221-2; Paasikivi's diary entry, 1 June 1948, *Paasikiven päiväkirjat*, 1:624. Text of the reduction treaty in *Suomen ja Neuvostoliiton Suhteet 1948-1983*, 18-19. The Moscow-based *New Times* magazine cited the reduction as "indicative of the success of Soviet foreign policy"; *New Times*, 16 and 25 June 1948, 15; see Paasivirta, *Suomen kuva Yhdysvalloissa*, 150.

if successful, such a coup would not necessarily have enhanced
Moscow's security interests because of the political backlash it might
have provoked in the West. Given that they had a military base,
Porkkala, on the southern coast of Finland, and had just concluded the
FCMA Treaty, Soviet security aims along its northwestern border were,
indeed, relatively well satisfied. To aim for more might have either
provoked a strong western response or, at the minimum, caused
Sweden to abandon its neutral position. In that sense, the choice for
the USSR was between accepting a large neutral zone—part of which
was to a degree under Soviet control—or pushing the Iron Curtain
North of the Baltic Sea.[57] Thus ideological considerations took a back
seat in Soviet policy vis-à-vis Finland. In 1948 the Soviets seemed to
be more interested in their own national security than in their
"ideological responsibility" to support a leftist takeover in Finland.
In fact, as recent research has shown, Soviet policy overall was
arguably far less aggressive and ideologically motivated than has been
previously assumed. In relations with the Czech, French, Greek,
Hungarian, Italian, Polish, and other national Communist leaders,
Stalin did not invariably push the revolution ahead at full steam.
Rather, he often evidenced a genuine lack of interest in his ideological
compatriots' efforts to gain power and gave his support to the more
radical local Communists only when it was evident that such a course
was likely to succeed relatively easily and presented the best available
way to secure the USSR's national security interests. In the case of
Finland, Stalin's ambivalence would have been especially justifiable
given the relative weakness of the Finnish Communists that would not
allow them to stage a serious bid for power.[58]

In addition, the Soviets saw the utility of a Finnish Solution in their
dealings with the West. In the heated Cold War climate of the day,
Finland stood as a sole example of Soviet "reasonableness." Indeed,
in early May Soviet Foreign Minister Vjacheslav Molotov told
Ambassador Smith in Moscow that the FCMA Treaty was " a

---

[57] On this point see, Kevin Devlin, "Finland in 1948," 441-2.

[58] Compare with Peter Stavrakis, *Moscow and Greek Communism, 1944-1949*
(Ithaca, NY, 1989); Charles Gati, *Hungary and the Soviet Bloc* (Durham, NC, 1986);
John Coutovidis and Jaime Reynolds, *Poland, 1939-1947* (Leicester, England,
1986); and Karel Kaplan, *The Short March: The Communist Takeover of
Czechoslovakia, 1945-1948* (London, 1987). On Soviet relations with the Italian
and French Communist parties, see Paolo Spriano, *Stalin and the European
Communists* (London, 1985).

convincing example of the lack of aggressiveness in Soviet foreign policy." In striking contrast to the recent Czech coup d'état and the crackdowns in Eastern Europe, Soviet relations with Finland served to symbolize, however feebly, the possibility of coexistence at a time of ever-increasing Cold War tensions.[59] American officials, however, would have none of that. Instead, in early May 1948 the Americans went on the offensive in Finland, hoping to affect the outcome of the July elections. Believing that the Soviets were about to reduce Finland's reparations as a means of affecting the elections in SKP/SKDL's favor, Warren thought that the U.S. should respond in kind. Therefore, he recommended that export licenses to Finland should be granted quickly and that the U.S. should reopen the discussions of a future $40 million credit to Finland. Warren also told Torsten Vahervuori of the Finnish Foreign Ministry that the FCMA Treaty would not affect U.S.-Finnish trade relations and that the Export-Import Bank would soon make a move regarding Finland. "This," Vahervuori wrote in a memorandum to President Paasikivi, "would be the surest sign that Finland had regained any trust it may have lost [in the West]." And sure enough, on May 26, 1948, a week before the 50% reduction in Finland's reparations payments to the USSR was made public, the Commerce Department announced the approval of over $4 million worth of export licenses to Finland.[60]

This action was not simply a result of American hopes to score a victory in Finland. Finns themselves were quick to capitalize on the Soviet-American confrontation and the evident eagerness in Washington to give aid to those allegedly threatened by communism. Thus, while the Finnish minister to the U.S., K.T. Jutila, went to great lengths in early June 1948 to express gratitude for the recent granting of export licenses, he at the same time hinted about the possibility of a "little Marshall Plan for Finland." In response, Assistant Secretary of Commerce William Thorp gave quiet assurances that a "favorable

---

[59] Smith to Secretary of State, 4 May 1948; quoted in Allison, *Finland's Relations with the Soviet Union*, 30.

[60] Warren to Secretary of State, 9 May 1948, SD, RG 59, 660d.119/5-948, NA; Heikkilä, 254-55; Memorandum by T. Vahervuori, 12 L:Yhdysvallat, 1948, UMA. The CIA also maintained that the USSR reduced the reparations as a measure "to win Finnish favor at the polls"; "CIA Review of the World Situation," 17 June 1948, *National Security Council's Minutes of Meetings with Special Advisory Reports, 1947-1977* (UPA microfilms, reel 1).

outcome" in the July elections would have an important impact on the credit and aid Finland were to receive from the U.S.[61]

So it did. The Communist defeat in the July elections and their removal from the cabinet forced a gradual remolding of the image of Finland as the "next domino." The picture that now emerged was, however, by no means a clear one. On the one hand, some viewed the Finnish case as a victory; because there had not been a Communist takeover in Finland the Finns had "contained" Soviet expansion. On the other hand, many remained suspicious of long-range Soviet objectives vis-à-vis Finland. The policy that thus emerged—a diplomatic non-policy combined with relatively extensive economic aid outside the European Recovery Program—was a unique one in that it clearly recognized the specific circumstances in Finland by accepting its foreign policy collaboration with the USSR. Because American policy towards Finland was only a small part of the larger Cold War policy vis-à-vis the USSR, however, it would never be totally free from the long-term threat perceptions prevalent in Washington. Given that the Soviet Union's ultimate goal was assumed to be world dominance, many argued that the Kremlin would not be satisfied with such an ideological heretic as Finland on its border.

This did not prevent Secretary of State Marshall from viewing Finland as a success. Outlining recent events in Europe during a meeting with President Truman and Secretary of the Navy James Forrestal on July 19, Marshall concentrated on western triumphs, implying that the tide was turning against the Soviet Union. He argued that the Americans had been victorious in turning back the Communist tide in Greece, Italy, and France, where the local Communist parties had suffered losses in recent elections. Moreover, Marshall added, "the Soviets had been reversed in Finland" as well. The very top-level of Washington's decision-making hierarchy saw Finland linked to the larger picture of American containment policies in Europe. And, as Marshall's comment seems to indicate, the Secretary of State was very eager to take credit for the victories of the local non-Communist parties.[62] That Finland was in its own class is,

---

[61] Memorandum of conversation, 8 June 1948, SD, RG 59, 660d.119/6-848, NA.

[62] James Forrestal's diary entry, 19 July 1948, *The Forrestal Diaries,* ed. by Walter Millis (New York, 1951), 459. On U.S. policies vis-à-vis Greece, Italy and France, see Wittner, *American Intervention in Greece*; Jones, *"A New Kind of War"*; Miller, *The United States and Italy*; Smith, *The United States, Italy, and NATO*; Frank Costigliola, *France and the United States: The Cold Alliance since World War II* (New

however, clearest when looking at American economic policies towards Finland during the second half of 1948. Already on the eve of the July elections Minister Warren had promised Finnish officials that, given a Communist defeat, Finland would not be put in the same category with the USSR's East European satellites when it came down to designing American economic policy. In the wake of the elections Warren then said that the U.S. had "decided" that Finland was a democracy and indicated that the Americans would look very favorably upon future Finnish loan requests from the Export-Import Bank. This promise was realized when the U.S. issued a $5 million cotton credit on September 1, 1948, and the Export-Import Bank granted a $10 million loan to the Finnish woodworking industry two months later.[63]

Nevertheless, the favorable economic policies and the obvious satisfaction with the election results were balanced by a much more pessimistic and sinister view about the future of Finland. The most negative opinion came from Howard Donovan, the chargé d'affaires in Moscow. He argued that, despite their seeming peacefulness, the USSR and the Finnish Communists would, sooner or later, try to take over Finland. As he put it, "Finland will continue as [a] problem child which Kremlin intends to deal with whenever and as soon as suitable opportunity arises." In other words, although much of the evidence available pointed to the contrary, Donovan believed that the Soviets would—when the time was ripe—absorb Finland completely into their orbit. To many Americans Finland was still a *potential* Soviet satellite and lay permanently in the danger zone.[64]

York, 1989); Edward Rice-Maximim, "The United States and the French Left, 1945-1949: View from the State Department," *Journal of Contemporary History* 19 (October 1984): 729-47.

[63] Bruno Kivikoski to Paasikivi, 2 July 1948, JKPK, VAY 4460, VA; Paasikivi's diary entry, 14 July 1948, *Paasikiven päiväkirjat*, 1:631; Heikkilä, 255-8. A table of approvals and rejections of export licenses to Eastern Europe (including Finland) through 1948 is in Heikkilä, 258. In addition, Finland was seen as a relatively "safe" investment for American business; see *Business Week*, 10 July 1948, 101. Also see Väyrynen, "Finland in Western Policy," 94.

[64] Donovan to Secretary of State, 9 July 1948, *FRUS, 1948*, 4:784-5. This nagging fear—the conviction that Finland was (permanently) on the "danger zone"—also made the secretary of state decide that any civil aviation agreement with Finland "should be subject to cancellation on short notice"; Marshall to Douglas (London), SD, RG 59, 711.60d27/7-2948, NA. The pessimists could have cited Soviet media as evidence of the willingness of the USSR to take over Finland. The new Social Democratic prime minister, K.A.Fagerholm, was criticized as wanting "to direct that

It would remain that way for some time to come. Given its unique position between East and West, Finland's situation would not be completely settled for years to come. Nevertheless, the "Finnish Solution" provided an important sounding board for American policymakers when set against two other, in many ways more dramatic, events of 1948.

The Finnish Crisis in Comparative Perspective

Finland's 1948 spring crisis did not take place in isolation. In order to place it into its proper framework, I will draw some tentative comparisons between the events in Finland, the Prague coup of February 1948, and the Tito-Stalin break that became public in the summer of 1948. The main interest here is in the different policies of the U.S. and the USSR towards Finland, Czechoslovakia, and Yugoslavia; in the ways in which these policies fit into the larger framework of the Soviet-American confrontation; and in the "lessons" derived from them.

The Prague coup in February 1948 is a good example of the way lessons were learned in Washington. Between 1945 and 1948, the U.S. had gradually strengthened its stance on Czechoslovakia, responding to the clear trend in Czech internal policies towards nationalization and the growing strength of the Czech Communist Party (KSC). The decisions to cut down aid and trade to Czechoslovakia indicate that the United States had abandoned, or sought to abandon, Czechoslovakia to the Soviet sphere even before 1948. Ironically, American policies helped strengthen the local Communist Party and undermine President Eduard Benes' efforts to navigate a middle course between East and West.[65]

---

country into the orbit of the Marshall Plan, into the 'northern', 'Atlantic' and similar blocs which are being built up by the Anglo-Saxon imperialists"; *New Times*, 18 August 1948, 16-17.

[65] Many scholars have addressed the American reaction to the Czechoslovakian crisis. Here I am basing my analysis mostly on the following: Geir Lundestad, *The American Non-Policy Towards Eastern Europe: Universalism in an Area not of Essential Interest to the United States* (New York, 1975), 149-82; Lundestad, *The American "Empire" and Other Studies of U.S. Foreign Policy in Comparative Perspective* (Oxford, 1990), 143-73; Thomas G. Paterson, *Soviet American Confrontation: Postwar Reconstruction and the Origins of the Cold War* (Baltimore, 1973), 121-30; Yergin, *Shattered Peace*, 343-57; and Leffler, *A Preponderance of Power*, 20-36. For a more "traditionalist" viewpoint, see Walter Ullman, "Czechoslovakia's Crucial Years, 1945-1948: An American View," *East European*

To most American politicians the events in Czechoslovakia during the spring of 1948 confirmed the justifiability and necessity of the policy of containment. The Truman administration was ready and willing to use the "Czech model" to its advantage in order to pass legislation in Congress and, in effect, solidify bipartisan support for an increasingly open anti-Soviet foreign policy. The Czech spring crisis (along with the Finnish events) gave urgency to the Brussels Pact which was signed on March 17, 1948. On that same day Truman told a joint session of Congress that the USSR's "ruthless course of action, and the clear design to extend it to the remaining free nations of Europe has sent a shock-wave through the civilized world." The president added that "We have reached a point at which the position of the United States should be unmistakably clear."[66]

While the Czechoslovakian coup may have confirmed to many that there was a pattern in Soviet expansionist behavior that needed to be confronted, it is clear at the same time that the Soviets could not have succeeded in such an "elegant takeover" of Czechoslovakia without a significant pro-Soviet (or pro-Communist) sentiment and a very strong Communist party in that country. The Soviets had been, after all, the liberators of Prague in 1945 and had withdrawn their forces from the country by December of that year. While the ruthless policies during the short occupation period that followed took away much of the liberator's aura, it did not hurt the KSC significantly. Under Prime Minister Klement Gottwald's leadership the Communists won 38% of the votes in the May 1946 elections and were able to muster from a significantly stronger position than their Finnish counterparts who at the time controlled less than a quarter of the seats in the Finnish Diet. Moreover, although the KSC participated in a coalition (National Front) government, it did not face the same kind of opposition from other parties as the relatively isolated SKP did in Finland. On the contrary, Gottwald was able to successfully launch the so-called Construction (*Budovatelsky*) Program of 1947, a program

---

Quarterly, 1 (September 1967):217-30; and Ulam, *The United States in Prague, 1945-1948* (New York, 1978).

[66] Quoted in Yergin, *Shattered Peace*, 354. The events in Czechoslovakia were instrumental in enabling the passing of such acts as the Marshall Plan, the enactment of universal military training and restoration of selective service; ibid. William L. Thorp, a State Department official, remembered the Czech coup later on as a "godsend from the point of view of convincing Congress"; in William L. Thorp Oral History, HSTL, 120-1.

that aimed at the gradual nationalization of private businesses and industries.[67]

One could also argue that Benes was not as strong a leader as Finland's Paasikivi. Not only did Benes give in to Communist demands rather easily, but he in a sense legitimized their takeover in February by remaining as a puppet president. On the other hand, he was a man faced with essentially two options: giving in or risking a civil war and a potential Soviet intervention. Haunted by the ghost of Munich and the prospect of another western "sellout," Benes and his foreign minister, Jan Masaryk, may have viewed remaining in office as the only way to fight for the few remnants of democracy. Tragically, Benes died imprisoned at his country home at Sezimovo Usti on August 20, 1948.[68]

To be sure, one cannot disregard the impact of the Soviet threat on Czechoslovakian developments. Because of its geographical position at the center of East-Central Europe, Czechoslovakia was clearly of major strategic interest to the USSR. In Moscow it was considered a part of the Soviet orbit after World War II, and its subsequent rapid sovietization confirmed Stalin's keen interest in Czechoslovakia. And still, the fact remains that Czechoslovakia's inclusion in the eastern bloc was in part prompted by internal developments and not simply a result of Soviet aggressive designs. "The lesson of Czechoslovakia" learned in the United States—that it proved a pattern in Soviet behavior—was, it seems, to some extent an aberration.[69]

An added importance of Czechoslovakia and Finland lay in their respective propaganda values for Moscow and Washington. While the Czechoslovakian coup offered a "prototype" of Soviet behavior in Eastern Europe to the Americans, the Soviets could use Finland, because it did not conform with that prototype, as an example of how

---

[67] This account is mostly based on Karel Kaplan, *The Short March: The Communist Takeover in Czechoslovakia 1945-1948* (London, 1987). The term "elegant takeover" is from Paul Tigrid, "The Prague Coup of 1948: The Elegant Takeover," in *The Anatomy of Communist Takeovers*, 399-432. See also Jon Bloomfield, *Passive Revolution: Politics and the Czechoslovak Working Class, 1945-1948* (New York, 1979). The first Soviet FCMA treaty was actually signed with Czechoslovakia back in 1943; see Mastny, *Russia's Road to the Cold War*, 133-42.

[68] On Benes, see Edward Taborsky, *President Edward Benes: Between East and West, 1938-1948* (Stanford, 1981), esp. 211-34, 245-54. See also Leffler, *A Preponderance of Power*, 218-19.

[69] On the strategic importance of Czechoslovakia to the Soviet Union, see Josef Kalvoda, *Czechoslovakia's Role in Soviet Strategy* (Washington DC, 1978).

they only wanted to coexist with friendly neighbors, no matter what their social system was. It is no accident that Finland was later used as an example of the Soviet policy of peaceful coexistence.

On the other hand, Soviet behavior vis-à-vis Yugoslavia speaks of a clear animosity towards a challenger to the Kremlin's authority. Since 1945 Tito had pushed his country towards socialism at a rapid pace that far outran the other East European countries. As the Cold War ensued, the Yugoslav leader was often quicker on his ideological attacks on westerners than the Soviets themselves. Unlike his East European counterparts, Tito was also in complete control over his party and state. In addition, Yugoslavia was geographically in a very different position from most East European countries, sharing no common frontier with the USSR. This may have, in turn, strengthened Tito's own expansionist dreams, which found their clearest expression in the plans for a Balkan Federation that would have included Yugoslavia, Albania, and Bulgaria. Such a federation would have, however, been a potential competitor within the Soviet sphere and, beginning in January 1948, the Soviets began a series of attacks on the Yugoslavians' "nationalist deviation," aimed at discrediting, possibly removing, Tito and his regime which was acting too independently from Moscow's viewpoint. By June of 1948 an unprecedented break within the Communist bloc was a reality as the Cominform expelled the Yugoslav Communist party from its ranks.[70]

The subsequent success of the Yugoslav "heresy" was clearly a sign that nationalism had not died in those countries recently turned Communist. Put against the framework of increased repression, purges, and sovietization in the eastern bloc, the Tito-Stalin break also speaks to Stalin's ruthlessness and to a perceived need to keep the other East Europeans under control. Titoism became, indeed, even a greater evil than capitalism for the Soviet press during the late 1940s and early 1950s. In the end, the Tito-Stalin split turned out to be one of the greatest blunders of Soviet foreign policy during the early Cold War and a great indicator that, despite the internationalism preached in Moscow, the USSR often acted like a "traditional" empire—more concerned with controlling its sphere than with abstract ideological issues.[71]

---

[70] This is based on Joseph L. Nogee and Robert H. Donaldson, *Soviet Foreign Policy Since World War II* (New York, 1981), 220-2; and Adam Ulam, *Expansion and Coexistence*, 461-70. Also see, Wayne S. Vucinich, ed., *At the Brink of War and Peace: The Tito-Stalin Split in a Historic Perspective* (New York, 1982), passim.

[71] Ibid.

Even more than in Czechoslovakia, the Americans were caught by surprise in Yugoslavia. Before 1948 Tito was considered a more faithful follower of Stalin than virtually any other leader in Eastern Europe. The Yugoslavians' support for the Greek Communists had done nothing to undermine that image. Indeed, when the American chargé d'affaires in Belgrade, John Moors Cabot, had suggested in July 1947 that there were signs of a growing nationalist sentiment in Yugoslavia that might force a change in Soviet-Yugoslav relations in the future, Under Secretary of State Dean Acheson disregarded the suggestion as "rubbish." Most Americans learned of the squabbles within what was supposedly a Communist monolith only when Yugoslavia was expelled from the Comintern in June 1948. Therefore, the Tito-Stalin break offered a totally new prospect for Washington: perhaps there was a way to crack the monolith by supporting nationalism within Eastern Europe. As NSC 20 put it in August 1948: "The disaffection of Tito...has clearly demonstrated that it is possible for stresses in the Soviet-satellite relations to lead to a real weakening and disruption of the Russian domination."[72]

It was not that simple. After all, Tito went to great lengths to reinstate his strong commitment to communism and argued that he, rather than Stalin, was the true follower of Lenin's ideas. This was naturally not missed in the United States, where a CIA "Review of World Situation" of October 20, 1948, maintained that Yugoslavia" has gone out of its way to make it clear that it is none the less Communist...[It is] by no means certain that Yugoslav nationalism yet

---

[72] Robert M. Blum, "Surprised by Tito: The Anatomy of an Intelligence Failure," *Diplomatic History* 12 (1988): 39-59, esp. 42-3, 56. Cabot would remember this incident well beyond his retirement; see John M. Cabot, Oral History, HSTL; NSC 20/1: "United States Objectives With Respect to Russia," 18 August 1948, Documents of the National Security Council, 1947-1977 (UPA Microfilms 2/7). In the 1950s Cabot also served first as the U.S. minister and later as ambassador to Finland. It needs to be noted that George Kennan considered both the Czechoslovakian and Yugoslavian events as confirming the fact that the Soviets were about to encounter serious trouble from the nationalists in Eastern Europe; see John L. Gaddis, *Strategies of Containment: A Critical Appraisal of Postwar American National Security Policy* (New York, 1982), 42 ff. The most comprehensive recent study on U.S. policy toward Yugoslavia is Lorraine Lees, *Keeping Tito Afloat: The United States, Yugoslavia and the Cold War* (University Park, PA, 1997).

offers a real opening to U.S. influence. *The situation is still a rat hole to be watched, not an opportunity for decisive exploitation.*"[73]

Much like towards Finland, American policy towards Yugoslavia became an ambivalent one. On the one hand, the U.S. began to support Yugoslavia economically with loans and increased trade that equaled, and at times surpassed, loans and credits to Finland. This was done, it seems, in order to install a permanent break within the Communist monolith and to bring Yugoslavia to the western side. On the other hand, doubts about the correctness of such a policy never disappeared. After all, as long as Tito remained in power Yugoslavia was a Communist dictatorship, an embodiment of the ideological evil that the American foreign policy effort was geared to confront.[74]

On another level, the Yugoslav and Finnish cases represented interesting contrasts. First, in Yugoslavia an anti-Soviet Communist government was seeking to improve relations with and being courted by the West, while in Finland a western style democracy was enjoying relatively good relations with the USSR. Second, Yugoslavia and Finland came to embody two different future prospects for the Americans. Yugoslavia symbolized the hope that the Communist monolith in Eastern Europe could be broken by using the Titoist heresy as a tool. Finland, however, would soon come to symbolize a rather frightening prospect for Western Europe: that democracies could be swayed into accepting and respecting friendly relations with the Soviet Union as important and, perhaps even worse, "normal." In this sense, Finland and Yugoslavia represented European "wedge policy" for both the Soviet Union and the United States.[75]

---

[73] CIA "Review of World Situation," 20 October 1948, National Security Council, Minutes of Meetings with Special Advisory Reports, 1947-1977 (UPA Microfilms, Reel 1/3), emphasis added.

[74] See Henry W. Brands, Jr., "Redefining the Cold War: American Policy Toward Yugoslavia, 1948-1960," *Diplomatic History* 11 (1987): 41-53; Brands, *Specter of Neutralism: The United States and the Emergence of the Third World, 1947-1960* (New York, 1989), 141-80; Paterson, *Soviet-American Confrontation*, 139-43; and Leffler, *A Preponderance of Power*, 229-37.

[75] On wedge policy (mostly in Asia) during the early Cold War, see for example, Leffler, *A Preponderance of Power*, 293-8, 336-42; John Gaddis, *The Long Peace: Inquiries into the History of the Cold War* (New York, 1987), 147-94; David Mayers, *Cracking the Monolith: U.S. Policy Against the Sino-Soviet Alliance, 1949-1955* (Baton Rouge, 1986), passim.

On the Eve of Alliance Building

During the   spring crisis of 1948, Finland had almost been catapulted into the very heart of the Soviet-American confrontation. Contrary to widespread speculation, however, Finland had not become the latest acquisition of the growing Soviet-East European empire. The FCMA Treaty had not made Finland into a Soviet puppet. Nor was it followed by a Communist coup d'état a la Czechoslovakia. The view that the Finnish Solution did not fit into the uniform pattern of Soviet behavior was confirmed when, after Communist losses in the July elections and the creation of a completely non-Communist government in Helsinki, Moscow did not take "corrective action."

In 1948, Americans rejected the notion that Finland could be an indication of anything new in Soviet foreign policy. At best, the Finnish Solution was heralded as a victory in the Cold War in 1948, a successful case of containing Soviet expansion. Finland was in a sense rewarded by the extension of U.S. credits and the expansion of the amount of export licenses. But the Finnish case was not closed. American diplomats, military leaders and the NSC staff were certain that the USSR would not allow an ideological evil—however small and "friendly"—to   exist on its northwestern frontier indefinitely. Although it had abandoned military conquest and the manipulation of domestic Communists into an outright revolution, the Kremlin would get Finland sooner or later. Accordingly, American policy towards Finland in late 1948 had become an ambivalent one, a strange mixture of relief and fear. Americans were relieved over the lack of Soviet-Communist aggression in Finland, but they feared that, because the Soviets had not acted thus far, they were really up to something. While the USSR seemed to have abandoned revolutionary tactics, it must have chosen to draw Finland slowly into the Communist web by a mixture of fifth column campaigns and economic pressure.

In short, the American reaction to the Finnish Solution of 1948 was not clear-cut. There was no doubt that Finland was a success compared to Czechoslovakia. But the Finno-Soviet relationship, which the Kremlin seemed willing to exploit in its propaganda, created problems. Ironically, in 1948 Finland was in a sense a victory for both sides: a victory for the West because it did not follow the "Czech model" and a victory for the East because it satisfied the USSR's security needs. Because of this duality, Finland remained a problem child throughout the Cold War, but apparently less so for Moscow than for Washington.

5

If Finland Weren't Finland, Would Sweden Be Finland? The Finland Argument as a Rationale for Swedish Neutrality in the Early Cold War

Charles Silva

To the uninitiated, Swedish neutrality may seem somewhat puzzling. For example, over a thirty year period Swedish Social Democrat (SD) leaders stated emphatically that the country's neutrality policy precluded membership in the European Community (EC). Prime Minister Ingvar Carlsson declared as late as May 1990 in a leading Swedish daily that the caution necessary to ensure the neutrality policy's credibility was the reason Sweden had not applied for EC membership. Five months later the same Carlsson-led government proposed a package to handle the ongoing interest rate crisis. Among other measures, the package mentioned that the government was considering applying for membership in the EC. Despite neutrality's credibility, deep-seated opposition to the EC, and a near total absence of economic analysis over the impact of membership, Sweden joined the Community. It was that simple.

Part of the confusion over Swedish neutrality arises from a number of misrepresentations repeated by leading political figures and journalists. In a recent debate article on NATO membership, Swedish Foreign Minister Lena Hjelm-Wallén recounted that since the Second World War, Sweden's security policy has rested on two pillars: military nonalignment and an adequate defense, both aiming to keep Sweden out of armed conflict.[1] This statement is, however, not entirely true. A lapse occurred from roughly 1947 to 1949 when in fact the Swedish

---

[1] *Dagens Nyheter*, 13 June 1996.

Foreign Minister Östen Undén first proposed a defensive alliance with Norway and Denmark and then entertained various other possibilities for alternative security solutions in the postwar era. This lapse is indeed significant. In the words of Undén's biographer, it constituted a "unique departure from traditional neutrality policy."[2] The lapse is also important as it was the period when Finland became more emphasized as a motive for Swedish foreign policy.

The "Finland argument" claimed that Sweden should retain its neutrality in the postwar era as above all a means of encouraging milder Soviet treatment of Finland, even guaranteeing the latter's independence.[3] Swedish neutrality, according to this argument, is grounded primarily in Finland's interest. The main issue concerned whether an increased Swedish orientation toward the West would affect Russian relations with Finland. The Swedish turn toward the West could take different forms, but the Finland argument mainly concerned security and defense cooperation with the western powers, especially Swedish participation in an Atlantic alliance or a Scandinavian security arrangement. A related issue was whether a Russian occupation of Finland would automatically cause Sweden to apply for membership in the western alliance.

It goes without saying that Swedish foreign and security policies during the Cold War were affected by Finland's precarious situation vis-á-vis its large Russian neighbor. But the nature of this effect is complicated. Was Sweden's continued nonalignment the real guarantee of Finland's independence? Did the Swedish government believe that it was? Was Soviet treatment of Finland in general dependent on Moscow's relations with Stockholm? These questions cannot all be answered in such a short article. The focus will, therefore, be on illuminating how Swedish concern for Finland was manifested in discussions with the western powers during the years 1947-1951, in particular with the Americans. In what ways did the Finland argument appear in discussions with Washington and how was it received? Was it the main rationale for Swedish neutrality in

---

[2] Yngve Möller, *Östen Undén. En bigrafi* (Stockholm, 1986), 67.

[3] Please note that the "Finland argument" as used in this study refers to the specific postwar phenomena whereby Swedish concern for Soviet treatment of Finland was used as the rationale for Swedish neutrality policy. Although other examples of Swedish interest in Finland constitute significant background material, they are not meant to be encompassed by this term.

discussions with the United States? What weight was it given by the Swedish foreign policy elite themselves?[4]

Swedish Neutrality Policy

As mentioned, the official view is that Swedish neutrality rests on military nonalignment and an adequate defense, with the aim of keeping Sweden out of armed conflict. Historically the neutrality policy has not been so clear in practice, more often resembling an imprecise mixture of international law and national tradition, myth, and the actual implementation of neutrality in the face of external pressure. Swedish scholars have typically clarified some of this imprecision by distinguishing three separate terms: neutrality, nonalignment, and neutrality policy.

Unlike Switzerland whose permanent neutrality obligations stem from an international treaty, Swedish neutrality is a policy option only relevant in war. Given an outbreak of hostilities, Sweden may issue a neutrality declaration, expressing its wish to remain uninvolved. International law then clarifies what belligerent states can and cannot tolerate of the neutral, as well as what the neutral can and cannot do. For example, neutrals must not take measures favoring one or another combatant. They must also defend their territory against all violators. Failure to uphold these obligations may constitute a neutrality violation. In the worst case belligerents no longer feel obligated to

---

[4] This study relies primarily on recent research and debate in Sweden concerning the Finland argument. In the last decade a number of scholarly works have examined this issue and the related question of the Scandinavian Defense Union, basing their results on extensive research in the Swedish Foreign Office Archives (*Riksarkivet*) as well as State Department records (National Archives) in Washington and the Public Records Office in London. The results of previous research will, however, be supplemented by additional primary material including: the memoirs and diaries of Swedish decision makers, diplomatic correspondence between the Swedish embassy in Washington and the Foreign Office in Stockholm, and American diplomatic reports not previously examined in this context. Since the purpose of this study is not a comprehensive account of the Finland argument's appearance during the period, merely its use in discussions with representatives of western powers, instances where it surfaced in the Swedish press or other contexts will be discussed only as background material. It is additionally not possible, due to their inchoate state, to include the results of several doctoral dissertations in progress which take up various aspects of the Finland argument. See for example Sten Ottoson's forthcoming study of morality in Östen Undén's foreign policy, *Det kalla kriget, neutraliteten och moralen: normer och värden i svensk säkerhetspolitisk debatt 1945-1952*, Dept. of History, Uppsala University; also Olof Kronvall's forthcoming work on Swedish-Finnish relations during the Cold War, *Security and Insecurity: Perspectives on Finnish and Swedish Defense Policy*, Swedish Military College, Stockholm.

respect neutrality and the risk increases that the neutral will get dragged into the conflict. Although all these different neutrality conditions are set forth in major international agreements, essentially a neutrality declaration offers protection only when that country has emphatically asserted and won respect for its neutrality.[5]

One way to accomplish this is a peacetime policy of nonalignment. In the absence of war, Sweden's policy has typically been characterized as "military nonalignment." The idea is that the basic precondition for a credible declaration of neutrality, should war erupt, is that Sweden stays clear of alliances in peacetime. Nonalignment should be understood not as a goal in itself but merely as a long-term means of improving Sweden's security. An important component is its "military" emphasis, in effect advertising that Sweden is willing and able to defend its territorial integrity against potential aggressors. This lends a future neutrality declaration even greater credibility.

Strictly speaking, neutrality policy only concerns a neutral's conduct in response to belligerency. However, neutrality policy has commonly come to mean the sum total of foreign policy measures enacted in peacetime to strengthen the credibility of a declaration of neutrality in the event of conflict. A strong defense was previously named as one example. Other measures typically consist of self-imposed restrictions such as avoiding political or economic ties with other states that would automatically push the neutral into one belligerent side given hostilities. Other measures are confidence-enhancers designed to create such a strong impression among other powers that there is no doubt what Swedish policy will be in the event of war. The other powers thus have no reason to pre-emptively attack that country. Finally, neutrality policy may also include actions to reduce the general risk of war, such as lessening tension in global economics and politics or encouraging cooperation among Baltic neighbors.[6]

Swedish historians have further clarified Swedish neutrality by describing its changing nature. Johansson and Norman (1986)

---

[5] Alf W. Johansson and Torbjön Norman, "Den svenska neutralitetspolitiken i historiskt perspektiv," in *Neutralitet och försvar. Perspektiv på svensk säkerhetspolitik 1809*-1985, ed. B. Hugemark (Stockholm, 1986), 33-6. Neutrality conditions are regulated mainly by the agreements of the Hague Conference of 1907, especially the fifth and thirteenth conventions determining neutral states' rights and obligations in war. Sweden ratified these in 1909.

[6] Ibid., 11, 34.

distinguish historical from modern neutrality policy. Sweden's historical neutrality policy was based on conditions slowly evolving in the nineteenth century. These included an advantageous geographical and security position due to the loss of Finland (1809) and Norway (1905), the transition from an active to a passive foreign policy, and the shift in the nature of warfare itself toward total war. These factors tended to favor the neutrality policy by creating a situation where Sweden was isolated and strategically protected, unwilling to use its relatively weak military force abroad, and tended to emphasize the rule of law in international affairs. Modern neutrality policy is however based on additional factors, most of which appeared during or after the two major wars of this century. These include a strong military defense, economic gains made possible by wartime neutrality, the equating of neutrality with peace in the Nordic region (and the subsequent efforts to minimize great power interest there), and the growing emphasis of the Swedish government on freedom of action given different contingencies. Additionally the neutrality policy's development was favored by the particularly great support given it by Social Democracy, the party which came to dominate Swedish politics in the twentieth century.[7]

In addition, one could well argue that modern Swedish neutrality policy has been fairly elastic. This in part reflects the official view that Sweden as a sovereign state determines the nature of its neutrality policy itself. With the return of peace, Swedish neutrality ends and with it cease all obligations under international law. It has previously been discussed whether Sweden should enter into permanent neutrality obligations like the Swiss, but this option has been rejected by successive Swedish governments. Furthermore, neutrality as a guiding principle of foreign policy has not been written into the constitution. This would constitute a permanent binding of Swedish foreign policy in many different contingencies in an unforeseeable future, and is, therefore, seen as an unacceptable restriction on freedom of action. Thus, formally the foreign policy field of choice remains open as long as the government reserves the right to define autonomously the neutrality policy's content. In practice this has allowed decision makers to render membership in the EC both compatible and incompatible with the neutrality policy, depending on the perspective of the day.

---

[7] Ibid., 11-18, 22-8.

Swedish Relations with Finland

It is far beyond the scope of this study to attempt to describe the complex of factors which make up Finnish-Swedish relations. Some central elements shaping their postwar relations are historical, economic and cultural connections, realpolitical needs arising from their mutual proximity to a great power, and wartime experiences.

Long-term connections, while extremely important, are more difficult to gauge in terms of effect. As a former Swedish province with a large Swedish-speaking minority, Finland bears a great nostalgic and cultural weight in Sweden. Accompanying this is a whole matrix of bonds which arise from shared sentiments, ideological likeness, and everyday contacts between their peoples. This is often described as a sense of affinity among all Nordic peoples or a "spiritual kinship" based on a common social and cultural development, a shared outlook on life and common notions of freedom, justice and human dignity.[8]

Sweden and Finland's mutual fear of their Russian neighbor represents a much more salient common interest. In this respect, Finland's plight has historically manifested itself in a number a ways in Sweden: first in the desire to see Finland set free from Russian bonds; then in their mutual aim of self preservation facing a large hostile neighbor; and further in Sweden's interest as a democratic country in seeking to uphold Finnish democracy and independence. On the other hand, Finland also serves a more national-egoistic Swedish need as a security zone or cushion from Sweden's traditional archrival in the Baltic, Russia. Nothing made this more apparent than the outbreak of hostilities in Europe in 1939.

The Soviet attack on neutral Finland in November 1939 put Swedish foreign policy to the test. Formally Finland was left alone to defend herself. Yet instead of declaring neutrality Stockholm chose non-belligerent status, leaving the door open to help Finland. Sweden's pro-Finnish foreign minister, Rickard Sandler, was, however, forced out early in the Winter War and the new Swedish government of national unity under Per Albin Hansson made clear that military intervention on Finland's behalf was excluded. Nevertheless, Sweden

---

[8] Karl Molin, "Winning the Peace: Vision and Disappointment in Nordic Security Policy, 1945-49," in *Scandinavia During the Second World War*, ed. H. Nissen (Oslo, 1983), 365. This description is from public pronouncements of the Danish government.

both officially and unofficially gave considerable military and humanitarian help to Finland. This included large quantities of arms and allowing recruitment of volunteers from Sweden's own active reserves to fight alongside the Finns. This help was decisive in hindering Soviet conquest and annexation of Finland. The Swedish government was characteristically cautious about aiding Finland however. Official Finnish requests for military aid had been rejected on the basis of the Swedish people's underlying will for peace. Nevertheless the Winter War did cause public opinion to strongly respond to Finland's plight. This was in part due to certain forces in Sweden traditionally sympathetic to helping Finland against Russian encroachment. More important however was the Swedish public's firsthand contact with Finnish victims of the Russian advance, such as the over 80,000 refugees who sought shelter in Sweden.[9]

Swedish policy towards the larger conflagration of World War II, despite the official declaration of neutrality, greatly resembled the position taken in respect to Finland. Military intervention was out of the question even on behalf of fellow Scandinavians. Instead, freedom of action in foreign policy was emphasized, and the overarching aim of avoiding war received priority over all other goals including neutrality obligations. Important concessions were made to both belligerent sides, largely following the changing fortunes of war. Where not in conflict with the overarching goal of shielding Sweden from the war, both open and concealed help was offered to Denmark and Norway. As in the case of Finland, Sweden also received a great number of refugees from its two Scandinavian neighbors.[10] Some scholars feel, however, that Swedish concessions to the western powers

---

[9] Ibid., 29. On Finnish refugees in Sweden, see Berit Nøkelby, "Adjusting to Allied Victory," in *Scandinavia During the Second World War*, 317. This Swedish underlying will for peace can be understood as a kind of fundamental truth in policy during the whole Second World War; see Karl Molin, *Omstridd neutralitet: Experternas kritik av svensk utrikespolitiken 1948-1950* (Stockholm, 1991), 24. For Swedish policy toward Finland during the Winter War, see Krister Wahlbäck, *Finlandsfrågan i svensk politik 1937-1940* (Stockholm, 1964); and Alf W. Johansson, *Finlands sak, svensk politik och opinionen under vinterkriget 1939-1940* (Uddevalla, 1973).

[10] For Swedish foreign policy during the Second World War, see Alf W. Johansson, *Per Albin och kriget; sa mlingsregeringen och utrikespolitiken under andra världskriget* (Stockholm, 1984); and Alf W. Johansson, "Sverige och västmakterna 1939-1945," in *Stormaktstryck och småstatspolitik. Aspekter på svensk politik under andra världskriget*, ed. Stig Ekman (Stockholm, 1990).

were more restrained towards the end of the war, in particular out of consideration for Finland's future standing with the Kremlin.[11]

After the conclusion of the so-called March Peace in Moscow (March 13, 1940) ending the Winter War, Finland again fell into Swedish focus during attempts to form a state union between the two countries. Finland had learned from the war that it was impossible to stand alone against the Soviets—the outside help crucial to Finland's survival was proof enough. Sweden had long been aware of that particular strategic reality and had on several previous occasions pushed various plans for a common defense of the Nordic countries. It is perhaps not unusual that small nonaligned states seek security policy cooperation with other small neighbors in the same situation. Sweden had, for example, proposed a plan for a unified defense of Åland in the late 1930s, and ideas of a united greater Scandinavia under Swedish leadership had long been popular among right-wing circles in Sweden. Many of these "Nordic" proposals suffered similar fates too. The October 1940 state union plan for a common Finnish-Swedish defense failed, like its Åland predecessor, due to great power opposition.[12]

This led to another acute crisis for Swedish foreign policy when Finland joined in an informal alliance with Nazi Germany and partook as a co-belligerent in operation Barbarossa in the hopes of reconquering lost territories. The new military clash with the Soviets, though relatively calmer than the Winter War, endured for over four years. Sweden again played a significant role in negotiating between sides and trying to protect Finland.[13] From Stockholm's horizon, things could turn very sour for Finland this time around, perhaps leading to loss of its independence. Sweden would end up with the Russians on their eastern border and a dramatically worsened strategic situation. The Continuation War also showed the destabilizing effects

---

[11] According to this view, Stockholm wanted to avoid any measures which would give the Soviets the impression that Sweden was sliding away from neutrality towards some form of western alliance. Johansson and Norman, "Den svenska neutralitespolitiken i historiskt perspektiv," 30. See also Johansson, "Sverige och västmakterna 1939-1945," 89.

[12] Johansson and Norman, "Den svenska neutralitespolitiken i historiskt perspektiv," 34.

[13] Sweden allowed the transit of German troops from Norway to Finland, arguably in an attempt to aid the Finnish war effort. See Johansson, "Sverige och västmakterna 1939-1945," 79.

of Finland's foreign policy on the region, specifically by its appeal to an external great power to intervene in the North. Stockholm therefore urged the Finns to withdraw immediately from the war and began arranging preliminary contacts between the two warring parties. As the threat of Soviet occupation steadily increased, Stockholm also began to press Marshal Mannerheim to assume the presidency and sue for peace. A provisional peace treaty was in fact concluded by President Mannerheim in September 1944.[14]

Although Sweden's fear of a Soviet occupation of Finland had not been realized, the end of World War II meant a new strategic situation for the whole Baltic. The Russians now dominated the entire eastern half of that area, the small Baltic states had been annexed, and Finland faced a precarious existence within the Soviet sphere of interest. The clearly pre-eminent power emerging from the war, the United States, had actively moved to organize a new world body for peace, security and welfare, but it was far from clear what role the new organ would have. As Sweden prepared for entry into the UN, tension was already rapidly escalating between the former allies. The Swedish SD government, which had succeeded the wartime coalition, declared, therefore, in October 1945 that Sweden would join the new security organization and support its charter even in future conflicts where neutrality must be sacrificed for collective security needs. There was, however, one important reservation. If the UN divided into hostile camps, then Swedish policy must be to avoid being driven into one or the other side. Further, neutrality policy would remain a Swedish option given war between permanent members of the Security Council.[15]

Swedish politicians had in fact expected a continuation of the wartime allied collaboration into the postwar era. An essential part of this would be friendly relations between the U.S. and the Soviet Union. As long as wartime unity was maintained, Scandinavia's security could be assured through this great power cooperation. Herein the Scandinavians felt they could make a special contribution. The Labor parties had made impressive gains in many of the postwar Scandinavian elections. This, coupled with their nonaligned policies, raised hopes that the Scandinavian governments could function as a

---

[14] Nøkelby, "Adjusting to Allied Victory," 388-9.

[15] Johansson & Norman, "Den svenska neutralitetspolitiken i historiskt perspektiv," 31-2.

force to ease relations between East and West. Sweden therefore pursued a very cautious line towards Moscow in the immediate postwar. Contributing to this caution was an obvious national security interest in maintaining good relations with the dominant Baltic power. Two widely criticized Swedish decisions exemplify this prudence: the repatriation of Baltic refugees in December 1945 and the bilateral agreement with Moscow (March 1946) granting one billion kronor in export credits.[16]

As for Finland's fate, the official Swedish view at the end of the war was that Finland had in many respects managed better than other countries in the Russian sphere. Stockholm believed a Soviet occupation unlikely. This would have the doubly negative effect of damaging relations with the West and potentially pushing the Scandinavians into the arms of the British. Internal developments in Finland were cause for hope as well. The political situation seemed to be stabilizing and a new course was being plotted in relations with the Soviets, one less tainted by events of the past. Finland's economic position was not as rosy, however. Here Sweden could play a major role as a reliable source of supplies and financial assistance. For Stockholm it was easier to give aid and trade than get involved in Finland's political problems. It was further hoped that these contacts would help anchor Finland to the West.[17]

Challenges to Swedish Foreign Policy, 1947-48

From the summer of 1945, Swedish foreign policy was carried forward for the next seventeen years by the same man. Probably few Swedes would have guessed that the Social Democrat who took the helm of the Foreign Office in the summer of 1945 would become the father of modern Swedish neutrality. Östen Undén, an expert on international law and former Swedish representative to the League of Nations, was a staunch critic of Sweden's wartime neutrality. A warm friend of collective security since the 1920s, Undén had argued as early as 1943 of the necessity of a universal peacemaking organization with effective powers. If such an organization were created, Sweden would certainly seek membership and forsake the neutrality policy. This Undén had stated on several occasions. War

---

[16] Molin, *Omstridd neutralitet*, 19; see also Molin, "Winning the Peace," 340-1.

[17] Kent Zetterberg, *I skuggan av Stalin. En säkerhetspolitisk balansgång. Sveriges bevakning av Finland's öde, 1944-49 (Stockholm, 1995),* 31-2, 45.

had taught Sweden that neutrality was a frail shield when the whole world was aburst. Ultimately, collective security was the best guarantee for Sweden's peace, according to Undén.[18] Accordingly, support for the UN became the keystone of Undén's foreign policy when he led his nation into UN membership in December 1946.

Yet participation in collective security would also bring to the surface a fundamental dilemma of Swedish foreign policy, the tension between international solidarity within the UN context and the respected tradition of neutrality. As noted, the Swedish government had established parallel to UN membership a fallback policy if collective security failed. One of the conditions which would activate that fallback policy, the growth of competing alliance blocs within the UN, was already becoming apparent in 1947. Although this threatened to handicap the UN as a collective security institution, Undén continued to assert the organization's central role through 1948. A basic belief underlay his judgement. At the heart of the UN were two contradictory objectives: human rights grounded in democratic values and the principle of nonintervention in member states' internal affairs. The organization must, however, live with this internal contradiction to carry out its chief function of maintaining peace. Sweden was in a similar predicament. It was surrounded by a world fundamentally divided where coexistence appeared to be the only policy to prevent war. Sweden, therefore, ought to remain outside of bloc formations and instead actively promote peaceful cooperation free from ideological bias. Sweden like the UN must live with the contradiction between democratic commitment and pragmatic political needs.[19]

Through 1947-48, Undén was increasingly put on the defensive and forced to somehow reconcile the two potentially conflicting views in a single foreign policy—this in an atmosphere of worsening international tension and an increasingly sharp domestic debate on Swedish foreign policy.[20] Critics of the foreign minister began at this time a concerted campaign against the neutrality policy in the leading daily, *Dagens Nyheter*. Undén also had to take account of Swedish

---

[18] Molin, *Omstridd neutralitet*, 20.

[19] Ibid., 22.

[20] Karl Molin, "Neutralitetens dolda kris," in *Socialdemokratin och den svenska utrikespolitiken från Branting till Palme*, ed. Huldt and Misgeld (Stockholm, 1990), 76-7.

opinion which, with the emergence of the Cold War and the squeeze of opposing military blocs, became ever more attached to a policy of armed neutrality.[21] Public opinion was, however, deeply imbued with a fear of Russian expansionism.[22] Finally, 1948 was also one of the most heated election years in Swedish history.

Already in August 1947, Undén began to confront his critics by defending the postwar neutrality policy. In a highly publicized speech in Strömstad, the foreign minister pointed out that the policy was not a question of following a perfect line of indifference between the two competing blocs. Sweden's ambition should be to develop an objective, independent position on foreign policy issues. Neutrality policy was not apathy, it was independence of action. Sweden could very well end up in shifting political constellations with other countries depending on the relevant issue. This policy of autonomous decision making empowered Sweden with a means of demonstrating that it belonged to the democratic free community of nations, thus distancing itself from Communist and anti-democratic forces.[23]

Undén sought to counter critics who were demanding that Sweden take an ideological stance in the global conflict between western democracy and Soviet communism. He was emphatic in his assertion that Swedish neutrality policy should not be taken for *Gesinnungsneutralitet*, or ideological impartiality. Sweden's preference for western values like democracy was repeatedly stressed, as was Social Democracy's historical struggle against communism. Sweden's cultural belonging to the West was also accented. Yet significantly, Undén's portrait of Sweden's traditional affiliation with things western did not have any military-strategic implications. Peace was still the highest priority, even before that of democracy. Sweden's neutrality policy, unlike Sweden's ideological hue, had to be built on friendship with all governments irrespective of their political shade or form.[24]

The government further outlined its policy in a declaration to parliament in February 1948. Here the emphasis was on Sweden remaining free of ties and commitments. The majority of Swedes

---

[21] Möller, "Östen Undéns utrikespolitik," 65.

[22] Molin, "Winning the Peace," 340.

[23] Molin, *Omstridd neutralitet*, 22-3; see also Molin, "Neutralitets dolda kris," 77; and Möller, *Östen Undén*, 297.

[24] Molin, *Omstridd neutralitet*, 23.

wished to avoid membership in blocs and alliances. Further, should the UN be disabled in its security function because of bloc differences, Sweden must have the freedom to choose neutrality. Whether a neutrality policy would be practicable in future situations was impossible to foresee, so its feasibility could not with accuracy be determined in advance. But Sweden wished nevertheless to avoid any previous commitments which might remove that right to choose and potentially involve the country in a new war. This was the beginning of the now well known doctrine "nonalignment in peace, aiming at neutrality in war."[25]

The FCMA and Finland's Fate

Throughout 1946-47, the Swedish press carried alarming reports that Finland was slowly being swallowed up by the Russians. The main concern was that the Soviets would ultimately move in and fully occupy Finland or aid an internal coup led by the Finnish Communists. The latter had steadily been increasing in strength and attempting to infiltrate the state apparatus. There were also doubts whether the Allied Control Commission would be able to prevent a Soviet-inspired takeover. Although the Commission included the western powers, its role was in fact largely passive up to its dissolution under the terms of the Paris Peace Treaty of 1947.[26]

In February 1948, Stalin formally proposed a military alliance with Finland. After brief negotiations, the pact of Friendship, Cooperation and Mutual Assistance (FCMA) was signed in April. It was directed against German and western aggression, obligating Finland to prevent its territory from being used as a staging ground for attacks on the Soviet Union. In essence Finland was incorporated into the Soviet security sphere while retaining its political and economic independence.[27]

---

[25] Johansson & Norman, "Den svenska neutralitetspolitiken i historiskt perspektiv," 32-3.

[26] Zetterberg, *I skuggan av Stalin*, 46-54, 72-4.

[27] The treaty was very different from the agreements the Soviets made with other East European countries within its sphere. The preamble stated for example that Finland had the right to remain outside of great power conflicts. In Article II, Finland agreed to consult with the Soviet Union about military cooperation should it become apparent that Finland would be unable to prevent an invasion alone. Avoiding this risk of automatic consultations became a central focus of Finnish foreign policy throughout the Cold War until the treaty was disbanded in 1991.

Foreign Minister Undén's diary mentions several distressing reports about Finland received prior to the signing of the FCMA.[28] Some evidence indicates, however, that Undén was not terribly surprised by Stalin's announcement, it being "in the air" for some four months. Assured by rather mild Soviet behavior up until that time, Undén believed Moscow was not interested in pushing severe terms on the Finns. The main Russian interest was in patching holes in its defense system.[29] Indeed, from Stockholm's perspective, a coup in Helsinki would not have been very wise for several reasons. It would have chilled relations between Moscow and Stockholm and risked driving Sweden into some kind of defense cooperation or alliance with the western powers. Swedish Ambassador Sohlman had in fact, prior to the signing of the FCMA, pointed out to his Russian counterpart, Zorin, that Swedish policy was to remain aloof of bloc formations, this clearly said with an eye to current anti-western propaganda so prominent in the Russian press. The Kremlin would hopefully respond to this Swedish gesture by showing good will toward Finland and other small nations.[30]

The Swedish government did in fact see the FCMA negotiations as an example of fairly decent Soviet behavior. Things had gone better for Finland than expected, and the Kremlin had shown a greater will to compromise and reach a realistic and acceptable security agreement with its neighbor. The worst-case scenarios had proven wrong. Finland's special position had been given recognition by Moscow and its economic and commercial affairs left untouched.[31] In addition, the agreement was "extraordinarily favorable" in light of initial Russian proposals.[32] Undén's diary confirms that the foreign minister shared this view.[33]

---

[28] Undén diary, 21 February 1948 and 9 March 1948, Östen Undén Private Archive (hereafter Undén Archive), Royal Swedish Library, Stockholm. In addition, the Communist press in Sweden had maintained that the Russian-Finnish alliance was the natural result of Scandinavian affiliation with the "Marshall-Bevin bloc," probably much to the dislike of the government. See Stockholm to SecState, 12 March 1948, RG 263, Raymond Murphy Papers on International Communism (hereafter Murphy Papers), Box 71-73 on Sweden 1946-1951, National Archives (hereafter NA).

[29] Gerard Aalders, "Swedish Neutrality and the Cold War, 1945-49" (Ph.D. dissertation, Universitet van Nijmegen, Amsterdam, 1989), 69-70.

[30] Zetterberg, I skuggan av Stalin, 85-9.

[31] Ibid., 95.

[32] Molin, "Winning the Peace," 355.

[33] Undén's diary, 6 April 1948.

The War Scare and Sweden's Security Choice

The FCMA cannot of course be so handily isolated from its global historical context. For instance, the war scare during the first half of 1948 was a pronounced and very real phenomenon. The other relevant events are all well known and need not be discussed in depth here: Bevin's speech to Commons, the coup in Prague, Masaryk's sudden death, the creation of the Brussels Pact, Stalin's proposal to Paasikivi and rumors that Norway would be given a similar "offer," the strained situation in Berlin, and so forth. Although the international tension had its ebbs and peaks, the fear and risk of immediate war lived on. Indeed, the Prague coup alone caused great anxiety in the Nordic countries. It led to a very widespread belief that smaller states were in imminent danger and ought to seriously reconsider their security policies.[34]

This notion was registered in Sweden through a prominent media figure, Herbert Tingsten. In the leading daily, *Dagens Nyheter*, this zealously pro-American chief editor began a new phase in Swedish foreign policy debate. Starting in January 1948, Tingsten violently attacked the neutrality policy and campaigned for Swedish affiliation with a western defense alliance. Tingsten was no friend of the Finland argument either. In his view, it was just another example of Undén caving in to the Soviets, based on his own fear and weakness. Finland's fate would not be decided by the Russians. They were clearly a threat to Finland, but that threat was toothless. According to Tingsten, the American deterrence umbrella also protected Finland. Norway, for example, joined NATO without any Soviet reprisals on Finland. Tingsten meant that Sweden could and should do the same. Since neutrality policy was totally lacking in credibility, there was no reason to believe it had any bearing on the Kremlin's treatment of Finland.[35] Undén would in fact devote a lot of energy to refuting Tingsten's claims in the coming years.

---

[34] Molin, "Winning the Peace," 356.

[35] Alf W. Johansson, *Herbert Tingsten och det kalla kriget. Antikommunism och liberalism i Dagens Nyheter 1946-1952* (Stockholm, 1995), 199-201. Björklund also discusses the Finland argument's appearance particularly in the non-socialist press and in the person of Conservative leader Jarl Hjalmarson. He would become a prominent supporter of the argument in the coming decade. Frederika Björklund, "Samförstånd under oenighet. Svensk säkerhetspolitik debatt under det kalla kriget" (Ph.D. dissertation, Acta Universitatis Upsaliensis, Uppsala, 1992), 172-3, 176-7.

Another Undén project in the wake of rising East-West tension and the FCMA was the May 1948 initiative to create a Scandinavian Defense Union between Sweden, Norway and Denmark. According to the negotiations, it was to be in the form of a collective security guarantee in the event of an attack on any of the members. There is some consensus among historians that Undén was skeptical but proposed it anyway. The initial stimulus was fear that Norway was sliding into a western security alliance.[36] As Undén's biographer notes, the initiative constituted a serious break with traditional neutrality policy. Arguably, a neutral SDU without a link to a western alliance (as Undén fancied) was not such a revolutionary change in Swedish policy, merely an extension of that country's neutrality to all of Scandinavia.[37] It did, however, constitute something new—automatic Swedish defense commitments to another country. Negotiations, however, stranded over the issue of American weapons deliveries, leading ultimately to Danish and Norwegian membership in NATO.

A neutral Scandinavian bloc has a bit of an altruistic ring. Yet at the time of the discussions, Sweden was criticized for making a nationally self-serving proposal which chiefly sought to further Sweden's own security interests. As Finland's nearest neighbor, Sweden would immediately find itself on the Soviet border given any serious sharpening of the Cold War conflict in the North. Undén's response was that the world could benefit from the presence of several small "buffer" states, which in certain circumstances might contribute to reducing international tension. Nonalignment was not just good for Sweden, it was good for peace on earth.[38] The foreign minister also rejected the moral argument that Sweden would be betraying fellow

---

[36] Sverker Åström, *Ögonblick. Från ett halvsekel i UD-tränst (Stockholm, 1992)*, 72; and Molin, "Winning the Peace," 361; and Gerard Aalders, "The Failure of the Scandinavian Defence Union, 1948-1949" *Scandinavian Journal of History* 15 (1990): 133.

[37] Möller, "Östen Undéns utrikespolitik," in *Socialdemokratin och den svenska utrikespolitiken från Branting till Palme*, ed. Huldt and Misgeld, 67. Wilhelm Agrell points out another similarity: SDU military planning was based on resisting the same potential aggressor as the national Swedish defense strategy, the Soviet Union. See Wilhelm Agrell, *Den stora lögnen. Ett säkerhetspolitiskt dubbelspel i alltför många akter* (Stockholm, 1991), 73.

[38] Undén's views were related in a conversation to American Ambassador Freeman Matthews in June 1948. See Molin, "Winning the Peace," 360-1, and Molin, *Omstridd neutralitet*, 22.

democracies by not fighting beside them in a new war. A small country barely able to defend itself would actually be more of a burden than a benefit in war.[39]

Undén and Erlander on the Finland Question

The SDU is also interesting in its similarity to previous attempts to bind together the Nordic countries' security policies, especially those of Finland and Sweden before and during the Second World War. Undén had in fact inspired several of these, such as the aforementioned 1940 proposal. Characteristic of these suggestions was extending Swedish neutrality to embrace its neighbors, with the ultimate aim of limiting great power influence in the North.[40] Undén's views were, however, slightly different once Finland had already become a belligerent in World War II. All forms of Swedish intervention were decidedly rejected, and Undén felt Sweden should avoid taking any measures which ostensibly favored Finland.[41] Undén's biographer portrays him as "boldly realistic" concerning Finnish issues over a long period. While seeing the value of an independent Finland as a buffer against the Soviet Union, Undén's most consistent principle was to shun all foreign policy ties which increased the risk of pulling Sweden into a conflict. He, therefore, appreciated the new security situation in the Baltic at the end of the war, since it meant that Finland would have to develop its relations with the Soviets without the possibility of seeking military support from other powers.[42] This quite simply reduced the level of opportunity for great power involvement in Nordic affairs.

---

[39] Möller, "Östen Undéns utrikespolitik," 67-8.

[40] Möller, *Östen Undén*, 324. The 1940 proposal sought to limit German influence in Finland.

[41] Sweden's overriding intention then was to stay out of war. It was Undén's belief that intervention in the Winter War would lead to a marriage of this war with the general conflagration, making Sweden a theater for a great power interest struggle. According to Undén, not even for Finland's sake did the government have a right to jeopardize Sweden's fate. See Möller, *Östen Undén*, 182-3.

[42] Möller, *Östen Undén*, 172-88. The author describes in detail Undén's positions on various Swedish-Finnish issues in the 1930s and 1940s, including the problem of Åland and deliveries of war materials to Finland in 1936. One example of Undén's bold realism was the view that isolated Swedish help to Finland in the event of conflict is particularly dangerous. Another is the interpretation of the proposed state union as not just an attempt to limit German influence, but also a means of gaining control over Finnish foreign policy. During this period Undén was a member of parliament and held various government positions including cabinet minister.

Finland's overall significance in the mind of Undén is more difficult to judge. There are several reasons for this. As some scholars have suggested, the Finnish connection was one of the "great imponderables" of Swedish foreign policy. No one knew for certain what it meant or what significance it should be given. While Finnish issues were always important and sensitive in Stockholm, they could be enlarged or shrunk after one's needs.[43] Officially, Finland's place in Swedish decision making was too sensitive to clearly define. Even in internal documents it is discussed ambiguously, for example as "our special problem."[44]

Undén's private diary offers little insight on the importance he attached to Finland.[45] If the absence of notations about the Finland argument is indicative of its insignificance, then this notion certainly was not very prominent in the mind of the foreign minister. A 1946 visit by Herbert Hoover bears witness to Undén's reluctance to enter into a political discussion about Finland's fate.[46] Later, in March 1948, the foreign minister can be seen objecting to the Swedish crown prince who felt that developments in Finland should be given a more decisive role in Swedish deliberations on joining a western alliance.[47] One of the few mentions of the Finland argument by name is from an entry in February 1949. But Undén's views are not revealed here either, although there is some indication that the Finns were pressuring Sweden to use the neutrality argument.[48] Finally, Undén's diary

---

[43] Johansson, *Herbert Tingsten och det kalla kriget*, 199-200; and Sverker Åström, "Kommentarer till Karl Molin och Yngve Möller," in *Socialdemokratin och den svenska utrikespolitiken från Branting till Palme*, ed. Huldt and Misgeld, 90.

[44] Aminoff till Dahlman, 28 January 1949, RA, UD, 1920 års dossiersystem, HP1, vol. 624, Swedish State Archives, Stockholm.

[45] Undén diary; the period examined was 27 June 1945 to 12 February 1951.

[46] Ibid., 1 February 1946.

[47] Ibid., 24 March 1948. Undén believed this would become a thorn in his side. A subsequent entry from April, however, indicates that the prince, after seeing the mild results of the FCMA treaty, had accepted the government line. Sweden seemed to be "on the right track." Ibid., 23 April 1948.

[48] Ibid., 7 February 1949. This entry describes the visit of a Dr. Thörngren from Finland at the behest of Otto Järte (conservative politician and editor). The doctor reassured Undén that the Finns wholeheartedly approved of Swedish foreign policy. Norway was, however, cause for concern, and the doctor thought it worthwhile to make another attempt at selling a Scandinavian pact to the Russians. Undén remarked that Thörngren *also* felt Russian consideration of Sweden was an important factor in Soviet policy toward Finland (my emphasis). It is unclear who Undén intended as the first reference, but the context seems to indicate Järte.

indicates that the use of the Finland argument was at least still tolerated by Undén as late as May 1952.[49]

The diplomatic record offers a more detailed picture of the foreign minister's views. A first example finds Undén relating to the British ambassador in March 1948 that Stalin's FCMA proposal was no cause for any change in Swedish policy, relations with the Soviets being normal.[50] When the ambassador related the conversation to the American embassy in Stockholm, he noted that "Undén said he had always considered Finland to lie within the Russian sphere of influence and that events there could hardly cause surprise." Swedish policy toward the West, however, would continue to be economic cooperation within the European Recovery Program, but absolutely no political association with either great power bloc.[51]

One of Undén's most telling remarks about Finland came in response to a journalist's question while Undén was attending the ERP conference in Paris. The foreign minister commented that a repetition in Finland of the events in Czechoslovakia would be no cause for Sweden to change its present course. Swedish policy would not be influenced by events in Finland, regardless of whether there were a Communist coup or if Finland became a Soviet satellite.[52]

Yet a close colleague of Undén at the Foreign Office noted during this same period that the foreign minister appeared to be undergoing a westward shift in tone, perhaps as a result of concern for Finland's encounter with the Soviets. Sven Grafström, director of political affairs at the Foreign Office, confided to his own diary that Undén had gone much further than previously in emphasizing Swedish cooperation

---

[49] Ibid., 26 May 1952. This entry recounts a tea party with a group of British MPs, representatives of Swedish parties, and Undén. After a short exposé of Swedish foreign policy, Undén received questions. One British MP asked if all the Swedish parties were united around the official foreign policy. Undén referred the question to another party representative, Åke Holmbäck (Liberal), who underlined the Finland argument. Other party leaders present then confirmed this view. Undén appeared to tacitly approve of the Finland argument's use, at least when the non-socialists were behind it.

[50] Aalders, "Swedish Neutrality," 71. Undén made a similar statement after the signing of the FCMA; see Aalders, "The Failure of the Scandinavian Defence Union," 128.

[51] Stockholm to SecState, 3 March 1948, RG 263, Murphy Papers, Box 71-73 on Sweden 1946-1951, NA. The British ambassador drew the conclusion that Undén intended to maintain "unalterable adherence to strict neutrality."

[52] Stockholm to SecState, 5 April 1948, ibid.

within the Marshall Plan. Grafström even wondered if Undén realized how potent his words were given the strong political tone of the ERP talks at that time. Grafström's account is particularly valuable given his own typically critical view of Undén and official foreign policy.[53]

Gerard Aalders has also noted a further example of Undén's harsh realism with respect to Finland. In March 1949, the foreign minister related to Ambassador Boheman (then posted in Washington) that Boheman could make use of the Finland argument in his contacts with the State Department. Undén added however that the actual fate of Finland would not have any bearing on Swedish policy. Moreover, Undén considered a Soviet occupation of Finland as "purely hypothetical."[54]

Prime Minister Tage Erlander, unlike Undén, was not entirely skeptical of the Finland argument.[55] In his memoirs, Erlander devotes several pages to explaining what motivated the continuance of traditional neutrality policy in the postwar. The predominant reason he cites is the desire to stay out of war, a factor reinforced by the experiences of the Second World War. As a secondary explanation for policy, Erlander names Sweden's role in reducing tension by not allowing its territory to be placed along the East-West confrontation line. In this respect Sweden might even contribute positively to Finland's position. Erlander, however, then describes the Finland argument as *gångbart* ("practicable," "marketable") both at home in Sweden and in contacts with the western powers.[56] This certainly lends some credence to a more rhetorical explanation of the argument's appearance.

Erlander was of course well aware of Undén's doubts about the Finland argument. While it pleased and was useful to the Finns, the Finland argument could not alter the fundamentals. Sweden was still a small country, and small countries could not afford to harbor any illusions, especially about big neighbors. Sweden could ultimately do little to prevent a superpower from stretching out its sphere of interest. Erlander also indicated that Undén saw a certain risk in using the

---

[53] Sven Grafström, *Anteckningar 1945-1954*, 16 March 1948, ed. Stig Ekman (Stockholm, 1989). See also Zetterberg, *I skuggan av Stalin*, 91. Grafström was also the Swedish representative to the Program Committee of the OEEC.

[54] Aalders, "The Failure of the Scandinavian Defence Union," 129.

[55] Molin, *Omstridd neutralitet*, 42.

[56] Tage Erlander, *1949-1954* (Stockholm, 1974), 105-6.

Finland argument. Connecting Swedish foreign policy with events in Finland introduced a conditional element to neutrality policy decision making. This could engender a loss in credibility, especially if one followed the Finland argument to its logical conclusion (as the aforementioned journalist did with Undén). Sweden should moreover avoid becoming "a puppet in hands of superpowers."[57]

It is uncertain whether Erlander used the Finland argument at all in contacts with foreign diplomats. He at least did not appear to emphasize Finland in discussions with Denmark and Norway. At a February 1948 meeting of the Scandinavian foreign ministers, Erlander underlined Sweden's natural affinity for neutrality. The prime minister, however, preferred the term *obundenhet* ("free from commitment"). Asserting the impossibility of pursuing any other policy than neutrality, Erlander based his reasoning on the policy's broad support in parliament. But Finland was not mentioned as a rationale for Swedish neutrality (at least not in Undén's account of the event).[58]

A number of critical Swedish foreign policy documents from this period also totally lack any reference to Finland as a rationale for the neutrality policy. Inasmuch as Foreign Minister Undén penned these documents, they offer some evidence of his less than total faith in the Finland argument.

The first of these, a promemoria of April 2, 1948, is one of the most important statements on Swedish foreign policy of the period. To be distributed to other members of the government, it constitutes a detailed defense of neutrality policy. Among other things it stressed the policy's foundation in international law, its moral basis, and its widespread support among the Swedish people.[59] Clearly absent was any discussion of Finland's well-being. Undén was instead preoccupied with the thought that neutrality had spared Sweden the ravages of the last two world wars. Although the likelihood of remaining outside a future conflict was greatly reduced, this door still

---

[57] Ibid. See also Aalders, "The Failure of the Scandinavian Defence Union," 129.

[58] Undén diary, 9 February 1948. Note also Erlander's real political appraisal that all of Sweden's efforts to maintain her neutrality would be worthless if the Russians saw Swedish participation in the Marshall Plan as affiliation with the western bloc. The government had justified participation in the ERP as "purely" economic cooperation. See Tage Erlander, *1940-49* (Stockholm, 1973), 371.

[59] Molin, *Omstridd neutralitet*, 51.

had to be left open. Undén was essentially reiterating to colleagues that the old policy lines were still valid.[60]

The second significant case concerns a 1949 policy paper sent by Undén to all the heads of Swedish foreign missions. This seven page document is nothing less than a postwar neutrality handbook. It was intended to help Swedish diplomats explain the "strong reasons" for maintaining the neutrality policy. Besides pointing out the wartime benefits of the policy, it described precisely what negative effects alliance membership would incur. Nonalignment was named as the basic peacetime condition for a country which wished to remain neutral in war, and the document also emphasized Swedish neutrality policy's basis not in ideology but in international law. Once again, Finland was not mentioned at all as a rationale for nonalignment or as a reason for Swedish neutrality policy in general.[61]

The Swedish Military and Finland

It is difficult within the limited scope of this study to draw any definite conclusions about the military's opinion of the Finland argument. Yet, given their contacts with western officials, the views of the Swedish military on this issue may be useful as background material. Defense Minister Allan Vougt remarked rather undiplomatically to a visiting French minister in April 1948 that Sweden would not abandon neutrality even if the Russians seized Narvik.[62] Vougt was a Social Democrat member of government, thus scarcely representative of the traditionally very conservative Swedish military leadership. For this group, Finland had always been of the utmost importance. Though difficult to grasp, there existed a certain appeal in regarding Finland as the "eastern half of the kingdom." Many Swedish officers had developed a practical experience of this view from fighting alongside Finns as volunteers in the Winter War and War of Continuation. This undoubtedly created some decided impressions about Finland's fate, though it is more difficult to say exactly whether such impressions would have favored using Finland as a rationale for Swedish neutrality.

---

[60] Aalders, "The Failure of the Scandinavian Defence Union," 129; and Aalders, "Swedish Neutrality," 83, 184; see also Möller, *Östen Undén*, 324.

[61] Undén till samtliga beskickningschefer ang Sveriges utrikespolitik, mars 1949, L 108:6:37, Undén Archive.

[62] Stockholm to SecState, 26 April 1948, RG 263, Murphy Papers, Box 71-73 on Sweden 1946-1951, NA.

Yet, as previous research has shown, it was no great secret that among the military leadership there existed widespread opposition to Undén's neutrality policy. This was often combined with a determination to shift Swedish policy toward the western powers and some form of military alliance.[63] Commander of the Armed Forces Helge Jung often made fun of the neutrality policy, finding it "completely untenable." At times his public criticisms of neutrality totally undermined the basis of official policy.[64] Yet it is also clear that, at least in early 1949, Jung accepted at least partially the Finland argument. He remarked that, while it was not believed the SDU would lead to any Soviet reprisals against Finland, a more direct affiliation with the western bloc might worsen the Finnish situation.[65]

Other research has revealed a slightly different view among the navy leadership. Paul Cole cites a document from December 1948 which discusses information the British were receiving from Swedish Navy Commodore Tham. The latter felt that Finnish Prime Minister Fagerholm was exerting a strong influence on Undén, particularly in encouraging use of the Finland argument. Fagerholm was described as having a direct line to the Swedish foreign minister and was "using all his powers of persuasion with Undén" to deter the latter from "inviting Russia to occupy Finland." Tham felt that the Americans were only worsening the situation by trying to force Sweden into joining an alliance, something the Swedish people would not accept. Tham reasoned that American pressure was damaging to Scandinavian unity, which in turn distracted Swedish politicians and drove them to retreat into isolationism. This was ruining all hopes of Scandinavian unity and thus removing any chance of a Scandinavian alliance with the West.[66]

Other top military leaders represented a more traditional view of Finland's effect on Swedish policy. C.A. Ehrensvärd, then armed forces chief of staff, noted in a later study that there were strong reasons for a nonaligned policy in 1947-48. Finland's situation was the first of these. According to Ehrensvärd, it was of primary interest to Sweden to preserve Finland's position, Finland now as always

---

[63] Molin, "Neutralitets dolda kris," 80.

[64] Aalders, "Swedish Neutrality," 129-30; and Molin, *Omstridd neutralitet*, 71-81.

[65] Molin, *Omstridd neutralitet*, 42.

[66] Cole, *"Neutralité du jour*: The Conduct of Swedish Neutrality Policy Since 1945" (Ph.D. dissertation, Johns Hopkins University, Washington, D.C., 1990), 250.

serving as "Sweden's alarm clock in the east." Yet interestingly, Ehrensvärd also seems to imply that the Finland argument as used by Sweden had been encouraged by the Finnish leadership.[67]

The Finland Argument as Presented to the Western Powers

During the Second World War, Sweden had allowed violations of its neutrality to aid Finland. In the postwar era, anxiety over Finland's plight became instead an argument for maintaining the Swedish neutrality policy. Swedish diplomats readily explained to western audiences that Sweden had chosen nonalignment to encourage milder Soviet treatment of Finland, aiming at preventing an occupation and ensuring the latter's independence.

Previous research has shown that the Finland argument was taken up by Swedes with their American counterparts as early as February 1948.[68] It had also been discussed on various occasions in 1948 with British Foreign Minister Bevin who received it more sympathetically than the Americans.[69] Östen Undén had himself played the Finland card with American Secretary of State Marshall while at the Paris Marshall Plan talks in October 1948. According to Aalders, Marshall had difficulty responding to Undén at that time.[70]

The first detailed explanations of Finland's importance for Swedish policy appear with Ambassador Erik Boheman's arrival in Washington. Boheman visited the State Department on several occasions in late October 1948 to explain Swedish policy. According to Boheman, Sweden had cooperated loyally with the West on a number of issues including the ERP. Yet the Swedes were extremely reluctant to enter into any kind of military alliance, out of fear of Soviet countermeasures such as the prompt occupation of Finland. Not only would this be a catastrophe for the "persons of Swedish race" living in Finland, but it would also bring the Soviets right up to the Swedish border and force Sweden into permanent mobilization.

---

[67] C.A. Ehrensvärd, *Vett och vilja. Studie över svenska försvarsprinciper* (Stockholm, 1957), 97-9.

[68] Molin, *Omstridd neutralitet*, 42.

[69] Ambassador Boheman stressed the importance of Finland to Bevin on June 18, 1948, and Ambassador Gunnar Hägglöff used the Finland argument with Bevin later in October. Bevin was said to be sympathetic. He preferred an SDU with a western link, but felt that Sweden, out of consideration for Finland, had one good reason to remain outside the Atlantic pact. Aalders, "Swedish Neutrality," 144, 155.

[70] Ibid., 144.

Boheman concluded that the mild Soviet policy towards Finland thus far had been due to Soviet desire to avoid frightening Scandinavia into military cooperation with the West.[71]

Diplomatic reporting from Sweden's Washington embassy confirms the nature of Boheman's message to the Americans. In talks with Robert Lovett, the U.S. undersecretary of state, Boheman opined that if Sweden were to join a western military alliance, her territory would necessarily be coopted for the creation of allied bases. This would in turn lead to Soviet demands for similar rights on Finnish territory, perhaps even leading to an outright occupation. This would not only be a tough responsibility to shoulder because of Finland, but Sweden's strategic situation would also be dramatically worsened by the new Soviet positions.[72] In November Boheman was back at the State Department stressing Swedish concern for Finland. Yet this time he was careful not to describe Swedish policy as "neutrality." Furthermore, Boheman focused on other factors which put Sweden in a more positive light, such as the strong defense aimed exclusively against a Soviet attack. This was arguably an attempt by the Swedish ambassador to show that Sweden was capable of distinguishing between East and West in the global conflict.[73]

By early 1949, Boheman had even begun to use Finland's fate as a motive for the SDU. In talks with newly-appointed Secretary of State Dean Acheson, Boheman argued that a neutral Scandinavian bloc could help ensure Finland's independent position.[74] Throughout 1949 the Swedish ambassador found an ever wider audience for the Finland argument in the U.S. He made several trips around the country, holding public speeches and lectures, press conferences and interviews. In reports to Stockholm, Boheman claimed to be having great success in gaining sympathy for Sweden's foreign policy. The Finland card was, according to the ambassador, a big hit in America.[75] Sven Grafström, then Sweden's representative to the UN, also noted

---

[71] Cole, *"Neutralité du jour,"* 246-7.

[72] Boheman till Undén, 26 October 1948, RA, UD, 1920 års dossiersystem, HP1, vol. 623.

[73] Cole, *"Neutralité du jour,"* 247-9.

[74] Boheman till Kabinettsekr., 9 February 1949, RA, UD, 1920 års dossiersystem, HP1, vol. 624.

[75] Boheman till Undén, 31 May 1949, RA, UD, 1920 års dossiersystem, HP1, vol. 626.

using the Finland reasoning in a speech in Chicago, January 1950, in the "spirit of official policy."[76] Finally, in a report to Undén from June 1951, Boheman jubilantly proclaimed the great success of the Finland argument in winning American understanding for Swedish policy. American views toward Sweden were clearly undergoing a change, and Stockholm's main policy lines were now being accepted in Washington. This, according to Boheman, was mainly due to increasing respect for Swedish concerns about Finland as well as Sweden's strong military defense.[77]

There were, however, some instances where the very same Swedish diplomats ostensibly undermined the basis of the Finland argument. In one case from January 1949, Boheman portrayed the SDU to American counterparts not as a neutral group but rather the beginning of cooperation with the western powers. This was both in contrast to Sweden's official line during the SDU negotiations and the whole notion of Finland being rescued via Swedish neutrality.[78]

The American Reaction to the Finland Argument

Even before the end of the war, the U.S. had done studies that predicted the likelihood of dominant Soviet influence in Finland, which in turn would give Moscow greater leverage in relations with Sweden and Denmark than previously. By 1947, State Department reports stressed that Sweden had gone to great lengths in improving relations with Moscow *for the sake of Finland*, while at the same time realizing the dangers of too great a rapprochement with its large neighbor. It was further felt that Soviet influence in Sweden would naturally be curbed by Sweden's traditional orientation towards the West, based on shared values and trade.[79] As for Finland, Washington expected some concessions to be made to the Russians due to the war and Finland's exposed situation. The Finns were regarded, however, as tough independent types who, despite these necessary concessions, could be trusted to set clear limits on Soviet influence. American

---

[76] Grafström, *Anteckningar,* 947.

[77] Boheman till Undén, 14 June 1951, RA, UD, 1920 års dossiersystem, HP1, vol. 633.

[78] Molin, "Neutralitets dolda kris," 79.

[79] Geir Lundestad, *America, Scandinavia, and the Cold War 1945-1949* (Oslo, 1980) 40, 51.

policy would henceforth be to offer economic aid but refrain from policies openly challenging Soviet interests there.[80]

American policy toward Sweden, however, tended to follow a different path. As Molin correctly observes, Washington showed a strong dislike of Sweden's neutrality policy; but there was no single prevailing view among the Americans who had contact with Sweden at this time.[81] In fact, one can discern at least four different views, each of which has a corollary attitude about the Finland argument.

The first perspective is represented by individuals within the State Department who were sympathetic both to Swedish neutrality and Swedish claims of concern for Finland's plight. These forces often maintained that Swedish neutrality was valuable or at least acceptable. They included among others the head of the Policy Planning Staff, George Kennan, and also the American ambassador in Copenhagen, Josiah Marwell.[82] This group responded positively to the connection between Swedish foreign policy and Soviet treatment of Finland. Other "members," who at various times expressed support or understanding for Swedish concern for Finland, were OEEC Ambassador Averell Harriman and head of the State Department Division of Northern European Affairs, Benjamin Hulley.[83] This view was not, however, widespread in the American administration.

A second perspective is represented by those medium-level and senior diplomats whose views became ideologically charged by the Cold War. These were the doves who became hawks. John Hickerson, director of the Office of European Affairs, was representative of this type of transformation. In the fall of 1947, when the British military was pushing plans for encouraging Scandinavian military cooperation, Hickerson's response was less than enthusiastic. The northern area was deemed peripheral, Sweden was unlikely to jeopardize its traditional neutrality, and it was further felt that the Soviet reaction to such an initiative would be hostile, even leading to the complete absorption of

---

[80] Ibid., 108.

[81] Molin, "Neutralitets dolda kris," 78.

[82] Molin, *Omstridd neutralitet*, 29; Lundestad, *America, Scandinavia, and the Cold War*, 253.

[83] Averell Harriman, once visiting from Paris, confided to Undén on the Americans' great understanding for Swedish foreign policy, especially its importance for Finland. See Undén diary, 4 April 1949. For other sympathetic responses, see: Cole, "*Neutralité du jour*," 247; and Aminoff till Dahlman, 28 January 1949, RA, UD, 1920 års dossiersystem, HP1, vol. 624.

Finland.[84] Later, in March 1948, Hickerson again defended Swedish neutrality then under heavy attack in Washington.[85] By October 1948, Hickerson had been radically remade. In a conversation with Ambassador Boheman, Hickerson used straightforward language to describe how the State Department was not simply worried about Swedish neutrality policy, they were up in arms over it, even horrified by it. That Sweden would dare even use the word "neutrality" was an affront, implying that the global conflict was not really a contest between freedom and enslavement, just one between two different countries. Hickerson concluded that Swedish policy was indefensible and illusory.[86]

A third group is made up of the top leadership of American foreign policy. As Molin has noted, this group likely shared Hickerson's tougher attitude but was opposed to this kind of open pressure and arm-twisting. They thought it would do more harm than good. Marshall, for example, wanted to emphasize to Swedes that they were not being forced to choose between blocs. What they were choosing was instead the survival of free and democratic nations. Since these nations had a common interest in presenting a united front against aggressors, a "separate policy" such as neutrality would seem divisive and invite aggression. Swedish neutrality would also tend to weaken Norwegian and Danish resistance to the Soviet threat.[87] When Marshall met Undén during the ERP discussions in Paris, he condemned Swedish neutrality. But he did not respond to Undén's contention that Swedish affiliation with the West would lead to negative consequences for Finland. Lundestad argues that this was because the Finland argument was so particularly troublesome for American diplomats trying to sway Swedish policy towards the West.[88]

---

[84] Lundestad, *America, Scandinavia, and the Cold War*, 88-9.

[85] Hickerson to SecState, 22 March 1948, RG 59, Lot Files E1172, Box 19, NA. Hickerson, for example, stressed the new Swedish readiness to publicly take a tough stand on national defense issues and Scandinavian unity.

[86] Molin, *Omstridd neutralitet*, 29.

[87] Lundestad, *America, Scandinavia, and the Cold War*, 264; also Molin, "Neutralitets dolda kris," 78; and Memo SecState to President, 3 June 1948, U.S. Department of State, *Foreign Relations of the United States, 1948* (Hereafter *FRUS* followed by appropriate dates and volume), 3:134. See also Möller, *Östen Undén*, 334.

[88] Lundestad, *America, Scandinavia, and the Cold War*, 261.

The fourth group, represented by Ambassador Freeman Matthews and embassy Counsellor Hugh Cumming, is both the most intriguing and the most studied. From the moment of his arrival in Stockholm in December 1947, Matthews undertook a crusade to undermine every aspect of Swedish neutrality policy. His maxim became: "meet isolationism with isolation." What this meant was above all to make it nearly impossible for Sweden to get weapons deliveries from the U.S. Yet Matthews also wanted to use other policy areas to show the Swedes that countries interested in affiliation with the West received better treatment than those who refused. He intended to make the Swedes feel stuck out in the cold, with no friends to look after them especially in the event of war. In this spirit of isolate the isolationists, Matthews decided to never call on Undén but rather wait until the foreign minister called on him.[89]

Matthews had a special distaste for the Finland argument, calling it one of the "12 basic fallacies" of Swedish postwar policy thinking.[90] What the Swedes had somehow failed to see was that Soviet policy toward them was based on pure realpolitik—what the Kremlin perceived as its maximum economic, political and military advantage at the least cost. A friendly or neutral Swedish attitude had little impact on Soviet behavior. On the contrary, it would cost the neutral since the minimum price the Soviets charged for permitting Swedish neutrality was a large part of Swedish industrial output put to Soviet needs. To prevent this, Matthews wanted to take tougher measures against the Russians in the North. But the Swedish government stymied his efforts. Matthews thought that this was because Swedish public opinion could no longer be mobilized for Finland as it had been during the war, given the new predominance of Soviet military power. The majority of Swedes accepted that Finland was lost if the Soviets chose to occupy it. Even if Finland were swallowed up, it would only lead to the Swedes grasping more firmly than ever onto neutrality. This feeling of "comfortable isolation" was so widespread, according to Matthews, that it was even characteristic of those Swedes most friendly to the West.[91]

---

[89] Molin, "Neutralitets dolda kris," 78. See also Boheman till Undén, 26 February 1949, RA, UD, 1920 års dossiersystem, HP1, vol. 625.

[90] Matthews to SecState, 16 February 1948, *FRUS, 1948*, 3:24.

[91] Stockholm to SecState,18 March 1948, RG 263, Murphy Papers, Box 71-73 on Sweden 1946-1951, NA; see also Stockholm to SecState, 26 April 1948, ibid.; Stockholm to SecState, 19 December 1947, ibid.; and Zetterberg, *I skuggan av*

Matthews was unsure who was pulling the strings behind the Finland argument. Boheman was its chief spokesman, but it was most likely on someone else's instructions.[92] In another document, Matthews alleged that Finnish Prime Minister Fagerholm was "acting as Undén's stooge and beating the neutrality drum at the latter's request."[93] Matthews was also convinced that the Swedish press was overstating American sympathy for the neutrality policy, based on misrepresentations Boheman made to the media of his discussions with American counterparts. This especially concerned American understanding for Finland's delicate situation.[94] Undén was guilty of similar sins according to Matthews. Upon his return from Paris in March 1948, Undén had tried to hush the press and conceal his notorious statement of March 15. The foreign minister had achieved this by only allowing one interview and otherwise keeping the media totally ignorant of his views on recent international developments.[95]

To summarize thus far, there existed some diversity in the way individual American representatives reacted to Swedish use of the Finland argument. In some cases sympathy was shown for Finland's plight and Swedish neutrality was deemed acceptable, while in other cases the argument was rejected outright as immoral and reckless. Official American policy towards Sweden, however, did not reflect this same level of diversity. Policy represented rather a more stable, consensus view of Swedish neutrality and how to deal with it. To see, therefore, whether the Finland argument affected official American policy, three key documents on foreign policy from 1948 to 1952 must be examined.

The first of these, NSC 28/1, was produced by the National Security Council in September 1948.[96] NSC 28/1 reflected a number

---

Stalin, 78-9. Cumming too expressed doubts as to the credibility of the Finland argument. He wondered whether Swedes actually bought the argument themselves. See: Boheman till Hammarskjöld, 20 December 1949, RA, UD, 1920 års dossiersystem, HP1, vol. 628; also, Aalders, "Swedish Neutrality," 144.

[92] Cole, *"Neutralité du jour,"* 251.

[93] Aalders, "The Failure of the Scandinavian Defence Union," 140.

[94] Cole, *"Neutralité du jour,"* 247-9.

[95] Stockholm to SecState, 5 April 1948, RG 263, Murphy Papers, Box 71-73 on Sweden 1946-1951, NA.

[96] Following discussions within the National Security Council (NSC) with key departments, intelligence agencies and the military leadership participating, official U.S. policy was then set forth in NSC documents. These represented authoritative expressions of broad American interests and policy intentions. Once policy was

of key international events during the spring and summer of that year. It set out the fundamental American objectives in Scandinavia as ensuring that the three states remain independent and democratic, as well as willing and able to resist Soviet aggression. The chief Soviet threat was potential diplomatic pressure or in the worst case military attack. Sweden's policy was described as adherence to subjective neutrality, based on the conviction that neutrality could be maintained in the event of a future war. The U.S. aim was to make clear to Sweden its dissatisfaction with the apparent failure to distinguish between the West and the Soviet Union and further seek to influence Sweden towards eventual alignment with the western powers. Nevertheless, this policy was to be carried out to avoid unnecessary provocation of the Soviets. Military assistance would be determined by the Vandenberg Resolution, i.e., a restriction of Sweden's access to weapons and armaments.[97] One of the underlying aims of NSC 28/1 was to undermine the SDU negotiations by making it clear to Sweden that a neutral alliance could not rely on the U.S. as a source of armaments.

The next major statement of American objectives can be found in a State Department Policy Document from August 1949. This statement observed some positive Swedish developments in the field of economic cooperation with the West, but found Swedish political collaboration less than satisfactory. Public sentiment was noted as increasingly anti-Russian and anti-Communist, yet the government continued to resist joining any military efforts to strengthen West Europe. "Deeply imbedded" neutrality lay at the root of the problem. There was, however, some cause for optimism. NATO's creation had profoundly affected Sweden's strategic situation and mentality, and recent events such as the "ominous" Soviet FCMA initiative had "aroused" the Swedish people and led its government to depart from isolationist neutrality (in the SDU proposal). Yet the policy document concluded discouragingly that, in the absence of overt Russian aggression, no major changes were foreseen in Swedish policy in the near future. The consensus view was that Sweden could

---

adopted, it was then transmitted to relevant departments, agencies and embassies for implementation.

[97] NSC 28/1, The Position of the United States with Respect to Scandinavia, 4 September 1948, RG 273, Records of the National Security Council, Misc. Documents, Vol. 1, 1947-1948, NA.

not at present join the Atlantic alliance, but that external factors, especially Finland's fate, might change this situation and "force a decision" in the future. U.S. policy would, therefore, be to continue to help Sweden resist aggression, while not exerting pressure on Sweden to join NATO, despite the American view that neutrality was "dangerous and impractical."[98]

NSC 121 of January 1952 is the final significant policy document of this period. It in fact constitutes an important reappraisal of policy towards Sweden. Washington now appeared ready to accept the Swedish policy of nonalignment. The reasons cited were Swedish determination to defend its independence and territory, its contribution to European defense despite nonalignment, plus substantial informal cooperation with the West. To improve this cooperation, the National Security Council felt that a number of measures were appropriate including assisting Sweden in acquiring military equipment and strategic imports. It further stated that it was clearly in American interests to aid Swedish defense capability in all possible ways, the only reservation being that the U.S. should not create the impression that Sweden was reaping the benefits of alliance membership without undertaking corresponding obligations.[99]

American policy had undergone a change, but it is impossible to ascertain from these documents whether consideration for Sweden's policy toward Finland motivated that change. Finland is named only once, as a factor delaying Swedish entry into the western collective security system but which also had the potential to produce the opposite effect. NSC 121 appeared to point toward other more significant factors behind the change, such as an increasing tendency of Sweden to work informally with the western powers in achieving peacetime defense and military objectives. Consideration for Sweden's sensitivity towards Finland was, therefore, not a decisive factor in the change in U.S. policy.

---

[98] Relations of the United States with Sweden, Policy Statement of the Department of State, 15 August 1949, *FRUS, 1949*, 4:772-9.

[99] *Had There Been War...Preparation for the Reception of Military Assistance, 1949-1969*, Report of the Commission on Neutrality Policy, SOU 1994:11 (Stockholm, 1994), 111-116: NSC 121, The Position of the United States with Respect to Scandinavia and Finland, 8 January 1952.

The Soviet Reaction to Sweden's Finland Policy

This chapter has not dealt with the Soviet Union's actual handling of Finland during this period.[100] Nor is it within the bounds of this study to follow in any detail the Soviet reaction to Swedish neutrality policy. However some general observations can be made.

Despite the support given to Finland during the war, Sweden enjoyed a fairly calm relationship with the Soviets.[101] Moscow was nevertheless suspicious that Sweden's commercial and military dependence on the West might eventually push its foreign policy in the same direction. Swedish postwar military planning had also stirred up Soviet mistrust as had Social Democracy's ongoing battle with the Swedish Communists.[102] In reaction to these concerns, the Soviet press began an aggressive anti-Swedish campaign often depicting Sweden as on the verge of signing an alliance treaty with the western bloc.[103] Against this background, the Russian leadership also took diplomatic steps, warning Sweden about drawing closer to the West. [104]

The Kremlin further voiced its disapproval of the SDU. Opposition to northern collective security agreements was a familiar Soviet policy. The argument Moscow often used was that such pacts were never really neutral and ultimately would be directed against the Soviet Union. In the case of the SDU, Moscow feared it would merely become an extension of an Atlantic arrangement. Sweden was advised to abandon such plans. Ambassador Sohlman felt that the Soviets favored isolated neutrality on the part of all the Scandinavian countries. Some willingness to at least tolerate the SDU seems to have surfaced in February 1949, although the Soviets believed acceptance

---

[100] For studies in this area, see Maxim Korobochkin, "Soviet Policy Toward Finland and Norway, 1947-1949," *Scandinavian Journal of History* 20 (1995): 185-206; Mikko Majander, "The Limits of Sovereignty: Finland and the Question of the Marshall Plan in 1947," *Scandinavian Journal of History*, 19 (1994): 309-26; and Jukka Nevakivi, "A Decisive Armistice 1944-1947: Why Was Finland Not Sovietized?" *Scandinavian Journal of History* 19 (1994): 91-115.

[101] Molin, "Winning the Peace," 339-40.

[102] Undén diary, 11 May 1947.

[103] Möller, *Östen Undén*, 303; and Molin, "Neutralitets dolda kris," 82.

[104] According to a State Department report, Swedish Ambassador Sohlman had been summoned by Zorin, who expressed surprise and disappointment over Sweden's move westward. As proof of Sweden's shift, Zorin cited Undéns extended stay in Paris beyond the termination of the European Recovery Program talks. Zorin warned that a Swedish move westward would prove to be a great mistake. Stockholm to SecState, 18 March 1948, RG 263, Murphy Papers, Box 71-73 on Sweden 1946-1951, NA.

of the pact might lead to an increased anti-Soviet sentiment in Finland.[105]

The Kremlin nevertheless came to see Undén's presence in the Foreign Office as the ultimate guarantee of neutrality. As long as Undén remained, Sweden would continue its peacetime policy of nonalignment. Aalders reported that Undén too was proud that his policies had won so much favor with the men in the Kremlin.[106]

Previous Evaluations of the Finland Argument's Role

Several previous works have assessed the importance of the Finland argument and come to widely differing conclusions. In his biography of Undén, Yngve Möller sketches a cautious man with a cautious policy over a long period of time. Undén's views toward Finland were based on the harsh realism and cold logic characteristic of his policy for several decades. The Finland argument is not discussed in detail, but Möller suggests that concern for Finland's position was a way for non-socialist politicians to accept a nonaligned but western-oriented policy in the postwar era. This in effect prevented parliamentary criticism of Undén's neutrality policy.[107]

Dutch historian Gerard Aalders sharply disputes the argument that the issue of Finland ever actually influenced Undén. Though often used to justify Swedish neutrality, Finland played no role in the internal decision making of this government. Aalders supports his view by citing in particular the mild Swedish reactions to the FCMA. Yet, because of the pro-Finnish attitude of the Swedish public, official declarations suggested a greater importance of Finland in Swedish policy than was actually the case. It was mainly non-socialists who used the argument publicly however. The argument was also useful in selling Swedish policy abroad. Sweden could then use Finland as an alibi for its refusal to join the western alliance. Aalders recommends looking carefully at the difference between internal policy debates and public pronunciations. When Finland was taken into account in internal discussions, it was for Sweden's own national interest in keeping the Soviets far away from its border. Official statements in

---

[105] Aalders, "Swedish Neutrality," 77, 140; and Aalders, "The Failure of the Scandinavian Defence Union," 127-8. Aalders notes also that the question of the SDU was never directly discussed between Sweden and the Soviet Union.

[106] Aalders, "Swedish Neutrality," 140.

[107] Möller, *Östen Undén*, 307, 323-4, 340.

fact avoided the Finland argument as much as possible. It did not "fit with" official Swedish policy. The maintenance of Finland's independence was not of primary importance to Undén's policy. Finland was therefore not relevant to the proposal for a Scandinavian Defense Union. It could not be—it was not—part of Sweden's self interest.[108]

Swedish researcher Wilhelm Agrell continues much along Aalder's lines. He argues that the Finland argument had already in the early postwar years been used to justify Swedish restraint in contacts with the West. Agrell, however, assigns a greater role to Finnish politicians for the argument's reappearance during the crisis years 1947-48, in their exaggerations of the great risks Finland would face if Scandinavia slid into the western fold.

The Finland argument was then revitalized in the wake of the failed SDU negotiations. In the official view, the SDU proposal was not a real departure from neutrality policy, merely an honest attempt to export Swedish neutrality to its neighbors. Following the negotiations, however, it was difficult for the government to win credibility for a militarily impartial neutrality policy because western contacts had been discussed in the context of the SDU. Further discussions had also demolished the strategic argument for neutrality. Sweden could not on the one hand claim, in negotiations with its Scandinavian neighbors, that a Soviet attack against Scandinavia would most likely draw all three into the conflict, and then a couple months later assert that, with the aid of neutrality, Sweden would have a good chance of avoiding any future conflict.

According to Agrell, Sweden instead began to rely more heavily on the negative political effects a Swedish alignment with the West would have on relations with the Russians and the Soviet attitude toward Finland. This theme ran into problems as well, largely because of positions previously taken at SDU discussions. Significantly, Commander in Chief Helge Jung had emphasized the significance of a Scandinavian defense union in preserving Finland's position. That the Soviets did not move against Finland when Denmark and Norway joined NATO seemed to refute this claim. The Finland argument also lacked weight because Undén was less than a warm supporter of it.

---

[108] Aalders, "The Failure of the Scandinavian Defence Union," 128. The author cites private conversations with Erlander and diplomat Sverker Åström to support these points. See also: Aalders, "Swedish Neutrality," 71, 77, 86, 144-5.

The diplomats who played the Finland card in fact failed in their efforts to convince the western powers of any real Swedish concern for Finland. The argument, therefore, according to Agrell fits into a pattern of rhetorical window dressing, a consequence of the fact that Swedish policy contained elements impossible to reconcile or explain to foreigners.[109]

These irreconcilable elements of Swedish foreign policy and their effects are taken up in detail in the works of Karl Molin. In several studies, Molin argues that the refusal of the western powers to accept Swedish neutrality made it often a difficult task for the Swedish ambassadors in London and Washington to defend the official policy line. Many in the American administration in particular demanded that Sweden's ideological position as a western nation be matched by a corresponding political-military commitment to the western bloc. Leading figures within the Swedish military and foreign policy establishment also supported the American view, openly criticizing and casting doubt on Undén's neutrality policy.[110]

Among the staunchest critics of Undén's neutrality policy were in fact the very same ambassadors who had to defend the policy in Washington and London. This led to problems as they sought to justify the value of the neutrality policy. They did not share Undén's background, mentality or style. They did not speak in terms of bridge building between blocs or buffer zones. They relied instead on another argument to explain why the West should tolerate Swedish neutrality: Finland. Concern for the former Swedish province became a kind of respectable way of defending a neutrality policy they otherwise loathed. They did not sell the "neutrality for peace" argument of the Social Democrats, but rather neutrality for the sake of Sweden's former territory and friend. To talk of Swedish obligations to Finland was traditional conservative language, and it almost sounded altruistic. Molin also observes that these diplomats added force to their arguments by portraying Swedish policy as "in transition," i.e., that after a certain period of time a greater Swedish orientation toward the West would be forthcoming.[111]

Veteran diplomat Sverker Åström has in several works rejected any alternative interpretations of the Finland argument. In his memoirs he

---

[109] Agrell, *Den stora lögnen*, 75-6.

[110] Molin, "Neutralitets dolda kris," 79.

[111] Molin, *Omstridd neutralitet*, 41-2.

devotes an entire chapter to clearing up the muddle allegedly made by researchers. Åström argues that "interest without engagement" had been Sweden's traditional policy of concern for Finland. After the FCMA, Finland seemed to disappear from Stockholm's horizon. Finland was not at all in the picture when the SDU was discussed, nor was it named in internal government discussions on policy at the time. Åström cites two chief reasons for Finland's apparent absence. First, all the Swedish representatives discussing the SDU saw it as obvious that the Swedish proposal, based as it was on a neutral Scandinavia, would favor Finland. Finland's significance was so apparent and even imminent that it was unnecessary to state. Second, and of less importance according to Åström, was the fact that Finland's reorientation toward friendlier relations with Moscow meant that the Finns would be handling relations with the Kremlin on their own. Sweden, therefore, did not have to devote as much effort to discussing the ramifications for Helsinki of Swedish policy. Behind this development was the plain reality of the new security situation in the Baltic.[112]

Åström also dismisses the famous incident of March 1948 when Undén rejected the connection between Finland's fate and Swedish foreign policy. The whole event is played down in Åström's account as not reflecting any well-thought opinion of Undén's. The foreign minister's comment should be understood as an irritated response to a silly hypothetical question.[113] Åström also dismisses claims that the Finland argument was a convenient way for diplomats to describe Swedish neutrality in western capitals. He maintains that the Swedish government took the issue seriously. A Swedish alliance with the West would be seen in Moscow as an automatic advance of American strategic positions to a strategically significant Russian area. This would risk Russian reprisal on Finland, either in the form of pressure or an occupation. Åström means that there was consensus within the government on this point. Where opinions started to differ was on the question of whether a Soviet attack on Finland would automatically

---

[112] Åström, *Ögonblick*, 30-1, 72-3. Åström has been referred to in Swedish debates as "Mr. Neutrality," a reflection of his loyalty towards the official neutrality policy during many years of service at the Foreign Office.

[113] Ibid., 12.

lead to Sweden joining the western alliance. The Undénian response
was to leave both sides guessing.[114]

Historian Kent Zetterberg has written one of the few works that
looks in detail at Swedish-Finnish relations during this period. His
conclusion is that Finland was never forgotten. Since the Social
Democrats had formed their own government in the summer of 1945,
Östen Undén increasingly began to leave his mark on Sweden's
policy towards Finland. Undén saw it as an extremely important task
of Sweden to reduce tension in the Baltic Sea area and find a peaceful
equilibrium both in relation to East and West. In this respect relations
with Finland were of the greatest import. Finland was a Swedish
security interest of the highest priority, a fact Stockholm had
repeatedly made to Moscow during the war. For that reason Sweden
did not need to continually emphasize this point with counterparts in
the Kremlin. The Russians knew Sweden's position on the matter.
Zetterberg concludes that Swedish nonalignment policy during the
period 1944-56 was ultimately aimed at holding the Soviets back
from intervening in Finland and preventing the western powers from
becoming too involved in Scandinavian affairs. If the great powers
were kept at a distance from the North, even a small country like
Sweden could play a large role in the area. Finland was essential for
Sweden's plans to make the region a low-tension area and buffer zone
between East and West.[115]

Concluding Analysis

From the aforementioned research one can see at least two distinct
categories of explanation for understanding the role of the Finland
argument in Swedish foreign policy. The first group, scholars who
find the Finland argument legitimate, is informed by the "Nordic
Balance" perspective. This view sees the Nordic area as an exception
to the global pattern of Cold War. Despite NATO membership,
Denmark refused nuclear weapons and Norway rejected bases;
Sweden remained nonaligned, and even Finland had a quasi-neutral
status in spite of the FCMA treaty. Because the Nordic area had this
exceptional position, it served as a middle area between the two
conflicting blocs. One of the main aims of Swedish policy, according
to this view, was to keep the superpowers away from the Nordic area

---

[114] Ibid., 39-40.

[115] Zetterberg, *I skuggan av Stalin*, 12-13, 135.

and reduce tension in the Baltic. This explains the origin of the Finland argument. Finland, as part of this area, was a time-honored object of Swedish concern, and Finnish independence constituted a real Swedish security interest. The main audience for the Finland argument was the Soviet Union, whose continued good will would mean less demands on Helsinki. Sweden, according to this view, succeeded in its efforts vis-á-vis Moscow. This perspective's empirical foundation, indeed also its main weakness, is the unspoken but always present concern for Finland throughout Swedish history. In the postwar era, the Soviets did not need to be constantly reminded that Finland was an essential Swedish interest—it was well known.

The second perspective finds the Finland argument less credible. This view is informed by the belief that Swedish foreign policy during this period was essentially plagued by internal contradictions between potentially incompatible parts, for example between its political ideology (democracy) and its foreign policy (neutrality). In this view, the Nordic area is no exception to the Cold War pattern at all. On the contrary, because Sweden was part of the global conflict, it was forced into attempting to resolve these incompatible elements of its foreign policy. The inspiration behind the Finland argument was the attempt to reconcile Sweden's ideological-cultural attachment to western values with its independent, "detached" security policy (nonalignment). The Finland argument presented itself as the only rationale for nonalignment that Swedish diplomats and non-socialist leaders, themselves deeply critical of the neutrality policy, could accept as valid. The argument was primarily a rhetorical device whose main audience was the U.S. foreign policy establishment. Sweden did not, however, succeed in convincing the Americans that nonalignment was advantageous for Finland according to this perspective. Empirically, this view is grounded in Swedish and American diplomatic reporting. Its weakness is its failure to pinpoint the exact origin of the Finland argument among several Swedish actors.

There were a number of questions this study set out to answer, chief among them how Swedish concern for Finland was manifested in discussions with the western powers during the years 1947-51, in particular with the Americans. The empirical material has illuminated several essential facts in this respect. First, the Finland argument surfaced as an aspect of Swedish foreign policy primarily through the efforts of a small circle of Swedish diplomats posted in Washington and London. Ambassador to the U.S., Erik Boheman, used it repeatedly in contacts with Americans from 1948 through 1951. Foreign Minister Östen Undén, clearly skeptical of the argument, at least tolerated its use when defending Swedish neutrality policy before western representatives. The Finland card became the main rationale for Swedish neutrality policy in contacts with the United States. Other arguments in defense of nonalignment appeared, such as Sweden's strong military defense, but these were secondary to concern voiced for Finland's fate. Of all the arguments employed by Swedish diplomats in Washington, those which surfaced least were Undén's favorites, such as neutrality's peacemaking or buffer zone function. Most significantly, the Finland argument never appeared as an official government rationale for neutrality policy, as can be seen from a number of internal Swedish policy papers.

As for the argument's effect, Boheman and several other Swedish diplomats believed that it had caused a shift in the American leaders' attitude toward Sweden. Such a positive shift had indeed occurred by 1951-52, but American policy documents do not indicate that concern for Finland played a significant role in Washington's change of heart. There had always been American officials who were sympathetic to the Finland argument and Swedish neutrality. These forces were not the dominant influence on policy. It is clear from NSC documents that the shift in Washington's attitude was brought about mainly by Swedish defense efforts directed against the Soviets as well as increased informal cooperation with the West.

It is more complicated to establish what weight Finland was actually given by Swedish foreign policy decision makers. As noted, a difference existed between official policy and the views of individual leaders and diplomats. It is quite clear from the empirical material that the Finland argument was a contested issue within the government, noting in particular differences of opinion between Prime Minister Erlander and Foreign Minister Undén. Some researchers have claimed that concern for Finland was intrinsic in the minds of Swedish leaders and in relations with the Soviets. Empirically this is questionable. As noted, there were at least two occasions where government ministers, in one case the foreign minister himself, denied the significance of Finland to Swedish decision making. Were these both slips of the tongue? The material also convincingly documents Undén's history of doubt and hesitation about playing the Finland card, based on his fear that Swedish neutrality would be permanently bound to events in Finland. His worst fear was that an isolated Soviet occupation of

Finland would automatically overturn Swedish neutrality policy. Undén's diary ostensibly indicates that the argument was more tolerated than respected. This tends to support the theory that the Finland argument was rhetorical in essence, with a dual function of avoiding heated domestic debate on foreign policy and winning support for nonalignment in the West.

This material has also made apparent a number of new questions that future studies may address. For instance, Swedish concern for Finland's fate was obviously important in maintaining good Swedish-Finnish relations. Several documents have also indicated that the Finns themselves prodded Sweden to use the Finland card. But how much pressure was put on Undén and was it decisive in the decision to allow the argument's use in the West? Only a more comprehensive look at discussions between the two countries' leaders, based on both Swedish and Finnish archives, might reveal the extent of Helsinki's role as a stimulus. Further, one can imagine that there were risks for the Finns in intertwining Swedish-Soviet relations with Finland's own fate. For example, would the connection to Swedish neutrality encourage the Soviets to punish Finland whenever they were displeased with a particular Swedish policy? Did the Finns consider this risk?

Another set of open questions concerns the Soviet reaction to Swedish consideration of Finland. Did the Finland argument actually cause the Soviets to treat Finland differently? Some preliminary studies show that the Russians were opposed to a neutral SDU but in favor of separate Swedish neutrality. Nevertheless the rationale for the neutrality policy (ie., Finland's safety) could hardly have been publicly embraced by the Russians, Finland ostensibly being a free and independent country not under Moscow's thumb. Accepting the Finland argument would be like admitting that they themselves were the aggressors against Finland. A look at the Soviet archives might reveal the amount of leverage Moscow believed it had and could use against Sweden, based on threats to clamp down on Finland.

6

"The Road to Nowhere": Finland's Place in U.S. Cold War Policy

T. Michael Ruddy

In April 1954, Secretary of State John Foster Dulles dined with British Prime Minister Winston Churchill and Foreign Minister Anthony Eden. As the evening's conversation ranged across the spectrum of current international issues, at one point Dulles proposed a Finnish-style solution for Soviet dominance in Eastern Europe. Eden quickly discounted this possibility, noting that the Soviet Union granted Finland significant autonomy because it was "the road to nowhere," whereas the Soviet satellites were "the road to somewhere else."[1] Conspicuously absent from the minutes of this discussion was any response by Dulles to Eden's statement. The secretary apparently did not disagree with the foreign secretary's characterization of Finland. Herein lies an important basis upon which the Cold War relationship between the United States and Finland was constructed.

That Finland figured in America's postwar planning is evident from Dulles's suggestion of a Finnish solution, yet he, like his predecessors in the Truman administration, assigned Finland a low priority among American security concerns. Given its geographical position contiguous to the Soviet Union, little could be done to prevent Soviet domination. This judgment led to a degree of salutary

---

[1] John Foster Dulles, Memorandum of Dinner with Sir Winston Churchill, 12 April 1954, Folder: Meetings with President (4), Box 1, White House Memorandum Series, Papers of John Foster Dulles, Dwight D. Eisenhower Presidential Library (hereafter DDEL). John L. Gaddis mentions this dinner in a footnote in reference to Eisenhower-Dulles efforts to reduce Cold War tensions following Stalin's death; see Gaddis, "The Unexpected John Foster Dulles: Nuclear Weapons, Communism and the Russians," in *John Foster Dulles and the Diplomacy of the Cold War*, ed. Richard H. Immerman (Princeton, 1990), 68.

neglect, affording Helsinki the freedom to negotiate its own relationship with its superpower neighbor. If not totally removed from the Cold War rivalries, Finland enjoyed a significant degree of freedom to define its place within this bipolar geopolitical situation.

But Washington's conscious neglect did not mean that Finland was ignored by policymakers. As America defined its foreign policy objectives for Europe, which included an effective collective security system complemented by closer political and economic integration, the U.S. ultimately reached an understanding of the role neutrals could play in the postwar world. As one of these neutrals, Finland figured in the international equation. From a careful hands-off stance to cautious economic assistance to encouragement of Finland's participation as a more active member of the international community, a relationship between the two nations evolved that proved beneficial to both. By the time Dwight D. Eisenhower left the White House in 1961, a realistic and effective policy was in place that would essentially guide U.S. relations with Finland to the end of the Cold War. That policy was developed in the context of how Finland's unique circumstances could be coordinated with the aims of America's larger European policy.

Background to the Relationship: The Truman Years

In June 1944, Finland was a defeated nation, compelled by the victorious Soviets to accept a harsh armistice. Its very survival as an independent nation appeared in jeopardy when Juho K. Paasikivi became president in 1946. For ten years until his retirement in 1956, Paasikivi nurtured a foreign policy premised on the belief that Soviet interest in Finland was strategic and not ideological. He strove to convince the Kremlin that his country could be trusted and would in no way compromise Soviet security.[2]

To accomplish this, Paasikivi first negotiated a formal peace treaty. Signed in 1947, this pact required Finland to relinquish eleven percent of its territory, including the Karelian peninsula, the major city of Viipuri, and the Petsamo region on the Arctic Sea; to lease the port of Porkkala to the Soviet Union for fifty years; and to pay to the Soviet Union reparations of $300 million over six years (later extended to

---

[2] Roy Allison, *Finland's Relations with the Soviet Union* (New York, 1985), 12-18; John Vloyantes, "Finland," in *Europe's Neutral and Nonaligned States: Between NATO and the Warsaw Pact*, ed. S. Victor Papacosma and Mark R. Rubin (Wilmington, DE, 1989), 143-4.

eight). Finland further agreed to legalize the Finnish Communist party and to punish "war responsibles," officials who had been active in the government between 1939 and 1944 when Finland was at war with the Soviet Union.[3]

Despite the burdens imposed, this agreement safeguarded Finland's independence. But when, in the wake of the 1948 Communist coup in Czechoslovakia, Stalin demanded a mutual defense treaty along the lines of those he had already concluded with Hungary and Rumania, and later Bulgaria, Finland's future seemed in doubt. Once again, however, Paasikivi rose to the occasion and concluded an agreement that more precisely defined his country's relationship with the USSR and preserved its sovereignty, even though he accepted certain limitations on his country's freedom to act in the international arena. But these restrictions were largely what would be expected of a small nation in the shadows of a major power. According to the terms of the ten-year Treaty of Friendship, Cooperation, and Mutual Assistance (FCMA), Finland promised to resist an attack on its territory by Germany or any other country allied with Germany. In the event of an attack, Finland agreed to consult with the Soviet Union to determine the appropriate response for both nations. The signatories further promised to refrain from joining alliances aimed at one another.[4]

As Paasikivi fashioned the Finno-Soviet relationship, he conscientiously attempted to allay Soviet suspicions by minimizing his ties with the West. His country was in need of economic assistance. The Nazi forces had devastated large parts of northern Finland as they retreated. At great sacrifice, Finland had marshaled its resources to resettle 425,000 citizens who fled the Soviet-occupied Karelian Peninsula. And the Finnish economy, still not recovered from the hardships of World War II, had to concentrate more on fulfilling reparations than rebuilding its domestic economic life. This would ultimately leave Finland economically weak and heavily dependent on Soviet-bloc trade. Despite the need, Paasikivi was selective in the economic assistance he accepted from the West. Like the East European countries within the Soviet bloc, he declined an invitation to

---

[3] Allison, *Finland's Relations with the Soviet Union*, 171-3.

[4] Ibid., 20-5 and 174-5; Pekka K. Hamalainen, "The Finnish Solution," *The Wilson Quarterly* 10 (Autumn 1986): 68.

participate in the Marshall Plan, opting instead to receive $120 million in U.S. loans and credits from the World Bank and other agencies.[5]

The Truman administration initially watched this developing situation with trepidation. Wary of Finnish neutrality and fearing the impact of the FCMA treaty, officials doubted that Paasikivi's policies could preserve his country's independence in the long run. Still they realized that U.S. actions could be provocative and disrupt Finland's delicate balance with the Soviet Union. A 1948 policy evaluation warned that the U.S. should "not overlook the probable effect of [U.S. policy] on Soviet attitude toward and treatment of Finland" and warned that it was "axiomatic that the Soviets will be moved to consider counter-measures if they conclude that the implementation of United States policy jeopardizes an important Soviet political, economic or informational policy objective in Finland." The U.S., therefore, "should not heedlessly risk delivering the Finns to possible Soviet counter-actions overbalancing the expected advantage." The paper admitted that it was futile to challenge the Soviets on a "military plane," but predicted that a "continuing increase of stability in Europe will reinforce Finnish determination to remain free from bondage." It suggested that "judicious, but resolute measures of assistance will encourage Finland to persevere in its determination to maintain effective independence as a sovereign state."[6]

Finland and the Nordic Balance

This report drew a correlation between European stability, which was always a U.S. priority, and Finland's continued struggle to preserve its independence. Interestingly, despite Finland's commitment to neutrality, it not only was affected by the growing European stability, but unwittingly played a role in assuring that stability. During the negotiations leading to the North Atlantic Treaty (NAT), the cornerstone of Western Europe's collective security system, Finland became a passive participant in the Nordic balance that emerged and assured a secure and peaceful northern flank for Europe.

---

[5] Allison, *Finland's Relations with the Soviet Union*, 113; Arthur Spencer, "Finland Maintains Democracy," *Foreign Affairs* 31 (January 1953): 301-9.

[6] Draft revision of policy statement, Finland, RG 84, Secret File 1947-48, Box 2, U.S. National Archives (hereafter NA).

During the early treaty negotiations, when the U.S., joined by Great Britain, first explored the possibility of extending the alliance into Northern Europe, the response of the Nordic states was mixed. Finland wisely remained aloof from discussions. Norway was receptive, Denmark ambivalent, and Sweden adamantly opposed. In fact, Sweden resisted expansion of the alliance into any part of Scandinavia.

In an attempt to divert the alliance from the North, Sweden's foreign minister, Östen Undén, in 1948 proposed a union of Scandinavian states as an alternative to the NAT. He used Finland as one of the justifications for his proposal, arguing that the union would benefit the region as a whole since, should Sweden stray from neutrality, it would provoke the Soviet Union and consequently compromise Finland's independence. The Soviets, he reasoned, would be more prone to respect neutrality were it a common Scandinavian policy. This in turn would reduce the likelihood of a Soviet attack on the North in the event of general war. Alliance with the West would invite great power rivalry. Besides, according to his reading of the situation, the Scandinavians could count on protection from the West without assuming the risk. Even if they did not join the alliance, U.S. and British aid would be forthcoming in the event of an attack.[7]

Norway and Denmark were not totally convinced, but agreed to a series of meetings to discuss such a union. Ultimately, however, disagreements between Norway and Sweden proved irreconcilable. The three countries announced a shaky formula for union at Karlsbad, Sweden, in January 1949, by which Sweden reserved the right to withdraw should any member join the North Atlantic Pact, and Norway agreed to join only if the U.S. was willing to supply arms to this regional group.[8] In essence, Norway wanted a unilateral assurance from the West.

---

[7] Memorandum of Conversation by Secretary of State, 14 October 1948, *Foreign Relations of the United States, 1948*, 3:264-6 (hearafter *FRUS* followed by year and volume); Memorandum of Conversation by Acting Secretary of State, 26 October 1948, ibid., 3:268-9; Ambassador in Norway (Bay) to Secretary of State, 7 July 1948, ibid., 3:160-3. Sweden's role in the Scandinavian Defense Union negotiations based on Swedish sources is found in George Aalders, "The Failure of the Scandinavian Defense Union, 1948-1949," *Scandinavian Journal of History* 15 (1990): 125-53.

[8] Ambassador in Denmark (Marvel) to Acting Secretary of State, 10 January 1949, *FRUS, 1949*, 4:17.

This unilateral assurance was not to be. From early in the Scandinavian negotiations, Washington had made it known that it rejected "any one-way commitments" since they would undermine the goal of a cohesive North Atlantic defense community. Acting Secretary of State Robert Lovett had declared in November 1948 that every effort should be made to induce Norway and Denmark to join the North Atlantic Pact. He emphasized that the pact's viability would be threatened if nations unwilling to make commitments enjoyed the same benefits of alliance without incurring the obligations.[9] Non-alliance nations would not necessarily be denied U.S. support, particularly if the security of those nations was critical to U.S. and European security. However, nations with mutual commitments would receive precedence. The U.S. wanted the Scandinavians to foster no illusions about this.[10]

Persuaded by this unambiguous U.S. position, both Denmark and Norway joined the NAT, and from this decision sprang the Nordic balance. As alliance members, both Denmark and Norway prohibited stationing foreign forces on their territory in peacetime. As expected, Sweden persisted in its commitment to nonalignment, which in turn contributed to the Soviet Union's continued respect for neutral Finland's independence. Finland and Sweden together served as a buffer between the USSR and the alliance. William J. Taylor and Paul W. Cole have described this balance "as a carefully orchestrated zone within which the inherent tensions born out of superpower hostilities and capabilities [were] attenuated."[11]

The elements of the West's postwar collective security system were falling into place, and Finland was a part. As the U.S. monitored these developments, it grasped the symbiotic relationships that underpinned the situation and came to accept it as beneficial to the West's security interests. The U.S. recognized that Finland basically had no alternative

---

[9] Acting Secretary of State to Embassy in Sweden, 17 November 1948, *FRUS, 1948*, 3:272-3; see also John D. Hickerson to F.R. Hoyer Millar, 15 November 1948, RG 59, 840.20/11-1548, NA.

[10] Acting Secretary of State to Embassy in Norway, 14 January 1949, *FRUS, 1949*, 4:27; Memorandum of conversation by Counselor of Department (Bohlen), 8 February 1949, ibid., 4:69-73; Ambassador in Denmark (Marvel) to Secretary of State, 25 January 1949, ibid., 4:46; Geir Lundestad, *America, Scandinavia, and the Cold War, 1945-1949* (New York, 1980), 290-5.

[11] William J. Taylor, Jr., and Paul M. Cole (ed.), *Nordic Defense: Comparative Decision Making*, (Lexington, 1985), xix-xx.

to neutrality and that Sweden's and Finland's neutrality were mutually reinforcing. At the same time that this balance benefited Western European security, it contributed to a more confident American attitude about Finland's status. Washington's early doubts that Finland's neutrality would endure eased after 1952 when Finland successfully completed its reparations, its economy slowly began to revive, and Helsinki carefully expanded commercial ties with the West. Finland's determined adherence to democratic government and its undisputed affinity with the West further persuaded U.S. policymakers.[12]

American diplomats abroad reported Finland's steadily improving position. In April 1952, for example, John Cabot, U.S. minister to Finland, wired the State Department that there was "sufficiently definite" evidence that the Soviet Union was easing its pressure on Finland. Among the reasons he cited were that the Finns were "so sturdy and stubborn" that "browbeating doesn't pay" and that Soviet policy was now promoting a neutral northern bloc.[13]

Neutral Finland was instrumental in a Nordic stability that strengthened Europe's northern flank. Under the circumstances, Finland was making the best of a bad situation. The U.S., likewise, decided to make the best of that situation. A 1952 National Security Council Report (NSC 121) that defined America's policy toward Finland and Scandinavia remarked that "although the Finns value highly their independence and are intensely anti-Soviet, this country's freedom of action in its foreign relations is drastically curtailed by its proximity to Soviet power and by various treaty obligations." It was in the U.S. interest that Finland preserve its independence. But NSC

---

[12] The Position of the United States with Respect to Scandinavia and Finland, Report 121 (hereafter NSC 121), 8 January 1952, Papers of Harry S. Truman, Secretary's File, Folder: NSC Meeting 111, 16 January 1952, Box 216, Harry S. Truman Presidential Library (hereafter HSTL). Not only did the U.S. accept this situation because Sweden's and Finland's neutrality seemed mutually reinforcing, but Sweden, while publicly espousing nonalignment, was covertly cooperating with the U.S. and NATO on security matters. In response, the U.S. made Sweden eligible for important military assistance. See Paul M. Cole, *"Neutralité du Jour*: The Conduct of Swedish Security Policy Since 1945."* Ph.D. dissertation, Johns Hopkins University Nitze School of Advanced International Studies, Washington, 1990, 338-67; Cole, *U.S. Security Assistance to Non-NATO Countries: The Swedish Case and Post Communist Eastern Europe* (Santa Monica, 1992), 11-12.

[13] Report from American Legation in Helsinki, Diminishing of Soviet Pressure on Finland, 10 April 1952, RG 84, Finland Classified General Records: 1950-52, Box 4, NA.

121 returned to the old theme of hands off. The "key" to policy was to avoid measures that would "threaten the delicate balance of Finnish-Soviet relations and call forth drastic Soviet measures inimical to Finnish independence."

NSC 121 emphasized the difference between U.S. relations with Finland and the Scandinavian countries because of the "special relationship" with the USSR brought on by treaty obligations forced upon Finland. The "overwhelming majority of Finns…[identified] themselves with the West," but the situation prevented the U.S. from extending much more than "moral support through informational and cultural exchange, or economic support through carefully allotted credits and the maintenance of Finland's traditional pattern of trade predominantly with Western Europe and the Western Hemisphere." The problem here was the strategic goods the Finns were supplying the Soviet bloc. The U.S. understood that there was little or no immediate possibility that the Finns could reduce or eliminate this trade without serious consequences. NSC 121, therefore, advised that the U.S. impress upon the Finns that it was concerned about this trade, but that on a case by case basis it would "continue to export available materials necessary to the Finnish economy."[14]

The elements of future policy that would guide the U.S. relationship with Finland were spelled out here in NSC 121 just a few short months before Truman left office. Beginning with the recognition of Finland's precarious position and the fact that the Finns themselves were favorably disposed to the West, the U.S. charted a cautious course. It carefully aimed to utilize measured economic support to wean Finland from Soviet dependence, at the same time taking pains to avoid provoking the Soviet Union.

Finland and Eisenhower's Neutral Policy

Despite the inflammatory ideological rhetoric of the 1952 presidential election campaign, Eisenhower's administration deviated little from the course set by its predecessor.[15] In 1953, the National

---

[14] NSC 121.

[15] Liberation rhetoric particularly alarmed the Finns. During the 1952 U.S. presidential campaign, Finnish Prime Minister Urho Kekkonen told U.S. Minister to Finland John Cabot that he was "disturbed by some of the comments in the American campaign to the effect that America should aid the Soviet satellites. He said that he did not know exactly what was involved, but please to keep Finland out of any such aid." John Cabot memorandum of conversation, 17 September 1952, RG 84, Finland Classified General Records: 1950-52, Box 4, NA.

Security Council initiated a reassessment of Finnish policy that was noteworthy for considering Finland separate from the rest of Scandinavia (perhaps a tacit recognition that Finland could survive and, therefore, deserved closer scrutiny). NSC 5403 refined the tenets of NSC 121 and prescribed a policy that would remain in place until 1959. Like NSC 121, it explicitly recognized the "delicate balance" in Soviet-Finnish relations. It described America's objective to be the "continuance of an independent, economically healthy, and democratic Finland, basically oriented to the West (but with no attempt to incorporate Finland in a Western coalition), neither subject to undue reliance on Soviet Bloc trade nor vulnerable to Soviet economic pressures." But additionally, NSC 5403 emphasized Finland's strategic importance as a "land buffer" for Scandinavia, as well as its potential for providing the Soviets with advance air defense, early warning systems, and critical naval bases.[16]

NSC 5403 was much more optimistic than NSC 121 that Paasikivi's policies would succeed. Although the Communists controlled 22% of the seats in the *Eduskunta*, the Finnish parliament, they had not participated in the government since 1948. And it appeared unlikely that they would become part of the government in the foreseeable future, either by election or coup. Furthermore, given Finland's traditional animosity toward the Soviet Union, the report predicted that, in the event of general war, Finland would remain neutral and would resist providing any assistance to the Soviet cause. NSC 5403 doubted that the USSR would invade Finland "as a cold war move" because it had nothing to gain; still it might pressure Helsinki for bases and other concessions.

The study also paid considerably closer attention to the economic aspects of the relationship. Wartime devastation and reparations payments had saddled Finland with high industrial production costs, growing unemployment, and difficulties stabilizing the convertibility of its currency. A significant portion of its trade was with the East, making it uncomfortably dependent on the Soviet Union and vulnerable to Soviet economic pressure. NSC 5403 used forest products, Finland's major export to the West, to illustrate its point.

---

[16] National Security Council (hereafter NSC), Report 5403, U.S. Policy Toward Finland (hereafter NSC 5403), 12 January 1954, White House Office (hereafter WHO): Office of Special Assistant for National Security Affairs, National Security Council Series, Policy Papers Subseries, Folder: NSC 5403-US Policy Toward Finland (1), Box 8, DDEL.

Since 1951, world demand for and the price of these products had been dropping at the same time that Finnish trade with the Soviet bloc was rising from 20 percent of its exports in 1950 to 32 percent by 1953. The situation had not reached "crisis proportions," acknowledged the report, but it warranted "appropriate measures" to increase Finland's western trade and to address underlying cost and efficiency problems.[17]

NSC 5403's conclusions corresponded to a larger picture. Just as America's policy with Finland was being built on an understanding of Finland's position vis-à-vis the USSR, so Washington's approach to neutrals in general was coalescing around a more objective assessment of neutral states in world affairs. The U.S. began to view neutrals more as assets than liabilities in the Cold War rivalry with the USSR. This was far different from the public perceptions of the government's attitude toward neutrality.

Publicly, the Eisenhower administration seemed to vacillate between intolerance and confusion on the question of neutrality. Secretary of State John Foster Dulles, often the administration's foreign policy spokesman, consistently criticized neutrality, arguing in October 1955 that "barring exceptional cases, neutrality today is an obsolete conception." Later in 1956, he asserted that, except in exceptional circumstances, neutrality was an "obsolete," "immoral," and "short-sighted" conception.[18] Eisenhower at times contradicted his secretary. At a June 1956 news conference, he pointed out that the United States had been neutral for 150 years, that in 1956 neutrality meant avoiding any attachment to military alliances, and that "this [did] not necessarily mean...neutral as between right and wrong or decay and decency."[19]

H.W. Brands, in his much acclaimed work, *The Specter of Neutralism*, explained Dulles's remarks as politically motivated. "The secretary's sermonizing was designed to please conservatives, Republicans for the most part, who distrusted neutralists and continually threatened to block administration initiatives toward countries of the third world." Brands asserted that, while both Eisenhower and Dulles understood the moral dimension of neutralism,

---

[17] NSC 5403.

[18] *New York Times*, 11 October 1955 and 10 June 1956.

[19] U.S. President, *Public Papers of the Presidents of the United States: Dwight D. Eisenhower, 1956* (Washington, DC, 1959), 554-5.

they also recognized that great power politics was essentially amoral, a fact they could not publicly acknowledge without risking political repercussions.[20] Brands focused primarily on third world neutralism, but his observations apply equally to Europe. Eisenhower's remarks were more representative of U.S. policy than Dulles's statements. In the 1950s the U.S. was reaching a more mature, objective conception of neutralism and its place in international affairs.

By 1955, concern over neutralism had increased when Stalin's successor, Nikita Khrushchev, embarked on a program to exploit neutralism in Europe and the third world. He called for "peaceful coexistence" and in short order accepted an Austrian State Treaty mandating a neutralized Austria, traveled to Yugoslavia to heal the rift with Tito, and returned the port of Porkalla to Finland in return for an extension of the FCMA treaty. Washington tended to interpret peaceful coexistence as a tactic to undermine the solidarity of the West rather than accept it as a sincere gesture to reduce tensions. Khrushchev's campaign not only tempted the neutrals to improve relations with the USSR, but it had the potential to weaken the resolve of alliance members. Concerned about the repercussions, the Eisenhower White House charged the State Department with preparing a comprehensive study of neutralism worldwide.

The study, which reached the National Security Council in August, distinguished between *neutrality*, defined as the nation's "actual status" or "governmental policy," and *neutralism*, "essentially...an attitude or psychological tendency." The more "classical" neutralism that had long existed entailed a determination not to take sides in international rivalries, steering clear of emotional or ideological choices between competing forces. However, the report noted that since World War II a more pragmatic "quasi-neutralism" had become more prevalent, a "hodge-podge of attitudes and tendencies which, for one reason or another, tend[ed] to impede effective cooperation with other nations." This quasi-neutralism encompassed "any attitude which involve[d] a disinclination to cooperate with U.S. objectives in the cold war and in a possible hot

---

[20] H.W. Brands, *The Specter of Neutralism: The United States and the Emergence of the Third World, 1947-1960* (New York, 1989), 307. An alternative interpretation of Dulles's remarks is found in Jurg Martin Gabriel, *The American Conception of Neutrality After 1941* (New York, 1988), 186 and 286 (n91). He stressed Dulles's tendency to speak in generalities and suggested that "if Dulles had made specific reference to neutrals like Sweden and Austria, he might have made more sense."

war combined with either a similar disinclination or, at worst, hesitation to go so far as to cooperate with the USSR objectives."

A number of factors explained this proliferation of neutralism: fear of nuclear war, which was "unusually susceptible to exploitation by the Communists"; nationalism; negative reaction to U.S. leadership; a desire to attain security without responsibility; pacifism; selfish pursuit of special interests; and economic motivations. The report warned that the latent power of neutralism was great and was growing in parts of Europe, leading to a widespread and deep-seated reluctance to be associated with the U.S. in military hostilities. Communist strategy could certainly exploit this neutralism, while "the U.S. [stood] to gain more through active and unqualified cooperation with these European nations than it would gain as a result of their assuming a position of neutrality." Hence, the report recommended that policymakers seriously consider measures to check the spread of neutralism and counteract its influence.

All of this seemed to confirm officials' apprehensions that the Kremlin was benefiting from neutralism's growth. But at the same time that the report issued this warning, it cautioned that neutralism was a heterogeneous phenomenon and that many of the tendencies discussed were not adverse to American interests unless carried to the extreme. Furthermore, neutralism took different forms and varied from country to country. Combating it in certain countries, in fact, might be counterproductive to American interests.[21]

Finland was one of these exceptions. "Finnish neutralism," the State Department observed, "rest[ed] on an absence of alternatives to neutrality; despite pro-Western sympathies, most Finns fear[ed] a more active orientation toward the West would lead to swift and painful retribution." The more disturbing neutralism that existed in other countries, such as Finland's Scandinavian neighbors, Denmark and Norway, where neutralist sentiment resisted expanded roles in NATO and tended to be anti-U.S., was of little consequence among the Finnish people. Furthermore, Soviet interest in Finland differed from most other areas of non-Communist Europe. Elsewhere, the Kremlin encouraged neutrality because it tended to weaken American

---

[21] Neutralism in Europe, Summary Report, WHO: NSC Staff Papers, Planning Coordinating Group Series, Folder: #9 Bandung (2), Box 2, DDEL. The report was forwarded to the National Security Council in August 1955; Robert Murphy to Nelson A. Rockefeller, ibid., Folder: #9 Bandung (1).

influence. But in Finland, where the USSR was in an advantageous position, it discouraged neutralism and promoted "closer political and psychological affinity with the Soviet bloc." The Soviet Union was being "essentially pragmatic" in the pursuit of its own national interests.

The State Department analysis concluded that realistically there was little possibility that Finland's foreign policy would change in the foreseeable future and that to try to alter it might be contrary to American interests. But it was not entirely pessimistic about the situation. The litmus test for beneficial neutrality was a strong ideological identification with the West, demonstration of "solid resistance to Communist blandishments," and maintenance of a strong national defense establishment.[22] Finland possessed the first, exercised the second as far as could reasonably be expected, and lacked the third mainly due to restrictions imposed by agreements with the USSR.

This assessment of neutralism influenced both U.S. European policy in general and Finnish policy in particular. In general, it represented an escalating shift away from the perception of neutrals as a detriment to security interests toward a course that would exploit neutrality to the West's advantage. It found its way into much of the administration's strategic thinking. A 1956 document outlining "Basic National Security Policy" (NSC 5602/1), for example, advised that the U.S. "not exert pressure to make active allies of countries not so inclined, but...recognize that the independence of such countries from Communism serves U.S. interests even though they are not aligned with the United States." It recommended that Washington provide assistance to the neutrals on the basis of their ability to strengthen their independence and take "other feasible steps which will strengthen their capacity to do so."[23]

As for Finland in particular, the neutralism study reaffirmed Washington's evolving understanding of that nation and contributed to the outlook that, like other European neutrals, Finland might not just be tolerated, but might participate more actively in western affairs.

---

[22] Neutralism in Europe, Summary Report; "Neutralism" in Finland, 13 June 1955, WHO: NSC Staff Papers, Planning Coordinating Series, Folder: #9 Bandung (3), Box 2, DDEL.

[23] Basic National Security Policy, NSC 5602/1, 15 March 1956, *FRUS, 1955-57*, 19:251; the entire document is on 242-57.

As Finland's economic well-being improved and its independence became more secure, it would be less dependent on the Soviet bloc. As in the case of other neutrals, Washington forged economic links and championed European economic integration as a means of indirectly aligning them with the West. In contrast to other neutrals, however, economic assistance aimed at facilitating integration with the West proved more difficult in Finland's case. Finland's integration was longer in coming. Yet by the mid-1950s, the process as far as U.S. policy was concerned was set in motion.

Neutral Policy Implemented

When the National Security Council endorsed NSC 5403 in 1954, it delegated the Operations Coordinating Board (OCB) to monitor the implementation of that policy.[24] Between October 1954 and July 1959, this group issued eight progress reports that tracked the evolution of a coordinated economic and political effort to encourage an autonomous Finland within the western orbit.[25] During this time, officials adhered to established policy as they confronted Soviet diplomatic moves they feared were manipulating Finland to Soviet advantage as well as challenges to Finland's internal independence.

To gain an international advantage, the Soviet Union in the context of peaceful coexistence returned the port of Porkkala to Finland in 1955 in return for extending the FCMA treaty for twenty years. Suspicions of Soviet intentions abounded in Washington. Central Intelligence Agency director, Allen Dulles, to cite one instance, argued

---

[24] The OCB had been created by executive order on September 2, 1953. Designated "to provide for the integrated implementation of national security policies by the several agencies" of the federal government, it was composed of representatives of the Secretaries of State and Defense, the Directors of the Foreign Operations Administration and the Central Intelligence Agency, and the President. The working group on Finnish policy also had participation from the Treasury Department. Press Release, Executive Order Establishing the Operations Coordinating Board, 3 September, 1953, DDEL; Memorandum for the Secretary of the Treasury, 3 February 1954, WHO: NSC Staff Papers, OCB Central Files, Box 29, DDEL; Memorandum for Mr. Elmer B. Staats, Executive Officer, Operations Coordinating Board, 12 February 1954, ibid.

[25] Progress Reports on NSC 5403 are as follows: 20 October, 1954, WHO: NSC Staff Papers, OCB Central Files, Box 29, DDEL; 20 April, 1955, ibid.; 23 November 1955, ibid.; 3 July 1956, ibid.; 12 June 1957, ibid., Box 30; 2 January 1958, WHO: Office of Special Assistant for National Security Affairs, National Security Council Series, Policy Papers Subseries, Box 8, DDEL; 9 July 1958, ibid.; 1 July 1959, ibid. (Hereafter each report will be referred to as Progress Report followed by appropriate date.)

that the Soviet Union was trying to "use Finland as a lever to create a Scandinavian federation. The Soviet object was evidently to get Denmark and Norway out of NATO."[26] But based upon available information—the port was not as strategically important as it had been at the end of World War II—the OCB working group was not unduly alarmed. It had expected the return and doubted it would alter Finland's essential caution in its relations with the USSR. The United States carefully encouraged this Finnish propensity at the same time that it signaled its support for the direction Finnish policy was taking, for example by up-grading its diplomatic legation in Helsinki to embassy status in 1955.[27]

Rather than make an issue of Soviet actions, the U.S. improved its ties with Finland by supporting Finland's moves to participate more fully in the international community. In 1956, Finland joined the Nordic Council, a body founded in 1952 to promote cooperation among Nordic nations and, with the help of the United States, attained United Nations membership. In that same year, Paasikivi retired and was succeeded by Urho Kekkonen, who reaffirmed Paasikivi's policies, only with more activist, outward-oriented intentions.[28] OCB reports reflected U.S. satisfaction that America's posture was correct and effective, noting in 1956 that, although the Finns continued to foster good relations with the USSR, they displayed "greater boldness" in dealing with their neighbor. Closer ties with their Nordic neighbors and expanded economic coordination with the West, as well as the Finnish government's highly critical response to the 1956 Soviet invasion of Hungary in 1956, reflected this new boldness.[29]

In accordance with policy guidelines, however, the U.S. did not merely stand idly by and watch, but extended economic assistance to build links with the West and thus weaken dependence on the Soviet bloc. Throughout the 1950s, trade statistics improved. For example, exports to the West increased from 68.6% in 1953 to 74.2% by the

---

[26] Memorandum of discussion, 273d NSC meeting, 18 January 1956, *FRUS, 1955-57*, 10:67; see also, ibid., 27:484-5.

[27] Progress Report, 23 November 1955.

[28] For information on Kekkonen's policy, see Robert W. Matson, "Finlandization, an Ahistorical Analogy," *Research Studies* 51 (March 1983): 3-4. The Soviet Union opposed Finnish admission to the UN unless it was part of a "package deal" including some eastern bloc nations. *FRUS, 1952-54*, volume 4, has extensive material on this UN dispute. See also John Vloyantes, "Finland," 146.

[29] Progress Report, 12 June 1957.

end of 1955. Imports from the West increased from 65.5% to 73% as
Soviet bloc trade declined.[30] By late 1956, the OCB working group,
elated at "the happy state of our relations with Finland and her
improved political and economic status," considered disbanding since
it may no longer have been needed.[31]

But these gains were not achieved easily. A case in point was the
use of The Agricultural Trade Development and Assistance Act of
1954 to provide needed surplus agricultural goods to Finland.[32]
Finland paid for these products in its own currency. Consequently, by
June 1957, the U.S. Treasury had amassed $27.7 million in
Finnmarks. Although the U.S. was willing to continue these exports, it
worried about accepting Finnmarks that might lose value by inflation
or devaluation. This problem had to be solved if the shipments were to
continue. Washington tried several solutions, with mixed results.

One plan was to offer other nations aid in Finnmarks rather than
dollars. In 1957, the U.S. offered $12 million in Finnmarks to six
Asian countries to purchase small Finnish ships; $7 million for
prefabricated housing for air force family housing in Europe; and $1
million for paper products to Korea.[33] This met resistance not only
because the dollar was a sounder currency than the Finnmark, but also
because there were few Finnish products these other nations wanted
and the high cost of delivery impaired their competitiveness. By
January 1958, only Indonesia, of the six Asian countries involved in
the ship purchases, had made a firm commitment. As the U.S. was
working through these problems, as feared, the Finnmark was
devalued from 230 to 320 to the dollar, reducing the funds by 28%.
This devaluation made Finnish exports more attractive, but it was
costly to the United States.[34]

Another solution, to loan Finnmarks back to Finland, ran afoul of
loan restrictions imposed by the 1951 Battle Act which restricted U.S.

---

[30] Progress Report, 3 July 1956.

[31] Capt. D.W. Gladney to Staats, 28 November 1956, WHO: NSC Staff Papers,
OCB Central File, Box 30, DDEL.

[32] Public Law 480 authorized sale abroad for foreign currencies of surplus
agricultural commodities. Local currency proceeds were to be used for such purposes
as loans to promote multilateral trade and economic development; Public Law 480,
Agricultural Trade Development and Assistance Act of 1954, *U.S. Statutes at Large*
68, pt. 1 (1954): 454-9.

[33] Progress Report, 12 June 1957.

[34] Progress Report, 2 January 1958.

aid to nations exporting strategic goods to the Soviet bloc.[35] Conservative anti-Communists in Congress threatened to employ the act to tie the president's hands in his dealings with Finland. Since the end of World War II, Finland's economy had become unavoidably intertwined with the Soviet Union's. Even if Finland's trade with the West increased markedly, it would continue to be dependent to a great extent on eastern-bloc trade, some of which consisted of prohibited strategic items. There was concern, for example, when in 1955 Finland agreed to build two small tankers for the People's Republic of China. The Finns contended that "vital domestic labor and economic considerations" forced them to seek these markets.[36] But that did not satisfy many avid anti-Communists in Congress.

The administration accepted the fact that it could not expect Finland to sever such economic ties. It also understood that providing loans would bolster Finland's economy and reduce its vulnerability to Soviet intimidation. Therefore, on February 17, 1958, Eisenhower, at the recommendation of his National Security Council, signed a presidential determination sanctioning a $14 million loan to Finland on the basis of "overriding foreign policy considerations." A second presidential determination followed in December that added $5 million more in loans and made Finland eligible for future aid, provided it refrained from shipping Battle Act Category I goods— those most sensitive strategic items—to Soviet-bloc nations.[37]

Just as Washington's policy tried not to cross a line that would provoke the Soviet Union, likewise through much of this time the

---

[35] The Battle Act prohibited assistance to countries exporting items of "primary strategic significance" to the Communist bloc and discouraged other exports; Public Law 213, *Mutual Defense Assistance Control Act of 1951*, *U.S. Statutes at Large* 65 (1951): 644-7.

[36] Daily Intelligence Abstract #488, 1 November 1955, WHO: NSC Staff Papers, OCB Central Files Series, December 1954-February 1956, File: OCB 350.05 (File #2) (9), Box 111, DDEL; Intelligence Notes, 15 August 1956, File: OCB 350.05 (File #3) (6), February-October 1956, ibid. By mid-1956, concern still existed that the Finns continued to trade with "Red China," but there was some consolation that it included no more tankers; see minutes of NSC meeting, 19 July 1956, WHO: NSC Series, Folder: 291st Meeting, Box 8, DDEL; Jack K. McFall, Oral History Interview, HSTL.

[37] Progress Report, 2 January 1958; C. Douglas Dillon to President, 11 February 1958, WHO: Confidential Files, File: Mutual Security and Assistance Act, Box 39, DDEL; Memorandum for the Secretary of State from Dwight D. Eisenhower, 15 February 1958, ibid.; C. Douglas Dillon, Under Secretary of State for Economic Affairs, to Gen. C.P. Cabell, Acting Director, Central Intelligence Agency, 19 September 1958, Papers of Christian A. Herter, Box 5, DDEL.

Kremlin carefully refrained from interfering in Finland's internal affairs so long as Helsinki did not become too adventurous externally. This situation suited American interests. But in 1958 the situation changed, when, as a crisis once again brewed in Berlin, political events within Finland threatened the fragile relationship with the USSR. Khrushchev described the episode as the advent of a "night-frost" in Soviet-Finnish relations. In the aftermath of July parliamentary elections, President Kekkonen asked the moderate Social Democrat Karl Fagerholm to form a government. Fagerholm's five-party coalition excluded Communists, despite electoral gains by that party, and included two conservative Social Democrats who were supporters of Väino Tanner, one of the most prominent "war responsibles" who had been punished under the terms of the 1947 peace treaty. The Soviets expressed serious concern about this turn of events and employed diplomatic and economic pressure to influence Finnish politics. Faced with Soviet intimidation, Kekkonen withdrew support for Fagerholm's government, and in December a minority Agrarian Party government was formed without Social Democratic participation.[38]

Soviet attempts to sway Finnish politics prompted a reappraisal of American policy. The OCB's July 1958 progress report acknowledged the political problems and recognized that the Communists might benefit. But even though Communist membership in parliament had increased from 43 to 50, it judged that "the basic political situation [remained] unchanged."[39]

Ambassador Hickerson strongly disagreed. Upon receiving a copy of the report, he wrote to the OCB that he was "disturbed by what seem[ed] to be a rather complacent tone to the report," most notably its conclusion that the July parliamentary elections left the situation fundamentally unchanged. Not only did he fear increased Communist influence within the political system, but he argued that on-going economic problems and recent economic agreements with the Soviets threatened Finnish independence. He accused the OCB of tending to emphasize "operating problems in the economic field" while

---

[38] John P. Vloyantes, *Silk Glove Diplomacy: Finnish-Soviet Relations, 1944-1974* (Kent, 1975), 92-108; Allison, *Finland's Relations with the Soviet Union*, 138-40. Kekkonen's failure to support Fagerholm's efforts was due not only to Soviet intimidation, but also to the personal and political animosity he held toward Fagerholm.

[39] Progress Report, 9 July 1958.

downplaying important political developments. He admitted that Finnish political decisions were closely related to economic activities, but he believed a more "liberal definition of the contents of progress reports would avoid the risk of focusing on symptoms and overlooking causes." The situation in Finland was deteriorating, and there was no room for complacency.[40]

Subsequent Soviet actions substantiated Hickerson's concerns. The July 1959 progress report declared that "the Soviet initiative at this time stemmed not only from a decision to exploit a particularly favorable tactical situation in Finland, but probably also from the desire to arrest what they considered to be a general Western gravitation in Finnish policy, both economic and political." The USSR challenged Finland's gravitation toward the West. Soviet interference in internal Finnish politics was an alarming departure from the past. Therefore, the OCB recommended a review of American policy and reconsideration of steps the U.S. might take "to cope with the changed circumstances regarding Finland."[41]

This prompted a reassessment in 1959 (NSC 5914/1) and a subsequent revision in 1960 (NSC 6024). The new policy articulated by these two documents placed greater emphasis on Finland's geopolitical position in the world. Finland's pivotal place in the Nordic region and in western defense was underlined, as was the psychological value of a continued independent Finland:

> Complete Soviet domination of Finland would be a heavy blow to the posture of the Free World and could weaken the resistance of other small nations to Soviet Bloc pressures. In addition domination would put the USSR in control of advance air defense and early warning positions and additional naval bases on the Baltic. The continued denial of Finland to the USSR is thus psychologically and militarily important to the Free World.[42]

The events of 1958 sobered policymakers. Previously, the U.S. ambitiously strove for an independent, democratic, and western-oriented Finland "neither subject to undue reliance on Soviet Bloc

---

[40] John D. Hickerson to Jeremiah O'Connor, Operations Coordinator, Office of the Undersecretary, Department of State, 15 September 1958, WHO: Office of Special Assistant for National Security Affairs, NSC Series, Briefing Notes Subseries, Box 8, DDEL.

[41] Progress Report, 1 July 1959.

[42] NSC, "U.S. Policy Toward Finland," NSC 5914/1, WHO: Office of the Special Assistant for National Security Affairs, NSC Series, Policy Papers Subseries, Box 27, DDEL; NSC 6024, ibid., Box 29. Quote in text taken from NSC 6024.

trade nor vulnerable to Soviet economic pressures."[43] Khrushchev
may have been interested in peaceful coexistence, but as his reaction
to the 1958 elections demonstrated, there were limits to what the
Soviet Union would tolerate. Likewise, America's capacity to
influence the Finnish situation was also limited. Now, therefore, the
new policy outlined by the Eisenhower administration lowered
America's goal to preserving Finland "as free as possible from
vulnerability to Soviet pressures."[44]

Finland As America's Cold War Advantage

The successful pursuit of this Finnish policy furthered two broader
aims that gave the U.S. an advantage in its rivalry with the Soviet
Union. First, European integration could be described as both a means
and an end of American policy. It offered a means to incorporate the
neutrals within the western sphere without compelling them to align.
At the same time, integration that included the neutrals strengthened
Europe's collective security system since stability was based on more
than military alliances. Second, Dulles in particular envisioned a
Finnish solution as a paradigm for an acceptable relationship between
the USSR and its satellites. Even if realistically there was little hope
that Moscow would accept such an arrangement, the Finnish paradigm
offered diplomatic and propaganda advantages for the United States.

Integration, an integral part of America's postwar plans, was
intended to promote Europe's economic well-being as it reinforced
collective security. Washington insisted that the initiative had to come
from the Europeans themselves, but as a superpower it could
obviously influence the direction integration took, and it did so as
early as the Marshall Plan. In response to Marshall's offer, sixteen
nations, including neutrals, formed the Organization of European
Economic Cooperation (OEEC). From its beginnings as a body to
administer U.S. aid, it continued as an organization fostering
cooperation after that aid ended. The OEEC was followed
subsequently by bodies such as the European Coal and Steel
Community (ECSC) in 1950, the European Economic Community
(EEC) in 1957, and the European Free Trade Association (EFTA) in
1959.

---

[43] NSC 5403.
[44] NSC 5914/1.

The U.S. maintained that effective integrative institutions had to possess strong supranational authority to overcome the divisive forces of nationalism and had to be broad-based, to include neutrals as well as allies. In practice, Washington discovered that these two qualities were often in conflict. The OEEC, for example, had a broad membership, but lacked real power. The ECSC and EEC had the supranational power, but their membership was narrow, excluding neutrals. During both the Truman and Eisenhower administrations, therefore, Washington persistently balanced its support for these contrasting goals. With the plight of the neutrals in mind, it encouraged the evolution of strong institutions like the EEC, yet refrained from abandoning the OEEC and other bodies that encompassed neutral states.[45]

The effort to attract neutrals succeeded. Ireland, Sweden, and Austria were OEEC members. EFTA included the latter two. But Finland proved more perplexing. Since 1955, it had joined the Nordic Council and the United Nations, but hesitated to establish any formal ties with Western Europe until 1959, when Helsinki began to explore possible associate membership in EFTA, the creation of seven nations excluded from the EEC. As Helsinki wrestled with this pivotal decision, John D. Hickerson, U.S. ambassador to Finland, wrote to the State Department that the importance of EFTA to Finland could not be overemphasized. Finland's joining would be "a major step toward real independence and the establishment of further long-term and binding economic ties with the West," whereas if Finland backed down it would be "a major step toward greater dependence, political and economic, on the USSR."[46] In 1961, Finland did join as an associate member.

An independent Finland also offered another advantage for the United States beyond the contribution it could make to a strong, united Europe. America's neutral policy was in part a reaction to

---

[45] Dean Acheson, Truman's secretary of state, for example, opposed a 1952 proposal by British Prime Minister Anthony Eden that NATO take over many of the OEEC's functions. The OEEC, Acheson argued, was important to "maintain strong ties" between NATO and Europe's neutrals; Acheson to Eden, 21 March 1952, *FRUS, 1952-54,* 6:39-40. Later, when the ECSC began discussions leading to the creation of an economic community, the U.S. was heartened by the possibility of a strong integrative body, but was still not ready to abandon the OEEC; Dulles to British Foreign Secretary Harold Macmillan, 10 December 1955, *FRUS, 1955-57,* 4:362-64.

[46] Hickerson to Department of State, 16 July 1959, *FRUS, 1958-60,* 7:70.

Soviet attempts to exploit neutralism for its own purposes. Khrushchev tried to set up Finland as a showcase for relations with its neighbors. During a June 1957 visit to Helsinki, the Soviet leader praised Soviet-Finnish relations as an example of peaceful coexistence and contrasted this relationship with the less satisfactory relations with Scandinavia.[47] Ironically, however, at the same time, U.S. policy orchestrated by John Foster Dulles was attempting to turn the tables on the Kremlin and use Finland as a diplomatic weapon to challenge continued Soviet domination of Eastern Europe.

During the dinner conversation mentioned at the beginning of this essay, Dulles's suggestion that prompted Eden's description of Finland as the "road to nowhere" was that "something like a Finnish relationship might evolve" between the Soviet Union and its eastern satellites. This, Dulles proposed, might facilitate lasting peace in Europe.[48] This was not simply idle speculation on Dulles's part. On other occasions he had cited the Finnish option as a paradigm that might work to the West's advantage while addressing Soviet security concerns.

In September 1953 Dulles was analyzing America's security policies, which he believed required urgent reconsideration, especially in view of international obligations and budgetary considerations. In a memorandum reviewed by the president, the secretary proposed the possibility of a "broad zone of restricted armaments in Europe, with [the] Soviets withdrawn from [their] satellites and [the] U.S. from Europe." He noted that for such an initiative to be effective, it had to be coupled with other steps including control of nuclear weapons and opening of East-West trade. On the Soviet side, it would also require that the Communist Party end its "world revolution" mission and that the satellites be "politically freed, but oriented (friendly) to [the] U.S.S.R." He referred to Finland as the model for this relationship.[49]

---

[47] Progress Report, 12 June 1957.

[48] John Foster Dulles, Memorandum of Dinner with Sir Winston Churchill, 12 April 1954, Papers of John Foster Dulles, White House Memorandum Series, Folder: Meetings with President (4), DDEL; see also, John L. Gaddis, "The Unexpected John Foster Dulles," 67-8.

[49] Memorandum by the Secretary of State, 6 September 1953, *FRUS, 1952-54*, 2:457-60. John Gaddis, "The Unexpected John Foster Dulles," 67-9, cites this memorandum as evidence of a less rigid and more complex Dulles.

Later, during the 1955 Geneva summit, he suggested the possibility directly to Soviet diplomats. At a state dinner, he approached Nikolai A. Bulganin:

[Dulles] said that [the] US had no desire that [the] USSR "should be ringed by a group of hostile states. In order to avoid this, however, it was not necessary that they be satellites. There was the example of Finland for instance. Bulganin (who visibly froze up at this point) replied in effect that these countries have governments of their own choosing and that our expressed position on this point was not one which could be usefully pressed. This was a situation which could take care of itself with the passage of time.[50]

Even if the Soviet Union could not have reasonably been expected to accept such an arrangement, the paradigm had diplomatic and propaganda benefits the U.S. could exploit.

The idea, in fact, found its way into the revised policy on Finland in 1959 and 1960. Keeping Finland free from Soviet domination would serve a special purpose for U.S. foreign policy goals in the Cold War. "If Finland is able to preserve its present neutral status— that of a nation able to maintain its independence despite heavy Soviet pressure—it could serve as an example of what the United States might like to see achieved by the Soviet-dominated nations of Eastern Europe," NSC 5914/1 declared.[51] During one NSC session, Secretary of State Christian Herter, who had succeeded Dulles, questioned the advisability of including this broad policy goal in a report specific to Finland. He further wondered if indeed this reflected official thinking.[52] Despite Herter's concern, the statement remained in the final draft, a legacy of Dulles.

As much of the U.S. analysis of the Finnish situation since the beginning of the Cold War had emphasized, Finland was unique. Therefore, there was clearly doubt that what had transpired in Finland could be duplicated in the Soviet satellites. Nevertheless, serious consideration of this possibility, however remote, suggests that Finland occupied a place in American Cold War plans.[53]

---

[50] Memorandum for Record of the President's State Dinner, Geneva, 18 July 1955, *FRUS: 1955-57*, 5:372-3; see also, Memorandum of Conversation at President's Dinner, Geneva, 18 July 1955, ibid., 5:377.

[51] NSC 5914/1.

[52] Minutes of NSC Meeting, 1 October 1959, WHO: NSC Series, Folder: 420th Meeting, Box 8, DDEL.

[53] John Lukacs, in a 1992 retrospective vindicating Finlandization, underlines the success of this maligned policy, but emphasizes that it can in no way be used as a

Conclusion

The Finnish-U.S. relationship took root in the Truman years and flowered under Eisenhower. America's response to the 1947 peace treaty and the 1948 FCMA agreement set the tone for the future relationship, although at the time Truman officials worried that Finland could not survive as an independent state. During the 1950s, particularly after Finland had discharged its reparations obligations, the U.S. expanded this relationship with increasing confidence in Finland's ability to endure. Although much of the credit for Finland's survival has to go to Paasikivi and Kekkonen, U.S. policy had an influence. The U.S. response partially determined not only the extent to which Finland would become embroiled in the Cold War rivalry, but also how successful Finland would be in preserving its sovereignty and reducing its dependence on the Soviet Union as it moved closer to the West.

Finland was in a far stronger position in 1961 when Eisenhower stepped down than in 1953, and American national interests were served. After the "Night Frost Crisis," on only one other occasion did Finland seriously face absorption into the Soviet orbit, the so-called "Note Crisis" of October 1961, just a few months after John F. Kennedy's inauguration. Once again, in response to growing tensions in Berlin, Khrushchev unilaterally invoked the FCMA treaty and called for military consultation. This threatened to undermine the neutral position that Paasikivi and Kekkonen had constructed. But Kekkonen successfully avoided this eventuality, persuading the Soviets that if they withdrew their note, tensions in the Nordic region would ease, thus reducing the need for military preparation, not only in Finland and Sweden, but also in Denmark and Norway. With the passing of this crisis, Kekkonen even more determinedly pursued his more active neutrality.[54]

Finland scrupulously preserved its neutrality while taking a more active role in world affairs, especially in its relationship with Europe. It joined EFTA as an associate member in 1961 and by 1973 had developed a special relationship with the EEC. While the United States cannot take credit for this—indeed it was the Finnish leaders' skillful

---

precedent. Finland was a unique situation. John Lukacs, "Finland Vindicated," *Foreign Affairs* 71 (Fall 1992): 50-63.

[54] Vloyantes, "Finland," 147-9; Allison, *Finland's Relations with the Soviet Union*, 43-52; Vloyantes, *Silk Glove Hegemony*, 109-25.

diplomatic maneuvering that made this possible—the U.S. played a role in the background. The decision of the United States first under Truman and then Eisenhower to defer to Finland's wishes and not to force issues that might have injected Finland into the Cold War controversy provided a climate conducive for Finnish diplomacy to succeed.

The U.S. followed this policy because Finland's international situation left little alternative and because Finland was seen as "the road to nowhere." But at the same time, Washington managed this relationship with an eye toward promoting both its own and Europe's national security interests. And in this respect, U.S. policy largely prevailed. In particular, American policymakers related Finnish policy to three important initiatives, and they succeeded in the two most important of these. First, the U.S. sought to create an effective collective security system. The Nordic balance that evolved after only Denmark and Norway opted to join NATO reinforced this security system by creating a stable and secure area on Europe's northern periphery. Finland, the neutral on the Soviet border, was an essential component of this balance.

Second, America recognized that collective security could be enhanced by closer European union in the economic and political arenas, a belief Washington nurtured throughout the 1950s with its support for various European initiatives leading to the European Economic Community. Recognizing that it was risky to blatantly try to move Finland into these organizations, the U.S. took a circumspect approach, providing careful and directed economic assistance to Finland with the purpose of reducing Finland's economic dependence on the USSR. As Finland assumed a role of more active diplomacy after 1961, its relations with Europe became stronger, including participation in many of these organizations. Once again, U.S. interests had been achieved.

It was in the third initiative alone that American policy fell short. If Finland were to be promoted as an alternative to the closed sphere relationship that the Soviet Union had with its satellites, this was never achieved. Nevertheless, America's advocacy of the "Finland solution" underlined the fact that Washington was not blindly opposed to neutrality, but that neutrals did indeed have a place in the western security system. It, furthermore, served as a convenient propaganda weapon to expose the contradictions in Khrushchev's call for peaceful coexistence.

7

Finlandization: A Retrospective[1]

Robert W. Matson

Inhabitants of a beautiful northern land and heirs of a rich folkloric tradition, the Finns share many cultural traits with their Scandinavian neighbors. But the majority of Finland's people speak a language understood by hardly anyone else and they have often occupied an international position equally unique. Although they have learned to joke about the "privacy" of the Finnish tongue, they bemoan the widespread misunderstanding of what they consider to be their instructive diplomatic history since the Second World War.

In America almost everyone knows something about Finland, but the knowledge is episodic. Apart from the successes of its Olympic athletes and beauty contestants, Finland has captured the attention of Americans only when it has stood out against the presumed normal order of things—a posture calculated to bring misinterpretation as well as attention. During the Great Depression of the 1930s, for example, Finland was the only nation to keep the payments on its debt to the United States current ("that most acceptable of all public acts to the American democracy," the British ambassador at Washington observed wryly).[2] Then, in 1939, when Poland had been subjugated and Adolf Hitler's European foes seemed incapable of waging more than a "phony war" against him, the Finns responded with military vigor to an unprovoked Soviet attack and were accordingly cast in the role of David-versus-Goliath during the dramatic hundred-day

---

[1] This chapter is not only a retrospective of Finlandization from the post-Cold War perspective, but also of an essay I published in 1983 in *Washington State Research Studies*;"Finlandization, on A Historical Analogy," *Research Studies* 51 (March 1983): 1-11.

[2] Lothian to Halifax, 1 February 1940, FO 800/324, Individual Files, Public Record Office, London (hereafter cited as PRO).

"Winter War" which followed. But by the time the United States officially joined the war and the anti-Axis coalition was fully formed, events had pushed Finland across the line again and from 1941 to 1944 it occupied the unenviable position of a democratic state at war, as a somewhat reluctant ally of Germany, with two of the United Nations. Indeed, Helsinki was the only European capital where German troops could march past an active U.S. embassy and where American diplomats had to be concerned about damage from British air raids.

After the war, the ironies continued. Finland was the only portion of the old tsarist empire not reclaimed by the Red Army and the only European state bordering the USSR that did not become Communist. During the Cold War, though it was unquestionably within the Soviet geographic sphere, Finland was also linked to the democratic West— especially to the United States, where hundreds of thousands of persons of Finnish ancestry lived—by both sentiment and political doctrine. Max Jakobson, a distinguished Finnish scholar who served his country in several diplomatic posts, including at UN headquarters in New York, expressed the sense of this odd history well when he remarked somewhat ruefully that to those unfamiliar with Finland, its continued independent existence must have seemed "something like an Indian rope trick which defied the laws of nature."[3]

In fact, during the early stages of the Cold War, western journalists often expressed worries that Finland's independence would necessarily be short-lived. But when the Finns, in contrast to their borderland neighbors to the South, did not succumb to a one-party regime imposed from Moscow, the journalists simply turned their attention to other matters, having offered no satisfactory explanation for what had happened in Finland and leaving their readers with an unclear image of the Finnish identity. Nor were U.S. government officials, including those with responsibility for relations with Finland, much better informed than the general public. The Department of State discovered during World War II that it did not even have an analyst who could read the Finnish language. Though it temporarily solved that problem by retaining the services of Professor John

---

[3] Max Jakobson, "Finland's Foreign Policy," *International Affairs* 38 (April 1962): 196.

Wuorinen of Columbia University, it too seemed to forget about the Finns from about 1949 onward.[4]

Meanwhile, the Finns fashioned a foreign policy—first called the Paasikivi Line and later the Paasikivi-Kekkonen Line after the two principal postwar leaders—designed to maintain both political independence and good relations with the Soviet Union. Finland thus became the only place where something like President Franklin D. Roosevelt's vision of postwar Europe, described in the Yalta accords, emerged. Finland was a democratic country, friendly to the USSR but having open trade and cultural relations with the West and retaining its traditional social and political life. Though at first fearful of this policy, the historically anti-Russian Finns embarked upon it at the end of the war with assurances of continued East-West cooperation from U.S. officials. When the hoped-for cooperation gave way to increasing Cold War tensions, the Finns became somewhat elated at their unique success and began to cite the "lessons" the western democracies could learn from their experience. The intended pupils were not listening during the 1950s and 1960s, however. Then, to their dismay, in the 1970s the Finns were rediscovered by journalists who began to warn against what was sometimes labeled "the specter of Finlandization."[5]

Consequently, there are two interpretations of the meaning of the postwar experience of Finland. The virtually unanimous Finnish view (which, to be sure, is shared by many non-Finnish observers) considers the Paasikivi-Kekkonen Line a success. Its founder, Dr. Juho J. Paasikivi, was a crusty old gentleman who had been seasoned, but little mellowed, by long experience in both business and politics.

---

[4] Some of the typical postwar treatments were Laurin Zilliacus, "What Happened in Finland?" *Atlantic Monthly* 179 (May 1947): 69-74; Eric C. Bellquist, "Government and Politics in Northern Europe: an Account of Recent Developments," *Journal of Politics* 8 (August 1946): 361-92; Eric Dancy, "Finland Takes Stock," *Foreign Affairs* 24 (April 1946): 513-25; J. Hampden Jackson, "Finland Since the Armistice," *International Affairs* 24 (October 1948): 505-14; Arthur Spencer, "Finland Maintains Democracy," *Foreign Affairs* 31 (January 1953): 301-9. On John Wuorinen, see J.A. Morrison, "Can Finland Be Maneuvered Out of the War?" Research and Analysis Report #384, 31 December 1941, RG 59, Records of the Department of State, National Archives, Washington, D.C.

[5] Note, for instance, "Finns Want Closer Ties to West," *Business Week* 15 (June 1957): 121; "Finland's 60th Anniversary," *Scandinavian Review* 65 (December 1977): 9; and Walter Laqueur, "Europe: The Specter of Finlandization," *Commentary* 37 (December 1977): 37-41.

Coming to the presidency in 1946, he was convinced that the events of the twentieth century to date had amply demonstrated that there could be no security for Finland through either force of arms or an aloof practice of neutrality. Nevertheless, he was no pessimist and he welcomed the opportunity to test his theory that, propaganda notwithstanding, the Soviet interest in his country was mainly strategic rather than ideological. Unlike those who viewed submission and conflict as the only alternatives, he believed that it was possible to satisfy the security demands of the Soviet Union without sacrificing Finnish sovereignty. This was "our special foreign policy problem," he said, one "to which a solution must be found and on which the future of our nation depends." A political thinker with a profound knowledge of history and a scholar whose conversation abounded with classical and folkloric allusions, Paasikivi bent every effort to convert the Finns to what he considered a more realistic outlook. "In the future," he said in one radio address, "our foreign policies must never go against the USSR, and we must assure our eastern neighbor of our firmness in this conviction." His goal, however, was not subservience, but the development of "friendly and trustworthy relations between a free Finland and the Soviet Union."[6]

Although the Paasikivi Line was in accord with the policy urged upon the Finns and other European nations by U.S. diplomats at the end of the Second World War, it is clear that Paasikivi responded more to his own analysis than to pressure, and he did not abandon his course when the Americans adopted a more confrontational line as the Cold War set in. Fortunately, Paasikivi had some flexibility resulting from the absence of Soviet troops from his soil—the Finno-Soviet dimension of the Second World War having been settled through negotiation in 1944—and by generous economic aid from the United States in 1946 and 1947. The Finns were not forced into the role of victims in a competitive environment between a strong Soviet bloc and a strong West. They could, in fact, thrive in that atmosphere, provided that tensions did not increase to the point of crisis. But Finland had to be neutral in the Cold War. "It had become apparent," Foreign

---

[6] Juho K. Paasikivi, *Paasikiven Linja: Puheitä Vuosilta 1944-56* [The Paasikivi Line: Speeches, 1944-56] (Porvoo: 1962), 14; Annual Report on Finland, 1946, FO371/65918, N1455/159/56, Foreign Office Correspondence, PRO. A biographical portrait of Paasikivi is found in Marvin Rintala, *Four Finns* (Berkeley and Los Angeles, 1969), 93-112. On his foreign policy, see George Maude, *The Finnish Dilemma: Neutrality in the Shadow of Power* (London, 1976), chapters 1 and 2.

Minister Ralf Törngren recalled later, "that it would be mortally dangerous to Finland to serve as a forward part of an anti-Soviet coalition, first to be overrun in case of conflict, yet without any real influence over decisions on the issues of war and peace."[7]

Paasikivi's political strength and sagacity prevented internal disruptions as well. By the time he left office in 1956 the fruits of his policy were evident. Finland had paid its reparations to the Soviet Union and thus enjoyed a greater degree of economic latitude. On the other hand, the Soviets made concessions to the Finns and permitted them to join both the Nordic Council and the United Nations. Furthermore, the USSR removed its forces from the Porkkala Peninsula, which it had obtained as a naval base at the end of the war.

The emergence of Urho K. Kekkonen as the dominant figure in Finnish politics after Paasikivi assured that the Paasikivi Line would not be abandoned. But when Paasikivi appointed Kekkonen prime minister in 1950, the choice was not a widely popular one. A member of the Agrarian Party (later called the Centre Party) with the reputation of an opportunist, Kekkonen had run against Paasikivi for the presidency and had received the support of the left. Because of this and his popularity with members of the Soviet legation, some Finns nervously joked that his appointment would turn the country into "Kekkoslovakia."[8] But his dedication to the Paasikivi Line and his enormous self-confidence proved to be assets. In 1956 he succeeded Paasikivi in the presidency, though by a margin of only one vote in the electoral college. As president, he became Finland's most influential man, a role in which his powers in foreign policy were significant. His first goal was to obtain recognition of Finland's neutrality from the western powers, a recognition the Soviets had given, by implication at least, in a 1948 treaty of mutual aid and friendship, which cited as its main premise "Finland's desire to remain outside the conflicting interests of the Great Powers."[9] Kekkonen sought to help create an international climate in which Finland's standing would be more typical than it was during the Cold War—to point the Great Powers, in other words, toward détente.

---

[7] Ralf Törngren, "Neutrality of Finland," *Foreign Affairs* 39 (July 1961): 603.

[8] A. J. Fischer, "Finland and the Kremlin," *The Contemporary Review* 178 (May 1950): 286.

[9] Kalevi J. Holsti, "Strategy and Techniques of Influence in Soviet-Finnish Relations," *Western Political Quarterly* 17 (March 1964): 70. The text of the treaty is found in United Nations *Treaty Series* 49 (1948): 150-61.

To achieve these goals required great energy, and Kekkonen, a vigorous athlete as well as politician, seemed to have it. As a leader, he began to speak out on world affairs far more aggressively than Paasikivi had dared. He recommended, for instance, that Denmark, Norway and Iceland reconsider their NATO membership and perhaps withdraw to join Finland in establishing a truly neutral Nordic region. He also traveled widely, not only becoming the first Finnish president to visit the United States, but returning frequently and conferring with every U.S. president from John F. Kennedy to Gerald Ford. Obviously, he had larger goals than merely managing Finnish affairs with modest success.[10]

Furthermore, although there were incidents in Finnish-Soviet relations in 1958 and 1961, they were settled with no diminution of Finnish sovereignty. In fact, Kekkonen apparently convinced Nikita Khrushchev in 1961 that the Finnish, and not the Soviet, interpretation of the current European situation was correct. In short, Kekkonen abandoned Paasikivi's caution in foreign affairs and also his tendency to maintain a certain distance between Finnish and Soviet leaders. Embracing close cooperation, Kekkonen argued that the warmer Finnish-Soviet relations were, the more latitude Finland had to cultivate its ties with the West.

Whereas Paasikivi's main stage had been domestic, Kekkonen's was international. And, though this activism made Kekkonen controversial at first, it resulted in electoral victories. For, as Professor Keijo Korhonen of Helsinki University observed in 1975, "the Finnish people [had] grown accustomed to relying fully on his judgment, his experience, and his skill."[11] He was not only reelected in 1962, at the end of his first six-year term, but he sought and achieved an unprecedented third term in 1968. During this term, Finland's parliament, the *Eduskunta*, postponed the next general election from 1974 to 1978 and, well before that election, Kekkonen's victory was assured because several political parties had endorsed him. Most important of all, the Paasikivi-Kekkonen Line was

---

[10] John H. Hodgson, "Postwar Finnish Foreign Policy: Institutions and Personalities," *Western Political Quarterly* 15 (March 1962): 89-92.

[11] Keijo Korhonen, "The Foreign Policy of President Urho Kekkonen," *Contemporary Review* 27 (October 1975): 194.

accepted by virtually all parties and politicians as Finland's official foreign policy.[12]

At length, Kekkonen's claim that Finland was a model of successful coexistence with the Soviet Union stimulated the development of an alternative explanation, the concept eventually labeled "Finlandization," but this critique was some time in forming. Of course, the Paasikivi Line had some critics from the start, for it sounded a discordant note against the chorus of Cold War. In January 1953, the editors of the *Saturday Evening Post*, with clearly partisan motives, pictured it not as a considered policy, but one of desperation. "The Democratic Administration in Washington and the Labour Government in London," the *Post* charged, "helped to maneuver Finland into enslavement to the Russians."[13] If they expected, as seems obvious, a different approach from the incoming Eisenhower administration, however, they were disappointed.

Professor Wuorinen, in particular, launched a heroic literary effort. No doubt holding strong feelings of sympathy for Finland as a result of his Finnish heritage and his wartime work for the State Department, Wuorinen claimed to be an authoritative interpreter of the Finnish situation. But he dissented from the Paasikivi Line and sought to refute the thinking that underlay it. To Wuorinen, the USSR must be seen as a genuinely revolutionary force, determined "to overthrow the 'international bourgeoisie' and to create a Sovietized world order by whatever means necessary."[14] Defining Finland as "the northern-most segment of the Western defense frontier in Europe," he chided U.S. leaders for pursuing a "morally indefensible policy" which failed "to consider the precarious aspects of Finland's position— clearly the consequence of Soviet aggression and designs—a circumstance that undermines the security of the United States and should therefore be frankly recognized as a vital concern."[15] Repeatedly he urged a statement of policy that would "place a 'No Trespassing' sign, boldly lettered and facing East...along Finland's

---

[12] H. Peter Krosby, "Finland: The Politics of Economic Emergency," *Current History* 70 (April 1976): 176.

[13] "We Helped Make Finland an Economic Serf," *Saturday Evening Post*, 17 January 1953, 12.

[14] John H. Wuorinen, *A History of Finland* (New York, 1956), 450; Wuorinen, "Finland and the U.S.S.R.," *Journal of International Affairs* 16 (1962): 38.

[15] Wuorinen, *History of Finland*, 471; Wuorinen, "Finland," in *The Fate of East Central Europe*, ed. Stephen Kertesz (Notre Dame, IN, 1956), 357.

Soviet border, and that the line thus marked be openly recognized as a frontier to be defended."[16]

Though Wuorinen's prescription was precisely the opposite of that sought by Finnish leaders themselves, in the United States it harmonized with the prevailing public hostility toward the Soviet Union in the 1950s and 1960s and helped form a mythology about Finland which spread through large circulation periodicals such as *National Geographic* and *U.S. News and World Report*. Articles with titles such as "A Small Country Finds Out What It's Like to 'Coexist,'" "Finland: In the Giant's Shadow," and "Finland's Perilous Neutrality," stressed the misfortune of the Finns, lauded their courage, and suggested that their situation was untenable.[17] Historian Arthur M. Schlesinger, Jr., was apparently one who accepted this interpretation and accordingly misread Finland's own foreign policy. In 1961, when he was serving as a special assistant to President Kennedy, Schlesinger handled the arrangements for a visit by Kekkonen to the United States. The Finnish president, Schlesinger told Kennedy, seemed "to feel that Communism is the wave of the future and that Finland had better establish the best possible terms for survival in a world increasingly dominated by the Soviet Union." Thus, he recommended that Kennedy take a firm approach and attempt to bolster Kekkonen's faith in "the open society."[18]

Kekkonen was no doubt surprised by Kennedy's attitude, for he considered Finnish democracy to be at least as deeply rooted as American, but the conflicting interpretations of Finland were of little consequence in world affairs until the administration of President Richard M. Nixon began to pursue a policy of détente with the Soviet Union. The role of Finland in this démarche was shown by Kekkonen's trip to Washington in July 1970. Only a week earlier he had been in Moscow, and he carried with him an invitation to a

---

[16] Wuorinen, "Finland Stands Guard," *Foreign Affairs* 32 (July 1954): 660.

[17] "A Small Country Finds Out What It's Like to 'Coexist,'" *U.S. News & World Report*, 9 November 1959, 84; Don Cook, "Finland's Perilous Neutrality," *New Republic*, 1 January 1962, 7-9; "Finland: In the Giant's Shadow," *Time*, 9 June 1967, 46-8; William Graves, "Finland: Plucky Neighbor of Soviet Russia," *National Geographic* 133 (May 1968): 587-629.

[18] Arthur M. Schlesinger, Jr., Memorandum for the President, 13 October 1961, Box 9, Schlesinger Papers, John F. Kennedy Library.

general conference on European security to be held in Helsinki.[19] In marked contrast to Kennedy's approach of nine years earlier, Nixon praised Finland's foreign policy as neutral "not in a negative way but in a positive way, positive in working always for the cause of peace in the world and in reducing tensions between small and great powers." He also thanked the Finns for being the hosts for the Strategic Arms Limitation Talks in 1969.[20] It is probably too much to claim that Kekkonen was the true architect of détente, but he was then at the peak of his energies, and he regularly exercised his legendary powers of persuasion upon the incumbents of both the Kremlin and the White House. In Finland the leading newspaper, *Helsingin Sanomat*, commented editorially that it was obvious that the Americans understood the Finnish outlook better than they had in the past.[21]

The convergence of Urho Kekkonen's longtime goals and Richard Nixon's foreign policy made it necessary for the opponents of détente to comment critically upon the Paasikivi-Kekkonen Line. For this purpose, they seized the term "Finlandization," which had been coined in the 1960s by the German political scientist Richard Lowenthal. Lowenthal suggested that the Soviets no longer had expectations of the triumph of communism in Western Europe and also that their hold on Eastern Europe showed signs of weakening. If the NATO alliance also weakened for any reason, he thought that Western European nations might deal with the Soviet Union much as the Finns had done.[22] Lowenthal's "Finlandization" was neither a pejorative term nor a political theory, but the opponents of détente made it both. William F. Buckley recklessly redefined it as "a kind of inchoate subordination to Soviet policy," and Walter Laqueur advanced a formulation that sounded more sophisticated: "that process or state of affairs in which, under the cloak of maintaining friendly relations with the Soviet Union, the sovereignty of a country

---

[19] "Man on a Tightrope," *Newsweek*, 3 August 1970, 28; various articles, Leikelmäarkisto [clipping archive], 1970, Ulkopoliitinen Instituutti [The Foreign Policy Institute], Helsinki.

[20] "President Kekkonen of Finland Visits the United States," U.S. Department of State *Bulletin* 63 (17 August 1970): 195.

[21] "Toinen Vierailu" [Another Trip], *Helsingin Sanomat*, 22 July 1970, 6.

[22] Richard Lowenthal, "Has the Revolution A Future?" *Encounter* 24 (January 1965): 3-18 and (February 1965): 16-26; Lowenthal, "The Sparrow in the Cage," *Encounter* 32 (January 1969): 87-96 and (February 1969): 90-1.

becomes reduced."[23] Lowenthal reportedly was much distressed by this capture of his term for polemical purposes, but, like the Cold War era misunderstanding of Finnish foreign policy to which it was related, the polemical use of the term Finlandization passed into the journalistic folklore and was increasingly—and indiscriminately— used as though it were a reliable analogy. Although Finnish leaders and some scholars made attempts to offer an alternative positive interpretation of the term, it was the negative sense that stuck.[24]

So greatly did the spread of this terminology alter the conventional wisdom about Finland that, when ill health forced Urho Kekkonen to retire from the presidency in 1981, *Newsweek* remarked in its biographical portrait of him that he had "traveled frequently to the Soviet Union and became especially close to Nikita Khrushchev." The article was not balanced, however, by any reference to Kekkonen's many trips to the United States or to the visits of Presidents Johnson, Nixon and Ford to Finland.[25] The implication was that Finland was a self-made Soviet satellite, thanks to the Paasikivi-Kekkonen Line.

Proponents of the theory of Finlandization, however, offered little convincing evidence that Finland's sovereignty was in fact reduced beyond the constraints imposed by geography and history. The implication that a sinister process was under way rested on ethnocentric and ahistorical commentary. Finlandizationists averred that there were few crises in Finnish-Soviet relations only because the Finns had gradually become subservient to the point of anticipating Soviet wishes, making overt demands unnecessary. Thus, they argued, Finland was not truly a free country, although it retained the trappings of democracy. The long tenure of Urho Kekkonen in the presidency—seemingly comparable to contemporary strongmen like Tito of Yugoslavia and Castro of Cuba—offered a tantalizing proof. But such an argument rested on remarkable, though perhaps forgivable, ignorance of Finnish political tradition. The presidency of

---

[23] William F. Buckley, Jr., "The Finlandization Tactic," *National Review* 24 (19 August 1977): 958-9; Laqueur, "The Specter of Finlandization," 37.

[24] For example, "Losing an ism," *The Oregonian*, 5 January 1980, 14; C.L Sulzberger, "East or West of Finland," *New York Times*, 25 January 1975; "Prisoners of Geography," *The Times* (London), 3 November 1981. Note the comment in Fred Singleton, "The Myth of 'Finlandization,'" *International Affairs* 57 (Spring 1981): 1-2.

[25] "Goodbye to the Man in the Middle," *Newsweek*, 9 November 1981, 61.

Finland is not like that of the United States, nor is it a product of modern pressures from the East. The office is, rather, a relative of the constitutional monarchies of Scandinavia, and its occupant is not subject to the forces of checks and balances familiar to Americans. The tendency of Finns to give long terms of service and broad powers of national policy to their leaders owes much to the fact that their system of government retains many features from their centuries as an integral part of the realm of Sweden. And in Finland, as in Britain, the "constitution" is a developing set of precedents, not a single charter document.[26] Kekkonen, moreover, was a formidable wielder of political power who never cavilled at the use of the powers of his office for his personal ends. As one observer put it: "He consults with nobody, confides in no one, has no advisors who count for anything, and is capable of the most unpredictable and cynical political tricks." He used fear of Russia not, as Paasikivi had done, "to rally the Finnish nation but to scatter his political opponents."[27]

The 1961 "Note Crisis," in which Urho Kekkonen, while vacationing in Hawaii, received from Nikita Khrushchev a note proposing immediate Finnish-Soviet military consultations as provided for in the 1948 treaty in cases of possible threat to both powers, illustrated Kekkonen's style. Fearful that such consultations would destroy the role of the activist neutral he was attempting to play, he traveled to Siberia and convinced Khrushchev that the NATO exercises in the North Sea, which were the pretext of the note, were not really threatening. But Kekkonen then returned to Finland and used the air of crisis that had developed to maneuver his opponents out of the 1962 presidential election campaign. Electoral victories and decades in power did nothing to diminish his ego. After a 1980 visit by the imperious French President Giscard d'Estaing, a cartoonist depicted Kekkonen waving goodbye to the Frenchman while saying

---

[26] Jaakko Nousiainen, *The Finnish Political System*, trans. by John H. Hodgson (Cambridge, 1971), 145-50, 214-16. The *Eduskunta* had previously intervened in the presidency by selecting a president itself or by calling a previous electoral college back into session. The extension of Kekkonen's term, therefore, was within the Finnish political tradition, irrespective of whether it was wise; see Hodgson, "Postwar Finnish Foreign Policy," 80.

[27] Cook, "Finland's Perilous Neutrality," 7.

to members of his cabinet, "There goes a really great statesman—almost my equal."[28]

The Note Crisis also demonstrates the way Finlandizationists made selective and didactic use of the evidence. In his 1980 book *The Political Psychology of Appeasement*, Walter Laqueur declared that "the Soviet Union...threatened to invoke the 1948 treaty unless Kekkonen were reelected president."[29] That was indeed the self-serving interpretation of the crisis purveyed by Kekkonen himself, but in fact Khrushchev's note cited an allegedly threatening international situation, not internal Finnish politics. But to Laqueur and other Finlandizationists, the leaders of the USSR were aggressors and could have no legitimate fears of their own. Accordingly, he turned his sarcasm on Max Jakobson's 1971 candidacy for the post of secretary general of the United Nations, claiming that the Soviets opposed it because they suspected Jakobson of "taking neutrality seriously."[30]

Laqueur sought, in fact, to portray Finland's entire role in the UN as one of subservience to the Soviets. He noted, for instance, that the Finnish delegation did not vote to condemn the Soviet invasion of Hungary in 1956, but he failed to place that decision in the context of Finland's policy of abstaining from votes involving serious East-West confrontation. Nor did he acknowledge Finland's consistent identification in the UN—and in the world at large—with the causes of democracy and self-determination. In fact, the 1956 Hungarian crisis, which occurred during Finland's first season as a UN member, presented a serious problem at a delicate moment. There was no question whatever of sincere Finnish concern for the Hungarians. The Finnish Red Cross raised an unprecedented eighteen million Finnmarks for Hungarian relief in a single week. Ultimately, in the UN, the Finns voted for an Austrian compromise resolution that supported the Hungarians without specifically mentioning the

---

[28] *Ilta Sanomat* (Helsinki), 3 June 1980, 2. See also Krosby, "The Politics of Economic Emergency," 176; Holsti, "Strategy and Techniques of Influence," 63-8; Maude, *Finnish Dilemma*, 18-24, 60-6; and Anthony James, "A Northern Paradox: How Finland Survived the Cold War," *Contemporary Review* 264 (March 1994): 113-22.

[29] Walter Laqueur, *The Political Psychology of Appeasement: Finlandization and Other Unpopular Essays* (New Brunswick, 1980), 10.

[30] Ibid., 9.

USSR.[31] All of this, of course, Laqueur omitted. Other Finlandizationists, not content with such selective narrative, went as far as misstating Finnish-Soviet trade figures to support their claims of increasing Soviet economic influence over Finland and even redrawing maps to make it appear that roads and railroads had been built mainly to provide easy access to Finland for the Red Army.[32]

The salient point, unfortunately one easily missed, is that the Finlandization theory was not in fact about Finland itself; it was a critique of American and Western European leaders of the 1970s who sought to deal "realistically," as they put it, with the Soviets. Unwilling to credit the possibility of an authentic modus vivendi between a democratic state and the Soviet Union, the proponents of Finlandization sought evidence of Finnish independence in stormy relations with the Kremlin. In the absence of such turbulence, they concluded that the Finns had become servile, and they cited the case as evidence that the hope of détente with the Soviet Union was a dangerous illusion.[33] The Finns themselves were inevitably dissenters from such a world view, but there were other critics as well. One of the most redoubtable was the venerable Sovietologist and diplomat George F. Kennan, who held that the Finlandization argument was "absurdly overdrawn and unsuitable. The implications of this analogy do justice neither to Finland's actual position nor to Western Europe's potential one." To Kennan, the most remarkable feature of the Finnish-Soviet relationship was "its uniqueness," which tended to discredit all use of it as a model or analogy.[34] The fact that political commentators continued to use the analogy prompted Christopher

---

[31] Kent Forster, "Finland's Policy in the United Nations and the Paasikivi Line," *Journal of Central European Affairs* 21 (January 1962): 471, 475-6. Even so, Finland did not always abstain. In December 1982, for instance, it voted with the United States, Western Europe and the other Scandinavian countries against the Soviet bloc on a resolution linking Israel and South Africa in condemnation. See United Nations, Department of Public Information, Press Section, *Resolutions and Decisions Adopted by the General Assembly During the First Part of Its 37th Session* 1982, (A/37/595), 338-40.

[32] V.I. Punasalo, *The Reality of "Finlandization"* (London, 1978), 5-6, 8, 10; Christopher Hitchens and Jukka Rislakki, "The War of the Words," *New Statesman*, 16 January 1981, 10-11.

[33] For example, see Laqueur, "Euro-Neutralism," *Commentary*, 69 (June 1980): 21-7.

[34] George F. Kennan, "Europe's Problems, Europe's Choices," *Foreign Policy* 14 (Spring 1974): 3.

Hitchens by 1981 to label it "chimerical and dishonest" and to aver that "Finlandization" belonged with "appeasement" in a lexicon of disreputable terms that "involve distortions of history and the warping of current realities."[35] Clearly as much heat as light emanated from both sides of the argument. Perhaps the most balanced comment came from C.L. Sulzberger, who remarked that Finlandization had become "a political code word with many meanings."[36]

The resignation of Urho Kekkonen from the presidency of Finland in 1981 and the resignation of Mikhail Gorbachev from the presidency of a defunct Soviet Union exactly a decade later marked an era in which the concept of Finlandization was tested and finished. What direction would Finnish policy take after Kekkonen? How could his successors assure the Kremlin of their devotion to the Paasikivi-Kekkonen Line? Would they take steps to keep the lid on domestic political expression or be drawn into more active association with the Soviet bloc? If they allowed Finland to turn more decisively westward in orientation, what would be the Soviet reaction? Journalists raised questions such as these while the Finns went through the process of choosing a new president.

According to Finlandization theory, Soviet pressures should have sapped the energy of Finnish democracy. Finnish voters, whether as a result of overt fears of the USSR or the slow corrosion of their independence of thought by the seepage of pro-Soviet attitudes into the country under the guise of good relations, should have weighed their choice against the pleasure of the Kremlin. Nor would this have been difficult, for *Pravda*, to use the words of *Time* magazine, "baldly proclaimed its own favorite candidate," Ahti Karjalainen, president of the Bank of Finland and former foreign minister.[37] But Kekkonen's own Centre Party rejected this advice and handed its nomination to the speaker of the *Eduskunta*, Johannes Virolainen, who was known to be disliked in the Kremlin because he had been foreign minister during a brief incident in 1958 known as the "Night Frost Crisis."[38] In any case, Virolainen was defeated at the polls not by a candidate more

---

[35] Hitchens and Rislakki, "The War of the Words," 11.

[36] C.L. Sulzberger, "'Finlandization' Takes Strength," *International Herald Tribune*, 19 November 1981.

[37] "Making the Best of Deference," *Time*, 30 November 1981, 48.

[38] Finland, Ministry of Foreign Affairs, *Lehdistökatsaus* [Press Review], 23 November 1981.

friendly toward the Soviets, but by Mauno Koivisto, leader of the Social Democrats, the party most often reviled by Soviet spokesmen over the years. Finlandized Finns would surely not have voted for Koivisto. But as prime minister and one of the few politicians Kekkonen had not been able to keep down, Koivisto promised continued responsibility in the Presidential Palace.[39]

There was no question, of course, that any successful Finnish leader would base his foreign policy on the Paasikivi-Kekkonen Line, and President Koivisto made all of the necessary public statements and gestures in support of neutrality, good relations with the USSR and Finland's ties to the West. But he clearly saw the Line as a success—a fait accompli rather than a debate of continuing relevance or as an effort requiring ongoing nurture. Moreover, his personal style that, in comparison to Kekkonen's, was mild almost to the point of anonymity, did not embrace the use of the Kremlin as a political backstop. Nor did he see himself as a globe-trotting negotiator. Rather, he assumed the presidency with the promise of more normal politics and diplomacy during his term, including closer contacts between Finland and the other Nordic nations. And even as he began his term, political scientists noted the decline of the "artificial public consensus" that Kekkonen had fostered in support of his own hold on power.[40] Koivisto was fortunate enough to see what his predecessors could scarcely have imagined: the fall of the Soviet state itself. Yet in 1993, when he addressed the European Parliament, he did not use that event to explain the Finns' sense of security. Placing his own presidency in the context of those of Paasikivi and Kekkonen, he said, "We succeeded thanks to the hard work of the Finnish people, but also thanks to the favorable international arrangements we were able to conclude."[41]

Writers outside of Finland were less cautious than Koivisto. Supporters of the Paasikivi-Kekkonen Line quickly seized the opportunity to proclaim that events had proven them correct. In an article revealingly entitled "Finland Vindicated," for instance, John Lukacs reviewed the entire history of postwar Finnish-Soviet relations and asserted that the "limitations" imposed on Finland's freedom of

---

[39] Ibid., 19 January 1982.

[40] Ibid., 11 November 1981, 25 February 1982; "For Finns, Once-Taboo Topics Emerge into Open," *New York Times*, 17 May 1982.

[41] Ulkopoliittinen Instituutti, *Yearbook of Finnish Foreign Policy, 1993*, 68.

action by its proximity to the Soviet Union had proven to be "manageable and flexible...principally due to the moderation and wisdom of successive Finnish governments." Finnish foreign policy was vindicated even before the fall of the Soviet state, Lukacs contended, even though "this was not always understood in Washington."[42]

The Finlandizationists were neither impressed by this logic nor prepared to retreat from their position. In a brief and dismissive "Postscript to Finlandization," Laqueur reiterated the charge that "something was rotten in Helsinki" during the Cold War (the "something" being the alleged subservience of President Kekkonen to Soviet interests), and he continued to use his paradigm as part of the interpretive scheme of a large-scale synthesis, *Europe in Our Time: A History, 1945-1992.*[43] Laqueur's argument, taken with recent works by Finnish scholars and newly declassified documents, reveal not only Kekkonen's flaws, however, but also those of the whole theory of Finlandization. The test of the validity of Finlandization, ultimately, was not whether a renowned leader had clay feet but whether his policies sapped the vitality of the entire body politic. Clearly, the Finns were not Finlandized. Kekkonen's ambition, not good relations with the Soviet Union, was the dominant pressure in Finnish national politics during his tenure, and, if there were any obvious penetration of ideas and lifestyles from the outside, these came from the United States.

The conflict between these two interpretations is unlikely ever to be resolved, since it is an expression of a larger disagreement about the realities of the era of the Cold War. The argument, however, is now strictly historical; it no longer coincides with the discussion of current Finnish policy. For Finland, the post-Cold War era has brought different issues, such as the ramifications of membership in the European community, the new meaning of the Nordic group and the perplexities of dealing with a weakening neighbor to the East.[44] At the same time, the term Finlandization has appeared in a new positive

---

[42] John Lukacs, "Finland Vindicated," *Foreign Affairs* 71 (Fall 1992): 50.

[43] Laqueur, "A Postscript on Finlandization," *Commentary* 95 (January 1993): 53; Laqueur, *Europe in Our Time: A History, 1945-1992* (New York, 1992).

[44] See Jukka Valtasaari, "Changes in Europe and Russia," *Vital Speeches of the Day* 60 (15 April 1994): 395-7; and Risto Alapuro, "Finland, Thrown Out into the World Alone," *Scandinavian Studies* 64 (Fall 1992): 699-708.

sense, as simply a name for the uniqueness of Finland's experience during the Cold War, whatever the cause. It is this meaning that may well be the permanent one, although this will depend upon both the research that is done and developments in international affairs. Scholars, journalists and political leaders now ask whether Finlandization can serve as a model, not for Western Europe or America, but for the states emerging from the former Soviet bloc. Finnish leaders have been cautious about departing from their traditional dictum that their policy was "not for export," but they cannot suppress the question. Even as these words are written, a young Fulbright scholar is in Finland conducting detailed research into the relevance of Finlandization for Estonia. At the same time, "We look to Finland," a Latvian writer remarks, as "...an example to us—an example which we are striving towards."[45]

---

[45] Matti Huuhtanen, "Finland—a Model for the Baltic Republics?" *Scandinavian Review* 78 (Autumn 1990): 30.

Selected Bibliography

Allison, Roy. *Finland's Relations with the Soviet Union, 1944-1984*. New York, 1985.

Ausland, John C. *Nordic Security and the Great Powers*. Boulder, CO, 1987.

Berry, R. Michael. *American Foreign policy and the Finnish Exception: Ideological Preferences and Wartime Realities, 1941-1945*. Helsinki, 1987.

Brodin, Katarina. "The Policy of Neutrality: The Official Doctrines of Sweden and Finland. *Cooperation and Conflict* 1 (March 1968): 18-51.

_____. "The Issue of Finlandization." In *Finland and the United States: Diplomatic Relations Through Seventy Years*. Edited by Robert Rinehart, 98-103. Washington, D.C., 1993.

_____. "Yhdysvallat ja Paasikiven linja" [The United States and the Paasikivi Line]. *Ulkopolitiikka* 25 (1988): 27-37.

Gabriel, Jürg Martin. *The American Conception of Neutrality Since 1941*. New York, 1988.

Hakovirta, Harto. *East-West Conflict and European Neutrality*. Oxford, 1988.

Hamalainen, Pekka K. "The Finnish Solution." *The Wilson Quarterly* 10 (Autumn 1986): 59-75.

Hanhimäki, Jussi. *Containing Coexistence: America, Russia, and the "Finnish Solution," 1945-1956*. Kent, OH, 1997.

_____. "'Containment' in a Borderland: The United States and Finland, 1948-49." *Diplomatic History* 18 (Summer 1994): 353-74.

_____. "The First Line of Defense or a Springboard for Disintegration? European Neutrals in American Foreign and Security Policy, 1945-1961." *Diplomacy and Statecraft* 7 (1996): 378-403.

_____. "Self-Restraint as Containment: United States' Economic Policy, Finland, and the Soviet Union, 1945-1953." *The International History Review* 17 (May 1995): 287-305.

Jakobson, Max. *Finnish Neutrality: A Study of Finnish Foreign Policy Since the Second World War.* New York, 1968.

Kirby, David. *Finland in the Twentieth Century: A History and an Interpretation.* Minneapolis, 1981.

Krosby, Hans P. "Scandinavia and Finlandization." *Scandinavian Review* 63 (June 1975): 11-19.

Laqueur, Walter. "Europe: The Specter of Finlandization." *Commentary* 37 (December 1977): 37-41.

_____. *The Political Psychology of Appeasement: Finlandization and Other Unpopular Essays.* New Brunswick, NJ, 1980.

Lukacs, John. "Finland Vindicated." *Foreign Affairs* 71 (Fall 1992): 50-63.

Matson, Robert W. "Finlandization, an Ahistorical Analogy." *Research Studies* 51 (March 1983): 1-11.

Maude, George. *The Finnish Dilemma: Neutrality in the Shadow of Power.* London, 1976.

_____. "The Further Shores of Finlandization?" *Cooperation and Conflict* 17 (March 1982): 3-16.

_____. "Problems of Finnish Statecraft: The Aftermath of Legitimization." *Diplomacy and Statecraft* 1 (1990): 19-39.

Nevakivi, Jukka. "Finland and the Cold War." *Scandinavian Journal of History* 10 (1985): 211-24.

Olson, Keith W. "Finland: Between East and West." *The Wilson Quarterly* 10 (Autumn 1986): 45-58.

Petersson, Bo. "Changes of Wind or Winds of Change? Soviet Views on Finnish and Swedish Neutrality in the Postwar Era." *Nordic Journal of Soviet and East European Studies* 2 (1985): 61-85.

Polvinen, Tuomo. *Between East and West: Finland in International Politics, 1944-47.* Minneapolis, MN, 1986.

Rautkallio, Hannu. *Paasikivi vai Kekkonen. Suomi lännestä nähtynä 1945-1956* [Paasikivi or Kekkonen: Finland Viewed from the West, 1945-1956]. Helsinki, 1990.

Ruddy, T. Michael. "Confronting Cold War Neutralism: The Eisenhower Administration and Finland, a Case Study." In *The Romance of History: Essays in Honor of Lawrence S. Kaplan.* Edited by Scott L. Bills and E. Timothy Smith, 196-213. Kent, OH, 1997.

Singleton, Fred. "The Myth of 'Finlandization.'" *International Affairs* 57 (Spring 1981): 270-85.

Tarkka, Jukka. *Suomen kylmä sota. Miten heikkoudesta tuli voima* [Finland's Cold War: How Weakness Became a Strength]. Helsinki, 1992.

Värynen, Raimo. "Finland's Role in Western Policy Since the Second World War." *Cooperation and Conflict* 12 (June 1977): 87-108.

_____. *Stability and Change in Finnish Foreign Policy.* Helsinki, 1986.

Vihavainen, Timo. *Kansakunta rähmällään. Suomettumisen lyhyt historia.* Keuruu, 1991.

_____. "Neutrality and Non-Alignment: The Case of Finland." *The Non-Aligned World* 1 (July-September 1983): 346-60.

Vloyantes, John P. *Silk Glove Hegemony: Finnish-Soviet Relations, 1944-74.* Kent, OH, 1975.

_____. "Finland." In *Europe's Neutral and Nonaligned States: Between NATO and the Warsaw Pact.* Edited by S. Victor Papacosma and Mark R. Rubin, 137-59. Wilmington, DE, 1989.

Index